THE ROYAL DUKES AND PRINCESSES OF THE FAMILY OF GEORGE III.

Percy Hetherington Fitzgerald

A General Books LLC Publication.

CONTENTS

1

SECTION 1

THE
  KOYAL DUKES AND PRINCESSES
  OF THE
  FAMILY OF GEORGE III.
  CHAPTER I.
  EARLY LOVES OF THE KING.

At the age of twenty-three, having been born in 1738, the young Prince George came to the throne of England, being destined to rule sixty years, the longest reign hitherto known in this kingdom. At his coronation there were some eight of his royal relations alive. His uncle, William Augustus, Duke of Cumberland, celebrated or notorious for his connection with the battle of Culloden, was but forty years old, and lived till 1765. An aunt, the Princess Amelia, little heard of in comparison with her more interesting grandniece, died in 1786. Another aunt was the Princess Mary, who had been married, in 1746, to the Landgrave of Hesse-Cassel, and who died in 1771.

  VOL. I. B

Of the king's brothers, then living, there was Prince Edward, twenty years old, who was in the Navy, and who was created, in the fifth year of his accession, Duke of York and Albany, and who died in 1767. Another brother was Prince William

Henry, seventeen years old, created Duke of Gloucester, whose marriage in 1766 with a subject, Lady Waldcgrave, caused much family trouble. His son William, Duke of Gloucester, married his cousin, the Princess Mary. Another was Prince Henry, created Duke of Cumberland in 1766, two years after the Duke of Cumberland, of Culloden memory, and who also married a subject, Lady Ann Luttrell. His sister was Princess Augusta, married in 1764 to the Duke of Brunswick, whose children and connections seemed destined to misfortunes. The duke was a general of some reputation, but who suffered severely in the Revolution. Their second son, Duke Frederick, who succeeded to the duchy, fell at Quatre Bras, leaving a son, the third Duke Charles, and who was the half-crazy, diamond-loving prince still remembered. Of his daughters, one was the unfortunate Queen of Wirtemberg; while the career of Caroline, who became Queen of England, is familiar to all. Another sister of George III. was Caroline Matilda, married in 1766 to Christian VII., King of Denmark, whose tragic fate and wretched exile is one of the romances of royal history. Such were the members of the royal family, together with their more conspicuous descendants.

The fertility of this royal family, and their innumerable ramifications, has reached, by our time, to an extraordinary extent. The young king was to have a family of thirteen, seven sons and six daughters, of whom the fourth son, Edward, Duke of Kent, was to leave one daughter, our present Gracious Majesty, from whom has descended, within a period of little over forty years, a singularly large family, consisting at this moment of innumerable children, grandchildren, and great-grandchildren, and this though seven of her children have been married.

Of these early opening days of the new reign Mr. Walpole gives some vivacious sketches : " He [the king] left $50,000 between the Duke, Emily, and Mary : the Duke has given up his share. To Lady Yarmouth, a cabinet with the contents ; they call it $11,000. By a German deed, he gives the Duke, to the value of $180,000, placed on mortgages not immediately recoverable ! He gives him besides all his jewels in England, but had removed all his best to Hanover, which he makes Crown jewels, and his successor residuary legatee. My Lady Suffolk has given me a particular of his jewels, which plainly amount to $150,000." In November, 1760, he writes : "For the king himself, he seems all good nature, and wishing to satisfy everybody; all his speeches are obliging."

The account of the royal interment is dramatic : " Do you know, I had the curiosity to go to the burying t'other night. It is absolutely a noble sight. The prince's chamber, hung with purple, and a quantity of silver lamps the coffin under a canopy of purple velvet, and six vast chandeliers of silver on high stands, had a very good effect. The ambassador from Tripoli and his son were carried to see that chamber. The procession, through a line of foot-guards, every seventh man bearing a torch; the horse-guards lining the outsides, their officers with drawn sabres, and crape sashes, on horseback, the drums muffled, the fifes, bells tolling, and minute gunslall this was very solemn. But the charm was the entrance of the Abbey, where we were received by the dean and chapter, in rich robes, the choir and almsmen bearing torches; the whole Abbey so illuminated, that one saw it to greater advantage than by day; the tombs, long aisles, and fretted roof, all appearing distinctly, and with the happiest *chiaro oscuro*. There wanted nothing but incense and little chapels here and there, with priests saying mass for the repose of the defunct; yet one could not complain of its not being catholic enough. When we came to the chapel of Henry VII., all solemnity and decorum ceased|no order was observed; people sat or stood where they could or would; the yeomen of the guard were crying out for help, oppressed by the immense weight of the coffin. The bishop read sadly, and blundered in the prayers : the fine chapter, ' Man that is born of a woman,' was chanted, not read; and the anthem, besides being immeasurably tedious, would have served as well for a nuptial." This sketch of a royal duke, the hero of Culloden, is striking: " The real serious part was the figure of the Duke of Cumberland, heightened by a thousand melancholy circumstances. He had a dark- brown adonis, and a cloak of black cloth, with a train of five yards. Attending the funeral of a father could not be pleasant; his leg extremely bad, yet forced to stand upon it near two hours; his face bloated and distorted with his late paralytic stroke, which has affected, too,one of his eyes; and placed over the mouth of the vault, into which, in all probability, he must himself so soon descend|think how unpleasant a situation! He bore it all with a firm and unaffected countenance. Then returned the fear of catching cold; and the Duke of Cumberland, who was sinking with heat, felt himself weighed down, and turning round, found it was the Duke of Newcastle standing upon his train to avoid the chill of the marble. It was very theatric to look down into the vault where the coffins lay, attended by mourners with lights. Clavering, the groom of the bed-chamber, refused to sit up with the body, and was dismissed by the king's order."

" The first night the king went to the play, which was civilly on a Friday, not on the opera-night, as he used to do, the whole audience sang 'God save the King' in chorus. For the first act the press was so great at the door, that no ladies could go to the boxes, and only the servants appeared there, who kept places. At the end of the second act the whole mob broke in, and seated themselves; yet all this zeal is not likely to last, though he so well deserves it."

The young king had been fairly well educated considering his position, and was always distinguished for his sagacity and composure in addressing an audience. Miss Burney describes the clear voice and excellent elocution with which he read his answer to an address. When a child he and his brothers had been carefully instructed by Mr. Quin, under whose guidance a dramaticperformance had been given at Leicester House, the young princes taking the leading characters, and the private theatre of Leicester House was fitted up for the occasion. " Cato" was the play, and the cast as follows:

The cost of the lights, torches, and scaffolding used in the Abbey was Bet down at $1000, and the whole expense at upwards of $50,000. Two hundred performers were engaged in the music.

Portius . . . *Prince George.*
Juba . . . *Prince Edward.*
Cato . . . *Master Nugent.*
Sempronius . . *Master Evelyn.*
Lucius . . . *Master Montague.*
Decius . . . *Lord Milsington.*
Stphax . . . *Lord North's Son.*

Marcus . . . *Master Maddon.*
Marcia . . . *Princess Augusta.*
Lucia . . . *Princess Elizabeth.*
The prologue was spoken by the future king:
To speak with freedom, dignity, and ease,
To learn those arts, -which may hereafter please;
Wise authors say|let youth in earliest age,
Eehearse the poet's labours on the stage.
Nay more ! a nobler end is still behind,
The poet's labours elevate the mind;
Teach our young hearts with generous fire to burn,
And feel the virtuous sentiments we learn.
T' attain these glorious ends, what play so fit
As that, where all the powers of human wit
Combine, to dignify great Cato's name,
To deck his tomb, and consecrate his fame;
Where liberty|0 name for ever dear !
Breathes forth in ev'ry line, and bids us fear
Nor pains, nor death, to guard our sacred laws,
But bravely perish, in our country's cause,
Patriots indeed ! worthy that honest name,
Thro' every time and station still the same.
Should this superior to my years be thought,
Know|'tis the first great lesson I was taught.
What though a boy, it may with pride be said,
A boy in England born, in England bred,
Where freedom well becomes the earliest state,
For there the love of liberty's innate.

Yet more|before my eyes those heroes stand,
"Whom the great William brought to bless this land,
To guard with pious care, that generous plan,
Of power well bounded|which he first bsgan.
But while my great forefathers fire my mind,
The friends, the joy, the glory of mankind,
Can I forget, that there is one more dear ?
But he is present|and I must forbear.

The epilogue was spoken by Princess Augusta, afterwards Duchess of Brunswick, and Prince Edward, late
Duke of York:
Princess Augusta.

The Prologue's fill'd with such fine phrases,
George will alone have all the praises,
Unless we can (to get in vogue)
Contrive to speak an epilogue.

    Prince Edward.
    George has, 'tis true, vouchsafed to mention
His future gracious intention,
In such heroic strains, that no man
Will e'er deny his soul is Roman.
But what have you or I to say to
The pompous sentiments of Cato ?
George is to have imperial sway,
Our task is only to obey.
And, trust me, I'll not thwart his will,
But be his faithful Juba still.
|Tho', sister ! now the play is over,
I wish you'd get a better lover.

    Princess Augusta.
Why,|not to underrate your merit,
Others would court with different spirit;
And I|perhaps|might like another,
A little better than a brother,
Could I have one of England's breeding;
But 'tis a point they're all agreed in,
That I must wed a foreigner,
And cross the sea|the Lord knows where;
Yet, let me go where'er I will,
England shall have my wishes stilL

    Prince Edward.
    In England born, my inclination,
Like yours, is wedded to the nation;
And future times, I hope, will see
Me General, in reality.
Indeed ! I wish to serve this land,
It is my father's strict command :
And none he ever gave, will be
More cheerfully obey'd by me.

After the play some lines were spoken by Master Nugent and Prince George, in
their respective characters of Cato and Portius :
    Cato *to* Portius.

While I, exalted by my prince's grace,
In borrow'd pomp assume old *Cato's* place,
Tho' ill may suit his form with beardless youth,
Yet shall his soul beam forth in honest truth;
And thou, indulgent to my real part,
Accept this tribute from a faithful heart, etc.

The king was ever fond of the stage. There was a picture painted of the scene, and an engraving from the picture, an attractive one. The piece selected seems above their strength. It is not often that we light on records of such juvenile pastimes in the royal family, and such are always interesting.

The first time that his royal highness appeared at the theatre as Prince of Wales, a remarkable occurrence took place, which drew the whole attention of the audience towards him. " In the entertainment there was a dove-house represented, which was attacked by a ruffian, with an intent to destroy the emblems of innocence; the doves being frightened, flew about in disorder, one fell on the stage, and another taking two or three turns, flew into the prince's box, and

2

SECTION 2

fell down by his side. The whole audience testified their enjoyment of this singular occurrence, by loud clapping. The prince expressed a wish to keep the dove, but it was restored to the owners by his attendants."

An odd incident of this early time that deserves record was the arrival of Omar Efiendi, the new ambassador for Algiers, who on June 3rd had an audience of the king to deliver his credentials. He brought over, as a present, twenty-four fine horses, a lion, two tigers, and some curious sheep. " He was very desirous of having the lion and tigers led before the king in procession, such being the custom, he declared, in his own country; his request, however, could not be granted; the fine horses and curious sheep were, however, admitted into the procession. But here he wished that the animals might actually be driven into the presence of the king, that he might report to his master that he had delivered them with his own hands. On being informed that this could not be granted, as the horses could not ascend the stairs, he wished to be informed whether, as the horses could not ascend to the king, the king could not descend to them. The animals were then driven into the royal garden, and his majesty viewed them from the window of the palace. The ambassador was then admitted into the royal presence, and he apologised to his majesty for his not being attended with the lion and the tigers ; but his majesty, in a happy manner, diverted the discourse, by expressing his grief that his excellency had such a bad day for his public entry. " No, Sire," said the ambassador, "it is not a bad day, it is a very fine,it is a glorious day for me, when I have the honour to behold so great a monarch as your majesty."

The king, when he was informed of the accession of Peter III., exclaimed : " Well, there are now nine of us in Europe, the third of our respective names;" as the following proves I George III., King of England; Charles III., King of Spain; Augustus III., King of Poland; Frederick III., King of Prussia; Charles Emanuel III., King of Sardinia; Mustapha III., Emperor of the Turks; Peter III., Emperor of Russia ; Francis III., Duke of Modena ; Frederick III., Duke of Saxe-Gotha.

One of those legends that are almost invariably associated with a Court, and have a mixed flavour of romance, is that of the beautiful Quakeress Hannah Lightfoot, who was reported to have engaged the affections of the young prince before he came to the throne. There is a curious air of melodrama over the story, which is thus recounted. The scene appears to have been the site of the present passage or arcade at the back of the opera-house : " I well remember the shop," says an old inhabitant, " which, after the decease of the old folks, was kept by their son until the recent destruction. It was a linendraper's, and, as the principal part of the business lay with the country market people, the proprietors were accustomed to keep a cask of good ale, a glass of which was always offered to their customers.

" The royal family proceeded to the theatres in chairs, preceded only by a few footmen, and followed by about a dozen yeomen. On these occasions the linens were taken out of the eastern window, and Miss Wheeler sat in a chair to see the procession. The fame of her beautyattracted the notice of the prince, and there were not wanting those who were ready to fan the flame and promote the connection. When the prince went to St. James's, the coach always passed that way, and seeing the young lady at the window occasionally, he became enamoured of her, and employed Miss Chudleigh, afterwards Duchess of Kingston, to concert an interview. The Court is said to have taken alarm at these circumstances ; and Miss Chudleigh, seeing the danger likely to ensue, privately offered to become a medium of getting the young lady married. With this view she got acquainted with a person who was a friend of the Lightfoot family, named Axford, and who lived at that time on Ludgate Hill. This person consented to pay his addresses to Miss Lightfoot, and even nominally to marry her upon the assurance of receiving with her a considerable dower. Miss Lightfoot is supposed to have given in to the plan, for she was married at Keith's Chapel in 1754 ; for Miss Chudleigh, who had contrived the match (probably with the sanction of all parties), took her into a coach as she came out of the church door, and the husband pocketed the dower, but never saw his wife afterwards. The mother indeed heard from the daughter once or twice before she died, and Axford made inquiries after her at Weymouth, Windsor, and Kew; and once is even said to have presented a petition to the king on his knees as his majesty was riding one day in St. James's Park, but no certain account of her was ever known from the period of her marriage-day. She is said to have had a daughter, subsequently married to a gentleman of the name of Dal ton or Dalston, who afterwards received an appointment from the East IndiaCompany in Bengal, whither he went, and where he died, leaving three daughters."

On some persona, about the year 1820, making inquiries, members of the Axford family were found to be surviving, and the Editor of "The Monthly Magazine," a journal in which, some years later, Dickens published his first paper, discovered that the Axford family were'respectable grocers on Ludgate Hill. "We traced a son of the person alluded to in the letter, by his second wife, Miss Bartlett, and ascertained that the information of our correspondent is substantially correct- From him we learn that the lady lived six weeks with her husband, who was fondly attached to her, but one evening, when he happened to be from home, a coach and four came to the door, when she was conveyed into it and carried off at a gallop, no one knew whither. It appears the husband was inconsolable at first, and at different times applied for information about his wife at Weymouth and other places, but died after sixty years in total ignorance of her fate. It has, however, been reported that she had three sons by her lover, since high in the army ; that she was buried at Islington under another name, and even that she is still alive. He told me, when I last saw him, that he presented a petition at St. James's, which was not attended to ; also that he had received some money from Perryn's assignees on account of his wife. Isaac lived many years as a respectable grocer at Warminster, his native place, but retired from business before his death, which took place about five years ago, in the eighty-sixth year of his age. Many years after Hannah was taken away, her husband, believing her dead, was married again to a Miss Bartlett,of Keevel (N. Wilts), and by her succeeded to an estate at Chevrett of about $150 a year. On the report reviving, a few years since, of his first wife's being still living, a Mr. Bartlett (first cousin to Isaac's second wife) claimed the estate on the plea of the invalidity of this second marriage."

This question engaged the attention of Mr. Thorns, that diligent and thorough investigator, who collected the details just given and judicially pronounced on the controversy. He notes how all the accounts differ in innumerable pointslthe proper names, places, and timesland finally dismisses the prince's share in the matter as a pure invention. One argument which he presses, drawn from the irreproachable character of the king, is, it must be confessed, a forcible one. When writing on his son's disreputable connections with an actress, he says: " I thank Heaven, my morals and course of life have but little resembled those too prevalent in the present age ; and certainly of all the objects of this life, the one I have most at heart is to form my children that they may be useful examples and worthy of imitation."

And again : " Colonel Hotham has brought it to a conclusion, and has her consent to get the letters on her receiving $5000lundoubtedly an enormous sum; but I wish to get my son out of this shameful scrape. I desire you will therefore see Lieutenant-Colonel Hotham, and settle this with him. I am happy at being able to say that I never was personally engaged in such a transaction, which perhaps makes me feel this the stronger !"

Giving due weight to the unvaried steadiness of the
king's behaviour, it must be said that this is not quite conclusive, as will be seen.

There can be little doubt but that the leading facts of the story are truelviz. that a young Quakeress, married to the grocer, was admired by the young prince, and eloped in the mysterious way described. Now, as to the prince's share in the transaction. It must be remembered that he was of a highly susceptible nature, and that only a short time after he had conceived a violent passion for another subject, Lady Sarah Lennox, there being serious apprehensions that he would marry her. There is nothing unlikely, therefore, in a mere boy conceiving a passion for a person of such remarkable beauty as the Quakeress, and he might for a time have conceived the wild scheme of offering his hand, being too high principled to take any other course. Nothing, too, would have been more natural than that Lord Bute or others about the Court should have thought the best way of putting an end to the affair would have been to marry the young person to a respectable man in her own station of life; and it was equally likely that some of the dissolute nobles of the Court should have robbed the too-trusting grocer of his bride; or that the young woman herself, in disappointment at being robbed of her royal admirer, should have taken a disgust to Ludgate Hill. How natural, too, that her disappearance should have been set down to the account of the prince, who would be supposed to have prompted the transaction.

Another of the king's youthful attachments was to Lady Pembroke, whose stately beauty attracted admiration at his coronation, and whose mature attraction, nearly fifty years later, revived the old attachment|strongly shown when just recovered from, or verging on, his fits of madness. Mrs. Harcourt, in her diary, dwells on the annoyances of the family at this awkward *penchant.*

A more interesting romance, however, was associated with the Lady Sarah Lennox just mentioned, a beautiful girl of scarcely sixteen, to whom the susceptible prince was attached. There were hopes, well founded on his honourable character, that he would raise her to the throne; but reflection showed him that this would be a dangerous, if not impossible, step. He listened to the sound reasoning of those who had most influence with him, and consented, not merely to forego his design, but to at once select a princess from an influential foreign family, whose connections would be useful. The king is said to have never been forgiven by her brother, the duke ; though Colonel Lennox, who fought the Duke of York, was held in high favour. She consented, however|which fully supports the theory laid down|to be one of the train-bearers of the princess selected. The king, it is said, always looked fondly back to the old romance of his youth, and once, at the theatre, noting an actress, observed to the queen in a melancholy way : " She is like Lady Sarah still!"

This lady is described as being one of the most beautiful women of her time. The king sent her a message that amounted virtually to a proposal. " I think," he said to her female friend, " an English match would be better than a foreign. Pray tell Lady Sarah I said so." There have been various speculations as to the cause of the break off, but I believe the true reason

3

SECTION 3

to have been that his majesty never seriously contemplated such a match; and this is further shown by the little devices used by this beauty to carry on the affair. Thus she at one time dressed up as a shepherdess, at another disguised herself as a servant, in order to meet the king. All this points to a serious flirtation, and, it seems to me, supports the Hannah Lightfoot story : proving that the king at this time was rather adventurous in his admiration.

She was eventually married twice, first to Sir Charles Bunbury, next to Mr. Napier, brother of the well-known soldier, Sir Charles, and lived to be eighty- two. She died in the year 1826. She was actually the great-granddaughter of Charles II., so had royal blood in her veins. Sir Charles was a racing-man, fond of gambling, and the other pastimes of men of *ton*. When they were at Spa, in 1767, they both wrote to their friend Selwyn, then at Paris. Hers is a charming letter:

LADY SARAH BUNBURY TO GEORGE SELWYN.

Spa, July 18, 1767. Dear Sib,

You have always been so good to foreigners, that I take the liberty of recommending two ladies to your protection, who, though they are not French, really deserve as much attention as possible, and I flatter myself you will not refuse to attend them in London, where I fear they will be very much *sur le pav6,* having no acquaintance at all, and

London is now so empty it will be difficult to make any parties for them. But I own I think the Princess Powniatowska and Mademoiselle Kelbel, the ladies in question, too lucky if you will be their Ciceroni. I assure you they are very agreeable and pleasing, and you will like them vastly. I wish you would carry them to Richmond and Windsor, and show them as much of the *campagnes* as you can during their stay, which I hope will be very short, for we miss them sadly here, and are very impatient for their return.

I suppose Lord Carlisle is too much taken up with recovering his $800, to think of desiring him to pay these ladies any civilities. I really am so provoked at him for following your example, only in your faults, that I can hardly forgive him; but if I should find a moment's time, *seriously, I* should be vastly obliged to him if he would get the better of his indolence, and get acquainted with them. Tell him that I am sure he will admire Mademoiselle Kelbel, for that she is pretty and lively. She is such a great favourite of mine, that I shall be vastly disappointed if he does not admire her. Pray also tell him how much obliged Sir Charles and I are to him if he means to give us his picture, as I suppose he does by his telling us of it, and I am doubly obliged by Pollisson's picture being added. I cannot say Sir Charles seems to value it half as much as it deserves; Lord Carlisle's picture *only* would have contented him. It is amazing how little respect he has for dogs. As for me, I assure you I toad-eat a little cur that is here, only because his name is Raton.

The Duke of York is gone from Brussels to Com- piegne; when he will honour us with his company I do not know. The Prince and Princess of Brunswick came to Liege, and then suddenly went home. We always,

VOL. I.

you know, must find some reason for such sudden resolutions, and we suspect that it is owing to a Madame de Sehliben, who is here, and that the Prince does not choose to see; we have no sort of foundation for this suspicion, though ; it is only our fancy. This is a sad dull place, but I like it very well, for the country is pleasant always, and one may do as one pleases here, which is also always pleasant. Pray, Mr. Selwyn, write often to us, for you cannot think how much it will

oblige,

Your most obedient Servant,

Sarah Bunbuey.

P.S.lYou are too apt to be *distrait* not to believe my being so, and also my having wrote upon half a sheet of paper. Sir Charles desires his best compliments to you. The Princess Powniatowska will probably be arrived before you get this. She lives next door to Lord Spencer's.

4

SECTION 4

CHAPTER II.
FESTIVITIES AND PALACE LIFE.
The marriage of the young king was arranged in a prompt and businesslike fashion, owing, no doubt, to his own good sense and feeling, that it was expected by the nation, and that he should set an example of that excellent household and well-ordered family which has made its name so respected. Lord Harcourt was despatched to Mecklenburgh-Strelitz to ask the hand of the Princess Charlotte, and it was later reported that Colonel Grome had been sent previously to inspect that lady, with other candidate princesses, and found her at the Baths of Pyrmont in Waldeck, a little state which has so recently furnished another princess to the royal house of England. She was but seventeen. The emissary, Lord Harcourt, was deputed to bring home the bride. "After landing, she slept that night at his lordship's house; and a little after twelve o'clock on Tuesday, her majesty came to Rumford, where she stopped at Mr. Dutton's, wine merchant. The king'scoach and servants met her there, and she was by them served with coffee at his house.

" Her majesty was dressed entirely in the English taste. She wore a fly-cap, with rich laced lappets; a stomacher, ornamented with diamonds; and a gold brocade suit of clothes, with a white ground. They proceeded at a tolerable pace, attended by an incredible number of spectators, both on horse and foot, to the garden-gate of the palace, where her majesty was handed out of her coach by the Duke of Devonshire, as lord chamberlain, to the gate, where she was received by his royal highness the Duke of York. As her majesty alighted from her coach, his majesty descended the steps from the palace into the garden, and they met each other half way ; and as her majesty was going to pay her obeisance, the king took hold of her hand, raised her up, saluted it, and then led her upstairs. Afterwards, their majesties, her royal highness the Princess Dowager of Wales, and all his majesty's brothers and sisters, except the two youngest, dined together. After dinner, her majesty was pleased to show herself, with his majesty, in the gallery and other apartments fronting the park, to the people. On the road she was extremely courteous to an incredible number of spectators on horse and foot gathered on this occasion, showing herself, and bowing to all who seemed desirous of seeing her, and ordering the coach to go extremely slow through the towns and villages as she passed, that as many as would might have a full view of her.

" About eight o'clock in the evening the procession to the chapel began in the following order:

THE PROCESSION OF THE BRIDE.

Drums and Trumpets.

The Sergeant Trumpeter.

The Princess's Servants.

A Page.

A Quarter Waiter.

A Gentleman Usher between the two Senior Heralds.

Vice-Chamberlain.

Maids of Honour.

Ladies of the Bedchamber, not Peeresses.

Peeresses.

Unmarried Daughters of Peers. The King's Vice-Chamberlain|The King's Lord Chamberlain.

THE BRIDE,

In her Nuptial Habit, supported by their Royal Highnesses the Duke of York and Prince William, her Train borne by Ten Unmarried

Daughters of Dukes and Earls, viz.:

Lady Sarah Lenox, Lady Car. Russel, Lady Ann Hamilton, Lady Elizabeth Ker, Lady Harry Bentinck, Lady Car. Montagu,

Lady Elizabeth Keppel, Lady Louisa Greville,

Lady Elizabeth Harcourt, Lady S. Strangeways.

"Her serene highness having been in this manner conducted to the chapel, the lord chamberlain and vice-chamberlain, with the two heralds, returned to wait upon his majesty. They were then met by the King's Procession.

" The marriage ceremony took place, being performed by the Archbishop of Canterbury. The Duke of Cumberland gave her hand to his majesty, and immediately on the joining their hands the Park and Tower guns were fired." The ten bridesmaids to the queen were all dressed alike, in white lustring, with silver trimmings, ornamented with pearls, diamonds, etc., among whom was the beautiful, and we may presume disappointed, Lady Sarah, who was put to this curious trial.

The next exciting pageant of the opening of his new

5

SECTION 5

reign was of course the coronation, and as the same ceremonial ideas until late years were strictly observed, there is a curious sameness in the incidents, George IV.'s following that of his father's in the most minute particulars. The auspicious event took place on September 7, 1761. Mr. Walpole gives one of his pleasant sketches of the procession :

" It was in truth a brave sight. The sea of heads in Palace Yard, the guards, horse and foot, the scaffolds, balconies, and procession, exceeded imagination. The hall, when once illuminated, was noble, but they suffered the whole parade of it to return into it in the dark, that his majesty might be surprised with the quickness with which the sconces catched fire. The habit of peers is unbecoming to the last degree, but the peeresses made amends for all defects. Your daughter Richmond, Lady Kildare, and Lady Pembroke were as handsome as the Graces. Lady Rochford, Lady Holdernesse, and Lady Littleton looked exceedingly well in their day ; and for those of the days before, the Duchess of Queensbery, Lady Westmorland, and Lady Albemarle were surprising. Lady Harrington was noble at a distance, and so covered with diamonds, that you would have thought she had bid somebody or other, like Falstaff, 'rob me the exchequer.' Lady Northampton was very magnificent too, and looked prettier than I have seen her of late. Lady Spencer and Lady Bolingbroke were not the worst figures there. The Duchess of Ancaster marched alone after the queen with much majesty, and there were two new Scotch peeresses that pleased everybody, Lady Sutherland and Lady Dunmore. *Per contra,* were Lady P., who had put a wig on, and oldE., who had scratched hers off. The Dowager E. and a Lady S., with her tresses coal-black and her hair coal- white. Well, it was all delightful, but not half so charming as its being over!"

It was noticed of Archbishop Seeker, who officiated, that he had the honour of baptizing his majesty, confirming him when Prince of Wales, marrying him at St. James's, and crowning him at Westminster; besides which, he christened king George IV., the Duke of York, and some others of the royal family.

Soon after the coronation, the City of London, according to its old and honourable custom, offered the sovereign an entertainment, in token of greeting or reception, as magnificent as its resources allowed. The Lord Mayor's Day was selected for its solemnity, in order that his majesty and family might be gratified first by seeing a procession pass through the streets, and then proceed to the banquet. There was a pageant on the water of gilded barges or gondolas. It was curious that the mansion of a worthy Quaker, " friend Barclay," facing Bow Church, should have been selected for the king. And a daughter of Mr. Barclay's, in a letter, simply and naturally described what occurred during the royal stay. This account is so lively, and withal of such a Quakerly simplicity, that it will be welcome :

" About one o'clock papa and mamma, with sister Western to attend them, took their stands at the street door, where my two brothers had long been, to receive the nobility, above one hundred of whom were then waiting in the warehouse, from which place every appearance of merchandise was removed, and properly decorated for the purpose.

"As the royal family came, they were conducted into one of the counting-houses, which was transformed into a very pretty parlour for that purpose. The newspapers have doubtless informed you of the procession so I shall only say, that at half-past two o'clock their majesties arrived, which was two hours later than they intended ; but had you seen the crowd, you would have wondered how they ever got through it. A platform was raised in the street, on which, before their majesties alighted, my brothers spread a carpet, and as soon as they entered, the procession began. The queen came up first, handed by her chamberlain ; the king followed, with the rest of the royal family, agreeable to their rank; the master and mistress of the house, and then the quality. On the second pair of stairs was placed our own company, about forty in number, the chief of whom were of the Puritan order, and all in their orthodox habits. Next the drawing-room door was placed our own selves, I mean my papa's children, for, to the great mortification of our visitors, none else were allowed to enter the drawing-room; for as kissing the king's hand without kneeling was an honour never before conferred, his majesty chose to confine that mark of condescension to our own family, as a return for the trouble we had been at upon the occasion.

" But to proceed. After the royal pair had shown themselves to the populace for a few moments from the balcony, we were all introduced; and you may believe at that juncture we felt no small palpitations.

"His majesty met us at the door, which was a condescension we did not expect; at which place he saluted us with great politeness; and advancing to the uppercud of the room, we performed the ceremony of kissing the queen's hand, at the sight of whom we were all in raptures, not only from the brilliancy of her appearance, which was pleasing beyond description, but being throughout her whole person possessed of that inexpressible something that is beyond a set of features, and equally claims our attention.

" I suppose that you will not think the picture complete, unless the important article of dress be in part communicated; therefore, agreeable to the rules of painting, I shall begin with the head. Her hair, which is of a light colour, hung in what is called coronation ringlets, encompassed with a circle of diamonds, so beautiful in themselves, and so prettily disposed, as will admit of no description : her clothes, which were as rich as gold, silver, and silk could make them, was a suit from which fell a train, supported by a little page in scarlet and silver. The lustre of her stomacher was inconceivable, being one of the presents she received whilst Princess of Mecklenburg, on which was represented, by a vast profusion of diamonds placed on it, the magnificence attending so great a king, who, I must tell you, I think a very personable man: and the singular marks of honour by him bestowed on us, declare his heart disposed to administer all that pleasure and satisfaction that royalty can give: and nothing could have added to the scene, but that of conversing with the queen, who inquired if we could talk French for that purpose ; and so flattered our vanity, as to tell the lady in waiting, that the greatest mortification she had met with since her arrival in England, was her not being able to converse with us. I doubt not but that thenovelty of our appearance raised her curiosity; for amidst such profusion of glitter, we must look like a parcel of nuns. The same ceremony was performed of kissing the hand with the princess dowager, Amelia, Augusta, and the Dukes of Cumberland, York, and the other princes, who followed the king's example, in complimenting each of us with a kiss, but not till their majesties had left the room; for, you must know, there were proper apartments fitted up to give the rest of the royal family an opportunity of paying and receiving compliments ; and then we were at liberty to go in and out as we pleased ; but we could not bear the thoughts of absenting ourselves while we had one leg to stand on: and the feast prepared for our eyes supplied every other want, or at least rendered us insensible of any.

" As both the doors of the drawing-room were open the whole time, the people without had a very good opportunity of seeing : besides which, the queen was upstairs three times; and one of these opportunities was made use of for introducing my little darling, with Patty Barclay and Priscilla Bell, who were the only children admitted. At this sight I was so happy as to be present. You may be sure I was not a little anxious on account of my girl, who very unexpectedly remembered all instructions, but kissed the queen's hand with such a grace, that I thought the princess dowager would have smothered her with kisses; and on her return to the drawing-room, such a report was made of her to his majesty, that miss was sent for again, when she was so lucky as to afford the king great amusement, in particular by telling him she loved the king, though shemust not love fine things, and that her grandpapa would not allow her to make a courtesy.

" The king, you may observe, never sat down; nor did he taste anything during the whole time. Her majesty drank tea, which was brought her on a silver waiter by brother John, who delivered it to the lady in waiting, and she presented it kneeling; which to us, who had never seen that ceremony before, appeared as pretty as any of the parade. The rest of the royal family and nobility repaired to the place prepared for refreshments. Our kitchen, upon this occasion, was turned into a tearoom, and coffee and chocolate were prepared for above a hundred people, and four females to attend; besides, there was a cold collation of hams, fowls, tongues, hung-beef, etc., all served in small plates, for this repast was only designed for a bit, by way of staying the stomach. The dressers, after being covered with a fine cloth, were spread with white biscuits, rusks, etc. The floor, like the rest of the apartments, was covered with a carpet. In the decoration of this room I had like to have laid myself up in the morning. In the little parlour was a dessert of fruits and sweetmeats, and three men-servants to wait in the character of valets; for no servants in livery were suffered to appear.

" The leave they took of us was such as we might expect from our equals|full of apologies for the trouble they had given us, and returning thanks for the entertainment ; which they were so careful to have fully explained, that the queen came up to us as we were all standing on one side the door, and had every word interpreted, and left us in astonishment at her condescension ; my brothers attending them to the coachin the same manner they had received them, only with the additional honour of assisting the queen to get in. Some of us sat up to see them return from the hall, otherwise we should have seen nothing of the grandeur of the procession, as we could not have a view of it as they came; and it was worth our pains. Their majesties, thinking it a compliment from us, took great care to return it, by the notice they took of us as they passed. In short, they omitted nothing that could demonstrate respect. An instance of which the king gave by ordering twenty-four of the life guards, who were drawn up during his majesty's stay at Bow Churchyard, to be placed opposite our house all night, lest any of the canopy should be pulled down by the mob, in which there was one hundred yards of silk damask."

From a report furnished by the committee who were entrusted with the preparations, we gather what was the cost and even the mode in which City banquets were then served.

" The whole of the rooms were spread with Turkey carpet and blue cloth, and illuminated with near three thousand wax tapers, in chandeliers, lustres, girandoles, and sconces.

" A select band of music, consisting of fifty of the best hands, placed in a superb gallery, erected on purpose at the lower end of the hall, entertained their majesties with a concert during the time of dinner, under the direction of a gentleman justly celebrated for his great musical talents; whilst four other galleries| all covered with crimson and ornamented with festoons |exhibited to their majesties a most brilliant appearance of five hundred of the principal citizens of both sexes.

6

SECTION 6

" Their majesties' table was served with a new set of rich plate, purchased on this occasion, and covered with all the delicacies which the season could furnish, or expense procure, and prepared by the best hands. The whole number of guests within the hall, including the galleries, being upwards of twelve hundred; and that of the gentlemen pensioners, yeomen of the guard, horse and horse-grenadier-guards, and servants attendant upon their majesties and the royal family, and who were entertained at places provided in the neighbourhood, amounting to seven hundred and twenty-nine.

"And that this court may form some judgment of the entertainment, your committee have hereunto subjoined the bill of fare of their majesties' table, and the totals of several bills on this occasion, amounting to $6898 6s. 4d"

THE KING'S TABLE.

FIRST SERVICE.

$ *i. a.*

12 Dishes of olio, turtle, pottages, and soups . . 44 2 0 28 fish, viz. John Dories, red mullets, etc. . 44 2 0

7 roast venison 10 0 0

3 Westphalia hams consume, and richly ornamented . 660

2 Dishes pullets a la royale 220

2 tongues Espagniole 330

6 chickens a la reine . . . . .660 1 Tondron devaux a la Danzic . . . .110 1 Harrico 110

1 Dish popiets of veale glasse 140

2 Dishes fillets of lamb a la conte . . . .220 2 comports of squabs . . . . .220 2 fillets of beef marinate . . . . .300 2 of mutton a la mercorance 220

22 fine vegetables 16 16 0

SECOND SERVICE.

6 Dishes fine ortolans . 10 quails . . 10 notts .

1 Dish, wheat-ears

1 Goodevau patte

1 Perrigoe pie

1 Dish best chicks

4 Dishes woodcocks .

2 ,, pheasants

4 teal . .

4 snipes .

2 partridges

2 patty's royal.

$. d.

25 4 0

15 0 0

30 0 0

1 1 0

1 10 0

1 10 0

4 4

3 3

3 3

330

220

300

0 0 0 0

THIRD SERVICE.

1 Racout royal .... 8 Dishes fine green morrells 10 fine green peas 3 ,, asparagus heads . 3 fine fat livers 3 fine combs . 5 green truffles 5 artichokes a la provincale 5 mushrooms au blank 1 Dish cardons a la bcjamel . 1 knots of eggs . 1 ducks' tongues

3 Dishes of peths . . .

1 Dish of truffles in oil

4 Dishes of pallets

2 , ragout mille . . .

1 1 8 8

10 10
2 2 1 11
1 11 5 5
2 12 2 12 0 10 0 10
1 11 0 10

POUBTH SERVICE.

2 Curious ornamented cakes 2120
12 Dishes blancmange, representing different figures . 12 12 0
12 clear marbrays 1480
16 fine cut pastry 16 16 0
2 . mille fuelles. . . . 1 10 6

THE CEXTRE OF THE TABLE.

$ d-

1 Grand pyramid of demies of shell-fish of various sorts 220 32 Cold things of sorts, viz. temples, shapes, landscapes

in jellies, savory cakes, and almond gottees . . 33 12 0 3 Grand epergnes, filled with fine pickles, and garnished

round with plates of sorts, as laspicks, rolards, etc. 660

Total of the king's tahle . . $374 1 3

One of the first thoughts of the prudent monarch was the deliberate selection of proper residences for himself and his family. No Court in Europe was so indifferently lodged; and many a small duchy could boast of a finer palace than the King of England enjoyed. To this hour, if we except Windsor, there is scarcely a royal residence of fitting pretensions in the kingdom ; and the mean and straitened chambers of St. James's, and the shabby accommodations of Clarence and Marlborough Houses, are not worthy of so old and imposing a monarchy. The king set about looking for a house. He even went down to Essex to inspect Wanstead, and finally settled on the Queen's House.

Very early in his reign the young king showed his determination to reform the administration of his palace, and reduce the inordinate expenses of his establishment. He even took a courageous step in setting the example of abolishing a crying abuse, which was oppressing all persons of condition in the kingdom|viz. the levying by servants of what were called " vails." This nuisance, carried to ruinous extent, was at last reduced to limits ; but it is probable, as in the modern instance of the abolition of hotel fees, the employers had still to pay, but in another and more regulated form.

" It was the custom," we are told, " at all routs and parties, to give vails to servants, and it grew by degrees to such an excess, that Mr. Joseph Han way wrote a tract, entitled, ' Eight Letters to the Duke of Newcastle on the Custom of Vails-giving in England.' Mr. Hanway was instigated to this step by Sir Timothy Waldo, who one day dined with the Duke of Newcastle, and, on his leaving the house, was contributing to the support and insolence of a train of servants who lined the hall, and at last put a crown into the hand of the cook, who returned it, saying : ' Sir, I do not take silver.' 'Don't you, indeed ?' said the worthy baronet, putting his money in his pocket, ' then I do not give gold.' Mr. Hanway was once politely reproached by a friend in a high station for not coming oftener to dine with him. ' Indeed, my lord,' he replied, ' I cannot afford it.' On another occasion he was paying the servants of a friend, after a dinner to which their master had invited him, one by one as they appeared. 'Sir, your greatcoat,' said one, upon which he paid a shilling. ' Your hat,' said anotherla shilling; ' your stick ' I a shilling ; 'your umbrella'la shilling. ' Sir, your gloves.' ' Why, friend, you may keep the gloves,' said Mr. Hanway, 'they are not worth a shilling.' These heavy drains upon the finance of Mr. Hanway determined him immediately to write the letters already mentioned ; and the Duke of Newcastle took the earliest opportunity of submitting them to the perusal of his majesty. He immediately saw the impropriety of the custom, and he ordered the servants of the household to be called before him. His majesty first addressed himself to the headcook. ' You came into my service,' said the king, ' at a stipulated salary; the practice of vails-giving shall be abolished ;' and the news of this most unpleasant order soon spread through all the fraternity of the servants. The noblemen and gentry followed the example of his majesty."

In consequence, his majesty became very unpopular, as he was presently to learn in very disagreeable fashion on the occasion of a visit to the playhouse.

" Having gone in state to attend a performance of 'Richard III.' at Drury Lane, he was received with yells from a crowd of servants, some in livery, and some out, in which they were assisted by their fellow female servants, and particularly by the cooks and scullions, who came from the squares at the west-end of the town to give the king, as they termed it, 'a good basting,' openly abusing him for his interference with their privileges." The king was said to have borne the ill-mannered attack with the greatest good-humour till the very end of the performance. But it will be seen that he was destined to be frequently in conflict with the servants, and thus furnished Dr. Wolcot with some of his best weapons.

When peace was proclaimed in 1762, the new ambassadorlwho brought a new description of hat, which was presently adopted by many of the English nobility and bore his name.Iwas also to have experience of the rapacity of English innkeepers in a way that recalls a similar case of overcharge in our day, by a certain hotel at Dover. On the 12th of September, 1762, the Due de Ninervois arrived in England. Being

VOL. L D

obliged to stop for the night at Canterbury, the following bill was presented on his departure in the

morning:

$ s. d.

Tea, coffee, and chocolate 140
Supper for self and servants 15100
Bread and beer 300
Fruit . 2 15 0
Wine and punch 1088
Wax candles and charcoal 300
Broken glass and china 2 10 0

Lodging . .170

Tea, coffee, and chocolate for twelve persons .200
Chaise and horse for stage 2160

$44 10 8

It was about the year 1782 that his majesty's attention was once more directed to the abuses connected with the powerful body of menials. Already there had been what were called " footmen's riots " at the theatre, owing to their dissatisfaction at their being excluded from a gallery where they were allowed to see the performance gratis while waiting for their masters. At another time they considered they were held up to ridicule in the amusing comedy of " High Life Below Stairs," and they resented it by riots. Other abuses arose from the protection accorded to foreign ambassadors. It was a common custom at this period for persons under fear of an arrest to get their names enrolled, on payment of a trifling sum, as belonging to

The whole company, consisting of twelve persons, drank mostly port-wine; according to the quantity, it came to eleven shillings per bottle, and punch the same.

7

SECTION 7

the suite of a foreign ambassador; and this practice had risen to such a height, that nine persons out of ten who were arrested pleaded this privilege.

"The manner in which his majesty came to the knowledge of this glaring abuse arose from a transaction with a butcher in Smithfield, to whom the steward of his majesty had sold some sheep, which had been grazed on one of his farms at Windsor. The butcher was an unprincipled fellow, and would not pay the amount of the sheep, in consequence of which legal proceedings were instituted against him, but it was discovered that he was in the suite of the French ambassador. His majesty considered this such a gross evasion of all principle of justice, that he immediately issued the order alluded to, and it was signified in form to all the foreign ambassadors."

A serious scandal having arisen from the protection afforded by Count Haslaug, a disreputable foreign minister, to a delinquent, the king ordered that the domestics of ministers should be in future amenable to the laws of this country, and that they should be no longer under the protection or sanction of their masters. A less dignified interference, however, was attended by more serious consequences, and which, having a grotesque air, led to much ridicule and even persecution on the part of a witty libeller, who thenceforth almost made his livelihood by ridiculing the king and his family. " One day at the royal table an insect of an odious kind, which it is scarcely polite to name, was found in his majesty's plate. This 'disgusting occurrence'was laid to the account of the habits of the cooks, who were at once ordered, under pain of dismissal, to submit tohaving their heads shaved and wear wigs like their betters. The cooks made a spirited resistance, and, indeed, sent up remonstrances couched in scarcely anything but a respectful tone. The master cook, however, Mr. Dixon, who possessed very little remains of his youthful tresses, was not a whit less strenuous than the youngest beau of the kitchen. True, it was entitled a petition, but filled so full of arguments, not to call them reproaches, that there was visible no expression of humility beyond the first line ; but after many parleys they yielded. One young man, however, named Bear, refused, and was dismissed." His case was represented as one of hardship, and was greatly taken up in radical circles. It was this incident that prompted the coarse muse of Dr. Wolcot, who began to issue cantos of what he called " The Lousiad," which was eagerly bought.

THE PETITION OF THE COOKS.

Your majesty's firm friends and faithful cooks,
    Who in your palace merry live as grigs,
Have heard, with heavy hearts and downcast looks,

    That we must all be shaved, and put on wigs :
You, siru, who with such honour wear your crown,
Should never bring on ours disgraces down.

    Oh! tell us, sir, in loyalty so true,
    What dire designing ragamuffins said,
That we, your cooks, are such a nasty crew,

    Great sir, as to have crawlers in the head *l*
My liege, you cannot find through all our house,
Not if you give a guinea fort, a louse.

The incident of his rebuke to a prelate for giving Sunday entertainments is well known, though not, perhaps, the letter which conveyed the rebuke.

My Good Lord Pbelate,

I could not help giving you the notification of the grief and concern with which my breast was affected, at receiving an authentic information that routs have made their way into your palace. At the same time I must signify to you my sentiments on this subject, which hold these levities and vain dissipations as utterly inexpedient if not unlawful, to pass in a residence for many centuries devoted to Divine studies, religious retirement, and the extensive exercise of charity and benevolenceI add, in a place where so many of your predecessors have led their lives in such sanctity, as has thrown lustre upon the pure religion they professed and adorned.

From the dissatisfaction with which you must perceive I behold these improprieties, not to speak in harsher terms, and still more pious principles, I trust you will suppress them immediately ; so that I may not have occasion to show any further marks of my displeasure, or to interpose in a different manner. May God take your grace into His Almighty protection !

I remain, my Lord Primate,

Your gracious Friend,

G. K.

" The king rose between six and seven, and spent an hour in devotion before breakfast. Having taken his breakfast, he dressed, and attended to public business ; after which the children were brought to him for examination and instruction, when he dismissed them to the superintendence of the queen, who always employed herself in drawing and needlework.

"He passed his time between breakfast and dinnerin his study or on horseback; indeed, he was an excellent horseman. His courage was also the admiration of all those persons who were permitted to join in the royal hunt, and the most dangerous leaps were regarded by him with the utmost indifference.

" It is a point of etiquette, in the royal hunts, that no one be permitted to ride before his majesty, for which purpose the prickers are appointed to prevent a too near approach to the person of his majesty. It happened, however, during one of the chases, that a young sportsman, unable to govern his horse, rode past the king, and the heels of his horse threw some dirt into his majesty's face. The prickers were on the alert to resent this affront, but his majesty exclaimed in the most good- natured manner : ' Stop, stop ; never punish a man for what he cannot help.'

" His majesty never, till indisposition obliged him, omitted his annual visit (with the whole of his family) to the races at Ascot Heath, at which place he gave a plate of one hundred guineas, to be run for on the first day, by such horses as had regularly hunted with his own hounds the preceding winter.

" At his table he was particularly temperate, seldom indulging in more than four glasses of wine. He passed the afternoon in reading some favourite author to her majesty.

" At supper he never went beyond a glass of wine and water, after which meal the happy pair joined in private devotion and gratitude to God for their mutual blessings. Sometimes reading a portion of some religious tract, and retiring at an early hour, when fashionable dissipation had scarcely begun her nocturnal orgies.

" There was no more methodical or businesslike administrator in his kingdom than his majesty. It was his invariable principle that it is system only which can carry a man successfully through the affairs of life ; and on once being asked how one of his ministers could possibly get through such a mass of business, he replied : ' He acts as I do; he always finishes one thing before he begins another.' The arrangements which his majesty made in August, 1785, for the remainder of the year, until their removal to town for the winter season, will show the precision with which he acted, and it was never known, unless some particular State affair interposed, that he ever omitted appearing at the appointed places according to the arrangement which he had previously made, which was as follows :

" At Windsor, the Queen's House, Sunday, Monday, and till Tuesday evening, when the king and queen came to Kew (since the decrease of days), for the greater convenience of his majesty's coming to town on Wednesdays to the leve"e. They remained at Kew on Wednesdays, Thursdays, and Fridays, and returned to Windsor on Saturday mornings. When the queen had no drawing- room at St. James's on Thursdays, the king and queen went to Windsor on Wednesday evenings, and returned to Kew the following evening. The junior branches of the royal family resided wholly at their several houses on Kew Green, and went to Windsor to visit their majesties occasionally. The Princess Royal and Princess Augusta had apartments for themselves and servants at Windsor Castle. The Prince of Wales had also a complete suite of apartments for his residence on the eastern side of the quadrangle. The princes resided occasionallyin the apartments which were some time before occupied by the Bishop of Osnaburg, and afterwards by Prince Edward.

" When the Queen's House at Windsor was completed, which was settled upon her as a part of her jointure, there was one singularity attending it, that many of the beds, quilts, and even carpets, were the work of her majesty, the princesses, maids of honour, and other females of the queen's own household, and were of the most exquisite taste and workmanship."

The reader will be interested in seeing an exact inventory of the king's private jewel-case in 1788, taken when he was seized with his first fit of insanity:

Windsor, Sunday, 30th November, 1788.lIn the centre upper drawer in the commode in the right-hand window in the saloon on the ground-floor apartments in the Queen's Lodge at Windsor, were his majesty's jewels, consisting of as follows, viz. : One diamond- hilted sword in a green case; a ditto in a black shagreen case; a ditto George, in a blue velvet case, belonging to the collar; a ditto in a black shagreen case; a ditto star in a green case; a ditto garter in a black shagreen box; two ditto buttons and loops in a black square box; a ditto Order of St. Patrick, in a green shagreen case; a ditto pair of buckles in a green shagreen case.

(Signed) George P.; Frederick.

Brudenell, Keeper of the Privy Purse.

The king's taste for music was highly cultivated,

8

SECTION 8

and the interest he took in it was genuine, as will be seen from the following unpublished letters :

THE KING TO LORD CARMARTHEN.

St. James's, March 23, 1786.

Lord Carmarthen's list of music for next Wednesday is very excellent, and meets with the approbation of those whose opinion on the subject he wished to know. His introducing Mrs. Billington, if he can get her to sing pathetic songs, and not over-grace them, will be

doing an essential service to the concert.

G. R.

THE SAME TO THE SAME.

Windsor, September 5, 1786.

"; pt. 9 A.M.

This morning I have received Lord Carmarthen's note, enclosing mood for Cr. de Keconitzky. I happen to know the archduchess's black gown is making, therefore she would not appear this day, otherwise the queen would have gone this day to town to receive them. I therefore think it will be less formal land consequently more agreeable to kiss incognital for the queen and me to receive them to-morrow evening, at half-past seven, at the Queen's House. Lord Carmarthen will therefore give notice of this to them. He, as well as Count de Havitzky, was desired to come with them, after having seen the archduke and archduchess. We will come into the other room, where we shall wish to see their suite. We shall keep them the evening and introduce them to *sterling music.*

f

His majesty, among other pleasing tastes, took a deep interest in agriculture, and his knowledge of farming was certainly of a practical kind. He, indeed, from his experiments, acquired the name of " Farmer George," and these experiments, if not more successful than those of many amateur fanners, were directed by enthusiasm. This taste was even brought on the stage in a good-humoured fashion, and the good-natured king was delighted with a character of agricultural taste |Frogmore|which the facetious Frederick Reynolds introduced into one of his comedies. Nay, he even became an author, and published in a periodical some letters on agriculture, which are scarcely known, and give him a place in the list of royal writers. Of the value of his remarks the practical agriculturist may pronounce.

January 1, 1787. Sir,

It is reasonable to expect that your laudable efforts for the improvement of husbandry, by publishing the Annals of Agriculture, must in time be crowned with success; therefore, it seems incumbent on all who think they have materials on this interesting subject worthy of the inspection of the public, to transmit them to you, who, if you view them in that light, will give them a place in that estimable work.

Without further preface, I shall mention that the dispute which has lately arisen on the subject of summer fallows, had made me secretly wish that Mr. Ducket, the able cultivator of Petersham, in Surrey, would have communicated his thoughts, not only on that subject, but would have benefited the public by a, full explanation of that course of husbandry which has rendered his farm at Petersham, which has now been above nineteen years in his hands, so flourishing, though his three predecessors had failed on it.

When he first entered on it, all the land, except the meadows, appeared to be hungry sand, and several acres were covered with gorse and brambles, which now produce excellent crops of corn.

As you have completed your sixth volume, and I find his great modesty prevents his standing forth among your correspondents, I will attempt to describe his mode of cultivation, rather than it shall longer remain unnoticed in your Annals.

Mr. Ducket's system of agriculture is a medium between the old and drill husbandry. He adopted his present mode of culture six years before he came to Petersham, on a small farm at Esher, as also at the late Duke of Newcastle's Villa of Claremount, where he used his three ploughs, but at that time hand-hoed all his corn.

His course of husbandry seems to be the employing clover, turnips, and rye as fallow crops, and as intermediate ones between wheat, barley, oats, and rye, changing these occasionally according to the nature and state of the land. Of these intermediate crops, those which serve only to fill up the winter interval are of the greatest use, for winter and spring food, and what these take from the ground is amply resupplied by the dung and treading of the cattle which feed on them; thus his ground, although never dormant, is continually replenished by a variety of manure, and thus unites the system of continued pasture with cultivation.

Mr. Ducket's implements of husbandry are, first, a trench-plough, which requires never less than four horses, and when he means to plough very deep, six horses: he ploughs an acre in one day. No additional strength would be required in strong soils, as they usually need not be ploughed so deep.

Second, a two-share plough, which, with four horses, ploughs two acres in one day.

Third, a drill, which he names a plough, as at seedtime it answers the purpose of one, and on this account prefers it to any drill of late invention that drops the seed; it requires but two horses; it will work three acres in one day ; although it makes five drills, it only completes two at every bout.

The first and second ploughs, he thinks, answer all the purposes that can be wanted of ploughs in husbandry. One deep ploughing with the trench-plough, to every other, or every third crop, with very shallow intermediate ploughings with the two-share plough, is the best method of using them, and from which he has derived the greatest benefit.

The advantages arising from this mode of practice, he describes thus: By a deep ploughing, fresh earth is brought up for the nourishment of the plants ; by not repeating it too often, the moisture is retained in the soil, being not too loose to draw off the wet, and yet not too hard to impede the penetration of the roots of the plants into it. The shallow ploughings with the two-share plough loosen the soil sufficiently for the seed to take root, until it has strength enough to penetrate into the first broken earth. Frequent ploughings, he thinks, bring up the buried seeds of annual weeds soabundantly, that in a grain crop it is difficult to destroy them. When the land is constantly ploughed to the same depth, the rain water is lodged between the loosened and unmoved earth, where it stagnates and injures, instead of assisting vegetation.

He seems now of opinion, that if he can get his ploughing finished two or three months before seedtime, and harrowed, the land may lay thus until the time of sowing, taking advantage of rains and other elementary aids to settle and consolidate the soil; the annual weeds have time to grow, which the drill (in preparing the soil thus managed for the seed) entirely destroys, and the crop of grain is kept during the summer cleaner from weeds than it would otherwise be. He has reaped by this method, in a dry summer, fine crops of grain, when others, not so treated, have perished through drought.

He prefers narrow furrows, his ploughs being constructed only to turn the furrow nine inches wide, consequently do not perform so much work in a day as some common ploughs, but the ground is better prepared for the drill, and the grain finds more nourishment.

He drills for all his crops, but sows the seeds broadcast (turnips excepted) as the seeds fall naturally into the drills, or what escape the hoe eradicates; turnips when eaten by the fly are well renewed by drilling. He has had good crops after the first sowings have been destroyed by the fly. Clover drilled among the corn he finds very advantageous, much seed being saved and the crop better secured from the fly, which feed on this plant as well as on turnips. If his clover fails, he sows bents broadcast when the corn is near in the ear, which, from the ground being loosened by the preceding drillings, are by the first rain washed into the earth, and insure him a crop of grass, but he prefers a crop of clover alone, being the better preparation for wheat.

His hoe machine is composed of two frames, in each of which five hoes are fixed; it is drawn by one horse, led by a boy, and worked by two men. If the ground works tolerably well, ten acres may be done in one day. If lands or ridges lay round or sharp, and the soil is stiff, the width of the machine, the number of hoes, and the strength, must be proportioned accordingly.

Mr. Ducket has lately adopted two new implements : the one for sowing is a frame on which are fixed five tin boxes, each holding about one pound of seed, which drops through the bottom of them into the drills. It is carried in a man's hand, and being continually shook, the seed is prevented from clogging the holes in the bottom of the boxes by a wire playing across them, and is thus dribbled regularly into the drills.

The other is for rolling the seed into the ground. It is composed of a frame containing five small rollers, each eight inches diameter, drawn by hand, the rollers filling the intervals of land between the rows of corn and pressing down the seeds.

He seems to think the frequency of manuring ought to depend on the quality, the state of the land, and the crop to grow upon it. Good stable and fold-yard dung he thinks the best dressing for strong tillage land, a compost of the aforesaid dung and turf or light loam

9

SECTION 9

for strong meadow land, and a compost of the said dung, stiff loam, and chalk, as also sheep-folding, for light soils.

He dungs for turnips, unless the preceding crop was dunged; for wheat he had rather dung on the seeds, that is, on clover, etc., which the wheat is to follow, after the ground has been trench-ploughed; he regularly trench-ploughs the clover lays, and throws the dung deep.

He is in general not sparing with seed, especially in land subject to weeds, and where the grain blights: the following are his common proportions to the acre:

Wheat, from two bushels to two bushels and one peck, and to two bushels and one half; barley, three bushels; oats, four bushels; rye, two bushels and one half for a crop; beans, two to three bushels; pease, three bushels ; tares, two bushels and one peck ; clover, ten to twelve pounds; turnips, two pounds.

I shall not take up more of your time, than to assure you that I am,

Sir, your most humble Servant,

Ralph Robinson.

Another letter follows, dated March 5.

It is well known, of course, how much the king's feelings were engaged in the prosecution of the American war, and how much mortification and anguish the recognition of the United States cost him. His manly and cordial reception of the first minister sent to England has a curious parallel in his equally generous declaration to Mr. Fox when he was obliged to receivehim as his adviser. In both instances he was loyal and true to the professions he made. Mr. Adams' simple, naturally told account of his first audience will be welcome to the reader, as well from its doing honour to the behaviour of the king as for its amusing touches of republican enjoyment in the state and honours of reception.

Bath Hotel, Westminster, June 9, 1783. Deae Sir, .

At one, on Wednesday, the 1st of June, the master of ceremonies called at my house, and went with me to the secretary of state's office, in Cleveland Row, where the Marquis of Carmarthen received me, and introduced me to Mr. Frazier, his under-secretary, who had been, as his lordship said, uninterruptedly in that office, through all the changes in administration, for thirty years, having first been appointed by the Earl of Holderness. After a short conversation upon the subject of importing my effects from Holland and France, free of duty, which Mr. Frazier himself introduced, Lord Carmarthen invited me to go with him in his coach to Court. When we arrived in the antechamber, the *CEil de Beuf* of St. James's, the master of the ceremonies met me, and attended me while the secretary of state went to take the commands of the king. Some gentlemen whom I had seen before came to make their compliments too ; until the Marquis of Carmarthen returned, and desired me to go with him to his majesty. I went with his lordship through the levee room into the king's closet; the door was shut, and I was left with his majesty and the secretary of state alone. I made the three reverenceslone at the door, another

about half way, and the third before the presence, according to the usage established at this and all the northern Courts of Europe, and then addressed myself to his majesty in the following words :

" Sir,|The United States of America have appointed me their minister plenipotentiary to your majesty, and have directed me to deliver to your majesty this letter, which contains the evidence of it. It is in obedience to their express commands that I have the honour to assure your majesty of their unanimous disposition and desire to cultivate the most friendly and liberal intercourse between your majesty's subjects and their citizens, and of their best wishes for your majesty's health and happiness and for that of your royal family.

" The appointment of a minister from the United States to your majesty's Court will form an epoch in the history of England and America. I think myself more fortunate than all my fellow citizens in having the distinguished honour to be the first to stand in your majesty's royal presence in a diplomatic character; and I shall esteem myself the happiest of men if I can be instrumental in recommending my country more and more to your majesty's royal benevolence, and of restoring an entire esteem, confidence, and affection, or, in better words, ' the old good nature, and the old good humour,' between people who, though separated by an ocean, and under different governments, have the same language, a similar religion, a kindred blood. I beg your majesty's permission to add, that although I have sometimes before been entrusted by my country, it was never in my whole life in a manner so agreeable to myself."

YOU I. E

The king listened to every word I said with dignity, it is true, but with an apparent emotion. Whether it was the nature of the interview or whether it was my visible agitation, for I felt more than I did or could express, that touched me, I cannot say; but he was much affected, and answered me with more tremor than I had spoken with, and said: " Sir, the circumstances of this audience are so extraordinary, the language you have now held is so extremely proper, and the feelings you have discovered so justly adapted to the occasion, that I must say that I not only receive with pleasure the assurance of the friendly disposition of the United States, but that I am very glad the choice has fallen upon you to be their minister. I wish you, sir, to believe, that it may be understood in America, that I have done nothing in the late contest but what I thought myself indispensably bound to do, by the duty which I owed to my people. I will be very frank with you. I was the last to conform to the separation; but the separation having been made, and having become inevitable, I have always said, as I say now, that I would be the first to meet the friendship of the United States as an independent Power. The moment I see such sentiment and language as yours prevail, and a disposition to give this country the preference, that moment I shall say, let the circumstances of language, religion, and blood have their natural and full effect."

I dare not say that these were the king's precise words, and it is even possible that I may have in some particular mistaken his meaning; for although his pronunciation is as distinct as I ever heard, he hesitatedsometimes between his periods, and between members of the same period. He was indeed much affected, and I was not less so, and therefore I cannot be certain that I was so attentive, heard so clearly, and understood so perfectly as to be confident of all his words or sense; and I think that all which he said to me should at present be kept secret in America, unless his majesty or his secretary of state should judge proper to report it.

The king then asked me whether I came last from France, and upon my answering in the affirmative, he put on an air of familiarity, and smiling, or rather laughing, said: " There is an opinion among some people that you are not the most attached of all your countrymen to the manners of France." I was surprised at this, because I thought it an indiscretion and a descent from his dignity. I was a little embarrassed, but determined not to deny the truth on one hand nor leave him to infer from it any attachment to England on the other. I threw off as much gravity as I could, and assumed an air of gaiety, and a tone of decision, as far as was decent, and said: " That opinion, sir, is not mistaken; I must avow to your majesty that I have no attachment but to my own country." The king replied as quick as lightning: " An honest man will never have any other."

The king then said a word or two to the secretary of state, which, being then between them, I did not hear, and then turned round and bowed to me, as is customary with all kings and princes when they give the signal to retire. I retreated, stepping backwards, as is the etiquette, and making my last reverence at the door ofthe chamber, I went my way. The master of the ceremonies joined me the moment of my coming out of the king's closet, and accompanied me through all the apartments, down to my carriage, several stages of servants, gentlemen porters, and under porters, roaring out like thunder as I went along: " Mr. Adams' servants! Mr. Adams' carriage !" etc.

With great and sincere esteem I have the honour to be, dear sir, your most obedient and humble servant,

John Adams.

10

SECTION 10

CHAPTER III.

THE NEW QUEEN.

N the young queen first set out on her new course of life, the stiff and gloomy code of the German Courts was enforced in all its severity. Her life was almost cheerless, and a starched etiquette ruled, even to the exclusion of all enjoyments. This discipline had an effect upon her character, and led to that sort of austerity, or absence of feeling, as it was believed to be, which was intensified by family distractions and disorders. Few parents have been so severely tried in this respect as this excellent king and queen, who through their whole lives kept duty before their eyes, and enforced prerogative, both parental and royal, with a sternness which perhaps intensified the disorders it was meant to repress. This German system Iwhich the king enforced thoroughly, though he " gloried in the name of Briton," and professed to be by birth and breeding a genuine English sovereignIwas chiefly accountable for the sufferings caused by his intractable sons; though, it must be said, the princesses, from first to last, from the beginning to the end, were the best of daughters.

11

SECTION 11

How judicious were the king's advice and directions, on her first arriving, may be seen from a letter of the queen's, written to her friend Lady Harcourt more than fifty years later.

" I am most truly sensible of the dear king's great
strictness, at my arrival in England, to prevent my
making many acquaintances; for he always used to say
that, in this country, it was difficult to know how to
draw a line, on account of the politics of the country;
and that there never could be kept up a society without
party, which was always dangerous for any woman to
take part in, but particularly so for the royal family;
and with truth do I assure you, that I am not only
sensible that he was right, but I feel thankful for it
from the bottom of my heart."

Lady Harcourt gives her this character : " Her understanding was of the first class; it was equally quick and solid. She liked wit in others, but checked it in herself. Her mind was highly cultivated, and her memory so retentive that she never forgot what she once knew. She had a talent for conversing, and much sweetness in her manner.

Hated flattery, and despised those who practised it. She was accomplished, and quick to judge."

Lady C. Campbell heard some characteristic tales of the queen and her earlier German manners, which have an air of truth.

" The Duchess of , a great favourite at Court,

besought Queen Charlotte to receive her niece, Mrs. ,

at the drawing-room, there having been reports bruited about which were injurious to that lady's reputation. The duchess implored the queen's clemency and indulgence on a point so wholly without any just foundation; and finally, when about to retire from the royal presence, she asked beseechingly : ' Oh madam ! what shall I say to my poor niece ?' to which Queen Charlotte replied : ' Say you did not dare make such a request to the queen.'

The Duchess of was so hurt by this unfeeling denial

to her entreaties, that she resigned her situation in the royal household.

"There are many other stories likewise told of Queen Charlotte, which do not bespeak much tenderness of heart. When Princess Charlotte was christened, Lady Townsend, who held the royal babe during the ceremony (being herself with child at the time), appeared much fatigued ; and the Princess of Wales whispered to the queen : 'Will your majesty command Lady Townsend to sit down ?' to which the queen replied, blowing her snuff from her fingers : ' She may stand, she may stand.' Again, I have heard that the queen seldom permitted her own children to sit down in her presence; and when she was playing at whist, one of the royal progeny has been known to fall asleep whilst standing behind the queen's chair."

I now begin the series of extracts from the interesting Harcourt Papers privately published by Mr. Harhoult of Nuneham, and which fill six volumes. By his kindness I have been privileged to draw at my discretion on this valuable collection, which, it is not too much to say, is the best testimony extant to the merits of this admirable royal family.

From the queen's letters may be drawn various little sketches showing her power of keen observation, and touched with a graphic power that is very agreeable.

" I have of late seen several ladies just returned from Paris, some very much improved in looks, & others far otherwise. M^{TM} Goldburn is quite Formidable by Three immense Feathers, which so directly run into my Eyes when she was presented, I was under the necessity of drawing myself back in order to avoid Mischief, & I rejoiced a little in lady Claremont's distress who presented Her. . . . Now let us *Compare Notes*. You talk of Loquacity as an Evil. I, on the Contrary, of *Taciturnity* as a drudgery; for the words of *Yes* & *No* is what I experience dayly; & if it goes a little further, I have the History & distresses of the Betties, Harries, &c. &c. &c. of the Families. Some People attribute it to shyness; & poor me attributes it to

S ss, & think myself quite a Phylosopher to bear it

with Patience; but as Necessity has no Law, I do not look upon this as a particular merit, for I am *Philosophe Malgre moi;* & you may apply our stile of Life to this :

' They *Eat,* they *Drank,* they *Slept,* What then?

They *Slept,* they *Eat,* they *Drank* again.'

" Yet after I have said this, tho' we are not *la Bande joyeuse,* we are *la Bande Contente, et c'est beau coup dire en pen de mots. . . .*

" Charlotte."

THE KINO TO LORD HARCOURT.

London, March 30th, 1796. My Lord,

It would be the truest mark of ignorance, were I to omit transmitting to so true a lover of works of artthe invaluable relics of antiquity which were left to me by such an acknowledged Virtuoso as Mr Sebastian Periwinkle, in Haverfordwest in Pembrokeshire, to whom they had been bequeathed by Mr Peregrine Pilkington, who had purchased them of a descendant of the Great Sir Walter Rawleigh, who is supposed to have collected them during his famous Sea Voyage. The only reward I can possibly expect from your Lordship is, that they may find a retreat in the magnificent museum I understand your Lordship is about to erect.

I have the honour to remain,

Your lordship's most humble and obedient Servant,

Timothy Trenchakd.

It will be a surprise to find that his majesty could indulge, with these favoured friends, in a sort of jesting that partook of the practical joke, somewhat laboured, it must be confessed, but showing an agreeable condescension. Rallying Lord Harcourt on his taste for antiquities, he assumed this character of " Timothy Trenchard," and again wrote to him, selecting the appropriate " 1st of April " for his jest:

My Lord,

By the advice of Timothy Trenchard, my Worthy friend & brother Antiquarian, I humbly presume to present your Lordship three most curious remains of antiquity, the one a Lock which would be most suitable for your Lordship's bed chamber or private study, as, if any one should get a false key, they could not use it if your Lordship should be within hearing, without being discovered.

I will not take up more of your time by explaining the particular merits of the two others, but subscribe

myself

Your Lordship's,

Marmaduke Spoonek.

The queen, too, would condescend to rhyme a little to show her affection for her friends at Nuneham.

" Left by Queen Charlotte on Earl Harcourt's table at Windsor, with a pair of old-fashioned gold-fringed gloves, 1791:

"Go, happy Gloves, bedeck Earl Harcourt's hand,

And let him know they come from Fairy-land,

Where antient Customs still support their Reignl

To Modernize them all attempts were vain.

' Go,' cries Queen Mab, ' some Noble owner seek,

Who has a proper taste for the Antique.'

" C."

It was the king's custom on an evening to read from his most admired authors to the queen, and in a short time she was not only able to converse fluently, but to write the English language. Another of her compositions was as follows :

Genteel is my Damon, engaging his air,
His face like the morn, is both ruddy and fair,
Soft love sits enthroned in the beam of his eyes,
He's manly, yet tender, he's fond, and yet wise.

He's ever good-humour'd, he's generous and gay,
His presence can always drive sorrow away,
No vanity sways him, no folly is seen,
But open his temper, and noble his mien.

By virtue illumin'd his actions appear,
His passions are calm, and his reason is clear,
An affable sweetness attends on his speech,
He's willing to learn, tho' he's able to teach.

He has promised to love me|his word I'll believe,
For his heart is too honest to let him deceive;
Then blame me, ye fair ones, if justly you can,
Since the picture I've drawn is exactly the man.

The selection of instructors and governesses for their children always exercised the thought of this excellent pair, and it became a matter of the most anxious consideration with them. Few parents in private station could have been so solicitous. Thus in 1792, when the princesses had reached the term of being considered " young ladies," and Lady Charlotte, who had brought them up from childhood, wishing to retire, the queen consulted her confidential friend on the matter.

ON THE CHOICE OF A GOVERNESS.

" Ldy Charlotte Finch finding herself of late very unwell, & feeling Her strength greatly to decrease, has begged leave to be excused giving so close an attendance upon the younger Princesses as she used to. I have ever heard the most Amiable Character of ldy Mary Parker. She is described to me as Cheerfull, sensible, ingenious, possessing many resources in Herself, used to a retired life, and well principled. You yourself have often spoke in Her favour; & should she answer the description, I think my choice in her could not be better.

" The attendance I require (for there are to be two) is that one of them always to attend of an Evening; & when we are not in Town to come by Dinner, to Dine, & stay with them all Day; & when poor dear Gooly isindisposed, to be in readiness to come & attend their lessons, & to watch that they prepare themselves in the afternoon for what is to be done next Day. Never to pass any incivilities or lightness in their behaviour; & to tell me openly & fairly every difficulty they meet with; & when I am not present to speak to Miss Gooly, who as sub-Governess is the only Person im-powered to direct, & who will ever be ready to assist them with Her Advice whenever it is necessary; and who it will be their Interest to Consult, as she hath known them ever since their Birth, & they are much attached to Her. The salary will be the same as that of the Elder Princesses ladies ; & whenever the younger ones appear in public they are of course to attend.

These were delivered by her majesty to the king in the early part of 1763, " in a most elegant valentine worked by her own hands."

" All this I beg my dear lady Harcourt to think over; & when well digested, to sound the Macclesfield Family, whether or not they will agree to lady Mary Parker being one of the ladies about the younger Princesses. I have secured one already & am sure that you will be pleased with my choice; but I do not name Her untill all is settled, in order to prevent disagreeable applications; & I think it right to add, that the lady who I am sure to have, is Married ; & that perhaps the unmarried one may at times be called upon to appear, when an increasing situation of the other prevents Her coming into Public; all this should be said, & be well understood, in order that no doubts and surprizes may arise hereafter, nor the attendance be looked upon as too much ; for I think it much better that both the pleasant & unpleasant side should be seen at once ; a fair statement on my side, makes me also hope that Nothing will be undertaken on the other side, without full consideration ; & here I leave off, my dear ld7 Harcourt, putting it in y Hands, as I am Certain it could not be in better ; the Event of this Commission I shall wait patiently ; & I do insist you will take the time the most convenient for you to execute it. I beg my best Compliments to Lrf Harcourt, & to *V* Vernon, & am

" Yr very affectionate Friend,

" Charlotte. "Windsor, the 20th Nov., 1792."

She added later: " One other thing occurs to me, which it would not be improper to insert in your letter to Lady M.P., that of health. Pray say, as strongly as you can, how necessary it is not to undertake being about Court without having a good share of that blessing; & you ought to know how to state this point, as both of us are acquainted with the inconveniences of the want of it in others."

SKETCH OF MADAME DE GENUS IN 1775.

" She has a pleasing appearance, neither Handsome nor Ugly, a pretty Figure, Her conversation Modest, reflections just, but totally void of all *pretensions* whatever, and what the French would call *(line Figure interessante)*. I saw Her for about an hour, not without great fear to appear before so great a Critick, being very sensible of my own deficiencies in everything ; but must own that I should not have been sorry, after a quarter of an Hour's Conversation, to see more of Her; She has, like every body else, two Characters. I neither *do accuse nor excuse Her,* but I own myself a great admirer of Her Works."

ANOTHER OF MADAME DE STAEL AT RICHMOND.

" Richmond seems to be this Summer a Colony of all Nations, Russians, Prussians, Spaniards, & Swedes, are all settled there. Amongst the latter, I must number Madame de Staehl, who is very much visited & liked by every body. Amongst her particularyties I must not omit to name that she carries a little bit of Stick in Her Hand, which lies by Her at Dinner, & when she speaks she plays with it in Her Hands, as very few people could suppose that a Sensible Woman like herself *pouvoit s'amuser, d'une telle*

Bariole. A lady in the Company, where she saw Her maneuvering with this would-be Fan, was determined to find out the meaning of it, & made acquaintance with the Femme de Chambre, who explained it to be *Necessaire d Madame pour lui fournier des Pensees & des Idees."*

Here are touches that show observation and wit:

" Lady Sidney, as usual, came to Windsor, but is always confined when she is wanted|*the Finger, the Bowels, the Head, & the Stomach,* are warring against one another, & make Her as useless as if she was not here. There is no Scandal; no Marriages to entertain you with. *Oh yes,* there is a Something that will make you happy; for I saw last night *Sir Robert & Lady Wigram,* Father & Mother of 20 Children, all alive ; their ages from 30 *years old to Jive months;* & he hopes to have 4 more to complete the two dozen. What is yr opinion ?

"We have led a dissipated, idle life ever since themonth of August; & by what you have read in the Newspapers, & perhaps heard by report also, gay & Merry. How it was I cannot tell; but amidst all this I found the Principal Person always was left out, *viz., Pleasure,* without whose attendance the attempt of enjoyment upon such occasions is fruitless."

"4 Dec. 1797.

"Well, My dear lady Harcourt, The King of Prussia is dead. Our Black Gowns just on, & our Thanksgiving being fixed before the arrival of the Berlin Post, for the 19th of this month, cannot be deferred, therefore our Sable is to be put by for that Day, & the Windsor Great Uniform both for Gentlemen & Ladies to be worn instead. The latter I have endeavoured to make as cheap as possible, by having a Dark Blue Sattin Fashionable Gown trimmed with Gold Fringe, & a White Crape Petticoat trimmed the same. I am always sorry to put Lri Harcourt out of His way, but this time all of us must submit to Higher Orders. The Sattin is made at Mr Ibbetson's. . . .

" Your ever sincere friend,

" Charlotte."

" My Lord,| .... I wish you would order Mr Cowden to make out an exact account of my travelling Expences the whole year through, *taking ten weeks off,* which I call the Weymouth weeks. I do not mean the expence of my own Horses, but merely the Post Horses, which, as far as I recollect, are 12 in number every time we go to London, Viz.|

" 4 for my Femme de Chambre.
" 4 for the Princesses Servants.
" 2 for the Pages.
" 2 for the under Servants.

"I have calculated myself that it comes to \$23 15s. per week; which I wish would be made in Cowden's account \$24. There may be, independent of what I have named, more Post Horses wanted which I do not know of; & therefore I beg that it may be stated in the fullest manner, & if it be possible to have it ready by Wednesday next at latest."

Here are glimpses of that domestic economy which reigned in the royal household
:

" My Lord,l .... I want you to exert your authority in dismissing my Footman, Oby, the Service as soon as possible, as His unquenchable Thirst ia now become so overpowering, that neither our absence nor presence can subdue it any more. Some messages of consequence being sent by Him to the apothecary's, were found in His Pockets when laying dead Drunk in the street a few days ago, luckily enough by the Duke of Cumberland, who knowing they were for the Family, sent them to Brandi; I do not want him to starve, but I will not have Him do any more Duty. This I hope will be an example to the others; but as I write a Tipling letter, I think it not amiss to mention that Stephenson has appeared twice a little *Bowzy,* the consequence of which was a fall from His Horse yesterday, by which He was very much bruised; & theSurgeon who came to bleed Him at the Duke of Cambridge's House, who very humanely took Him in, declared him to have been at least over dry, if not drunk. A reprimand to Him will be necessary; for should it happen again He must go also. . . .

" Charlotte. "Kew, 8th July, 1803."

VOL. I.

12

SECTION 12

CHAPTER IV.

MBS. DELANY AND MISS BUBNEY.

of the most gratifying proofs of the homely and simple tastes of the royal pair, was their appreciation of such of their subjects whose character had earned for them the respect and homage due to piety and principle. From this class were selected the king and queen's friends ; and, once selected, they continued through life in the warmest and most confidential relations with their royal patrons. Nothing could exceed the hearty affectionate sympathy extended by the king and queen to such persons as the venerable Mrs. Delany, Bishop Hurd, Earl Harcourt, the noble owner of Nune- ham, and others; and this regard was shared in the same cordial fashion by the princesses, on the ground that those whom their parents loved must be worthy objects of their affection.

Nothing is more pleasing or life-like than the sketches that have been preserved of the domestic life of king George and family, and one is struck by the unfailing good-humour and family affection, the goodsense, the patience and allowance, the simple tastes of "Farmer George" and his admirable wife and daughters. Little can be said for the elder sons, who seemed to have distinguished themselves by qualities the reverse of these, and brought disturbance and discord where all would have been peace and order. It is, of course, to Miss Burney that we owe the happiest sketches of their lifeǀexcellent, graphic, full of the art of observation, and of the true knowledge of character ; though coloured by feminine and a restless sense, that she was in a sphere where her talents were thrown away. These records, though often quoted, are not so familiar as one would suppose, from their length and cost; and it may be assumed that the general reading public know little more than that this clever girl was taken into the queen's service, saw much of the " snuffy old Swellenberg," and preserved many pleasant scenes wherein the queen and princesses worked, and the king came in for tea with his "What? what?" So, too, with the distressingly tragic time of the king's madness, the long tragic night when he wandered about restlessly, and found his way to the room where all were watching; the more agreeable sketches of their little progresses to country seats and favourite towns, and their innocent enjoyment of their holidays. It is, indeed, refreshing and pleasing to read the simple delight of the happy parents and the charming princesses, their good-humour, graciousness, and popularity. The affection of the royal family for the worthy Mrs. Delany is well known. She lived in a small house, given her by the king, close to Windsor Castle, where she was regularly visited by their majesties.

This good old lady was eager that her friend, the clever Miss Burney, should be introduced to them.

" We were all," the latter says, " in the middle of the room, and in some confusion, when the door of the drawing-room was again opened, and a large man, in deep mourning, appeared at it, entering and shutting it himself without speaking. A ghost could not more have scared me, when I discovered by its glitter on the black, a star! The general disorder had prevented his being seen, except by myself, who was always on the

watch, till Miss P , turning round, exclaimed, ' The

king ! Aunt, the king !'

" Everyone scampered out of the way, and Mrs. Delany advanced to meet his majesty, who, after quietly looking on till she saw him, approached and inquired how she did.

" I had now retreated to the wall, and purposed gliding softly, though speedily, out of the room; but before I had taken a single step, the king, in a loud whisper to Mrs. Delany, said, ' Is that Miss Burney ?' and on her answering, ' Yes, sir,' he bowed, and with a countenance of the most perfect good-humour, came close up to me.

" A most profound reverence on my part arrested the progress of my intended retreat. ' How long have you been come back, Miss Burney ?' ' Two days, sir.'

" He insisted she should sit down, though he stood himself, and began to give her an account of the Princess Elizabeth, who once again was recovering, and trying, at present, James's powders. She had been blooded, he said, twelve times in this last fortnight, and had lost seventy-five ounces of blood, besides undergoing blistering and other discipline. He spoke of her illness with the strongest emotion, and seemed quite filled with concern for her danger and sufferings.

" Mrs. Delany next inquired for the younger children. They had all, he said, the whooping-cough, and were soon to be removed to Kew.

" ' Not,' added he, ' for any other reason than change of air for themselves; though I am pretty certain I have never had the distemper myself, and the queen thinks she has not had it either; we shall take our chance. When the two eldest had it, I sent them away, and would not see them till it was over; but now there are so many of them that there would be no end to separations, so I let it take its course.'

" Mrs. Delany expressed a good deal of concern at his running this risk, but he laughed at it, and said he was much more afraid of catching the rheumatism, which has been threatening one of his shoulders lately. However, he added, he should hunt the next morning, in defiance of it.

" A good deal of talk then followed about his own health, and the extreme temperance by which he preserved it. The fault of his constitution, he said, was a tendency to excessive fat, which he kept, however, in order by the most vigorous exercise, and the strictest attention to a simple diet.

" When Mrs. Delany was beginning to praise his forbearance, he stopped her.

" ' No, no,' he cried, ' 'tis no virtue; I only prefer eating plain and little, to growing diseased and infirm.'

" During this discourse, I stood quietly in the place where he had first spoken to me.

" When the discourse upon health and strength was over, the king went up to the table, and looked at a book of prints, from Claude Lorraine, which had been brought down for Miss Dewes; but Mrs. Delany, by mistake, told him they were for me. He turned over a leaf or two, and then said: ' Pray, does Miss Burney draw, too ? ' The *too* was pronounced very civilly.

"'I believe not, sir,' answered Mrs. Delany; 'at least, she does not tell.'

" ' Oh I' cried he, laughing, ' that's nothing I She is not apt to tell; she never does tell, you know! Her father told me that himself. He told me the whole history of her " Evelina." And I never shall forget his face when he spoke of his feelings at first taking up the book Ihe looked quite frightened, just as if he was doing it that moment! I never can forget his face while I live !'

" Then coming up close to me, he said:

" ' But what ?Iwhat ?Ihow was it ?'

" ' Sir, ' cried I, not well understanding him.

" ' How came youIhow happened it ?Iwhat ?I what ?'

"' III only wrote, sir, for my own amusementI only in some odd, idle hours.'

" ' But your publishingIyour printingIhow was that ?'

" ' That was only, sirIonly because '

" I hesitated most abominably, not knowing how to tell him a long story, and growing terribly confused at these questionsIbesides, to say the truth, his own ' what ? what ?' so reminded me of those vile ' Probationary Odes,' that, in the midst of all my flutter, I was really hardly able to keep my countenance.

" The *What!* was then repeated with so earnest a look, that, forced to say something, I stammeringly answered:

" ' I thoughtIsirIit would look very well in print!'

" I do really flatter myself this is the silliest speech I ever made I

" While this was talking over, a violent thunder was made at the door. I was almost certain it was the queen. Once more I would have given anything to escape ; but in vain. I had been informed that nobody ever quitted the royal presence, after having been conversed with, till motioned to withdraw.

"Miss P , according to established etiquette on

these occasions, opened the door which she stood next, by putting her hand behind her, and slid out backwards, into the hall, to light the queen in. The door soon opened again, and her majesty entered.

" Immediately seeing the king, she made him a low 'curtsey, and cried :

" ' Oh, your majesty is here !'

"' Yes,' he cried, ' I ran here without speaking to anybody.'

" The queen had been at the Lower Lodge, to see the Princess Elizabeth, as the king had before told us.

" She then hastened up to Mrs. Delany, with both lier hands held out, saying :

" ' My dear Mrs. Delany, how are you ?'

" Instantly after I felt her eye on my face. I believe, too, she curtseyed to me; but though I saw the bend, Iwas too near-sighted to be sure it was intended for me. I immediately dropped a curtsey. She made one to me iii the same moment, and, with a very smiling countenance, came up to me; but she could not speak, for the king went on talking eagerly, and very gaily repeating to her every word I had said during our conversation upon ' Evelina,' its publication, etc. etc.

" Then he told her of Baretti's wager, saying : ' But she heard of a great many conjectures about the author, before it was known, and of Baretti, an admirable thing ! he laid a bet it must be a man, as no woman, he said, could have kept her own counsel!'

" The queen, laughing a little, exclaimed :

" ' Oh, that is quite too bad an affront to us ! Don't you think so ?' addressing herself to me, with great gentleness of voice and manner.

"I assented, and the king continued his relation, which she listened to with a look of some interest.

" The queen, again addressing me, said :

" ' But to betray to a father is no crimeldon't you think so ?'

" I agreed. The king then went on, and when he had finished his narration the queen took her seat. The king, meanwhile, came to me again, and said: ' Are you musical ? ' ' Not a performer, sir.'

" Then, going from me to the queen, he cried : ' She does not play.' I did not hear what the queen answered; she spoke in a low voice, and seemed much out of spirits. They now talked together a little while about the Princess Elizabeth, and the king mentioned having had a very promising account from her physician, Sir George Baker, and the queen soon brightened up. Theking then returned to me, and said : ' Are you sure you never play ? never touch the keys at all?' ' Never to acknowledge it, sir.' ' Oh ! that's it!' cried he; and flying to the queen, cried : ' She does playlbut not to acknowledge it!' I was now in a most horrible panic once more; pushed so very home I could answer no other than I did, for these categorical questions almost constrain categorical answers.

" The eager air with which he returned to me fully explained what was to follow. I hastily, therefore, spoke first, in order to stop him crying : ' I never, sir, played to anybody but myself!lnever !' He still, however, kept me in talk, and still upon music.

"' To me,' said he, ' it appears quite as strange to meet with people who have no ear for music, and cannot distinguish one air from another, as to meet with people who are dumb. Lady Bell Finch once told me that she had heard there was some difference between a psalm, a minuet, and a country dance, but she declared they all sounded alike to her! There arc people who have no eye for difference of colour. The Duke of Marlborough actually cannot tell scarlet from green !' He then told me an anecdote of his mistaking one of those colours for another, which was very laughable, but I do not remember it clearly enough to write it.

"The queen, then, ceasing to address me in particular, began a general sort of conversation, with a spirit and animation that I had not at all expected, and which seemed the result of the great and benevolent pleasure she took in giving entertainment to Mrs. Delany. The subject was the last drawing-room, which she had been in town to keep on Thursday, during the dense fog.

"' I assure you, ma'am,' cried she to Mrs. Delany, ' it was so dark there was no seeing anything, and no knowing anybody. And Lady Harcourt could be of no help to tell me who people were, for when it was light, she can't see; and now it was dark, I could not see myself. So it was in vain for me to go on in that manner without knowing which I had spoken to, and which was waiting for me ; so I said to Lady Harcourt: " We had better stop, and stand quite still, for I don't know anybody, no more than you do. But if we stand still, they will all come up in the end, and we must ask them who they are, and if I have spoken to them yet, or not: for it is very odd to do it, but what else can we manage ?"'

" Her accent is a little foreign, and very prettily so ; and her emphasis has that sort of changeability which gives an interest to everything she utters. But her language is rather peculiar than foreign.

"' Besides,' added she, with a very significant look, 'if we go on here in the dark, maybe I shall push against somebody, or somebody will push against mel which is the more likely to happen !'

" She then gave an account of some circumstances which attended the darkness, in a manner not only extremely lively, but mixed, at times, with an archness and humour that made it very entertaining. She chiefly addressed herself to Mrs. Delany, and to me, certainly, she would not, separately, have been so communicative ; but she contrived, with great delicacy, to include me in the little party, by frequently looking at me, and always with an expression that invited my participation in theconversation. And, indeed, though I did not join in words, I shared very openly in the pleasures of her recital.

" ' Well,' she continued, ' so there was standing by me a man that I could not see in the face ; but I saw the twisting of his bow; and I said to Lady Harcourt, " I am sure that must be nobody but the Duke of Dorset." "Dear," she says, "how can you tell that?" "Only ask," said I; and so it proved he.'

" ' Yes,' cried the king, ' he is pretty well again; he can smile again, now !'

" It seems his features had appeared to be fixed, or stiffened. It is said he has been obliged to hold his hand to his mouth, to hide it, ever since his strokel which he refuses to acknowledge was paralytic.

"The queen looked as if some comic notion had struck her, and, after smiling a little while to herself, said, with a sort of innocent archness, very pleasing :

" ' To be sure, it is very wrong to laugh at such thingslI know that; but yet, I could not help thinking, when his mouth was in that way, that it was very lucky people's happiness did not depend upon his smiles!'

" The queen then good-naturedly asked was she not going to write something more soon, when the king, suddenly coming up to us, inquired what was going forward.

" The queen readily repeated her kind speech. The king eagerly undertook to make my answer for me, crying: ' Oh I but she will write! she only waits for *inclination*lshe told me so.' Then, speaking to me, he said, ' What, is it not so ?'

" I only laughed a little; and he again said to the queen :

" ' She will write! She told me just now she had made no vow against it.'

" ' No, no,' cried the queen, ' I hope not indeed !'

"They afterwards spoke of Mr. Webb, a Windsor musician, who is master to the young princesses, and who has a nose, from some strange calamity, of so enormous a size that it covers all the middle of his face. I never saw so frightful a deformity. Mrs. Delany told the queen I had met with him, accidentally, when he

came to give a lesson to Miss P , and had been

quite startled by him.

"' I dare say so, ' said her majesty. ' I must tell Miss Burney a little trait of Sophia, about Mr. Webb.'

"A small table was before the queen, who always has it brought when she is seated, to put her tea or work upon, or, when she has neither, to look comfortable, I believe; for certainly it takes off much formality in a standing circle. And close to this, by the gracious motion of her head, she kept me.

"' When first,' continued she, ' Mr. Webb was to come to Sophia, I told her he had had some accident to disfigure his whole face, by making him an enormous nose; but I desired her to remember this was a misfortune, for which he ought to be pitied, and that she must be sure not to laugh at it, nor stare at it. And she minded this very well, and behaved always very properly. But, while Lady Cremorne was at the Lodge, she was with Sophia when Mr. Webb came to give her a lesson. As soon as he was named she coloured very red, and ran up to Lady Cremorne and said to her in awhisper: " Lady Cremorne, Mr. Webb has got a very great nose, but that is only to be pitiedlso mind you don't laugh I"'

" This little princess is just nine years old !

"The king joined us while the queen was telling this, and added: ' Poor Mr. Webb was very much discountenanced when he first saw me, and tried to hide his nose, by a great nosegay, or, I believe, only a branch, which he held before it; but really that had so odd a look that it was worse and more ridiculous than his nose. However, I hope he does not mind me, now, for I have seen him four or five times.'

" The king, then, looking at his watch, said : ' It is eight o'clock, and if we don't go now the children will be sent to the other house.'

"'Yes, your majesty,' cried the queen, instantly rising. N

" Mrs. Delany put on her majesty's cloak, and she took a very kind leave of her. She then curtseyed separately to us all, and the king handed her to the carriage. It is the custom for everybody they speak to to attend them out, but they would not suffer Mrs.

Delany to move. Miss P , Mr. Dewes, and his

little daughter, and myself, all accompanied them, and saw them in their coach, and received their last gracious nods.

" The queen, indeed, is a most charming woman. She appears to me full of sense and graciousness, mingled with delicacy of mind and liveliness of temper. She speaks English almost perfectly well, with great choice and copiousness of language, though now and then with foreign idiom, and frequently with a foreignaccent. Her manners have an easy dignity, with a most engaging simplicity, and she has all that fine high breeding which the mind, not the station, gives, of carefully avoiding to distress those who converse -with her, or studiously removing the embarrassment she cannot prevent.

" Their behaviour to each other speaks the most cordial confidence and happiness. The king seems to admire as much as he enjoys her conversation, and to covet her participation in everything he either sees or hears. The queen appears to feel the most grateful regard for him, and to make it her chief study to raise his consequence with others, by always marking that she considers herself, though queen to the nation, only, to him, the first and most obedient of subjects. Indeed, in their different ways, and allowing for the difference of their characters, they left me equally charmed both with their behaviour to each other and to myself."

It may be affirmed that the sketches of this scene and the touches of character are in the best style of comedy, and show dramatic power of a high order. The figure of the king is admirably drawn.

Miss Burney had made so good an impression that, on a vacancy, she was chosen to be one of the queen's ladies, or attendants. It is unfortunate that this clever and agreeable person should have not reconciled herself to the situation she had accepted, and should have all the time appeared to nourish grievances, suggesting that she was oppressed, overpowered by the duties of her service. Nothing could be more unfounded. Her labours were nothing in comparison with those of her royal mistress. The truth was she pined for admiration,flattery, and flirtation, which she had no opportunity of receiving in the sober discipline of the palace, where nearly all were married. Her airs and humours were good-naturedly borne with, as well as her infringements of etiquette. At last she foolishly withdrew, and lost what might have been valuable prospects, finally improvi- dently marrying a French *emigr$*. It was melancholy to note how her style seemed to decay with her situation, and the incisive powers of observation and clearness of touch in drawing gave place to the amazing bombast and rhapsody that is to be found in the memoirs of her father.

The queen's birthday was the occasion of the display of more of her amiable disposition. Miss Burney's sketch of the proceedings on this interesting occasion will be welcome:

" I was quite new dressed; for I find that, on the king's birthday and on the queen's, both real and nominal, two new attires, one half, the other full dressed, are expected from all attendants that come into the royal presence.

" This first labour was happily achieved in such good time, that I was just seated to my breakfastla delicate bit of roll, half-eaten, and a promising dish of tea, well stirredlwhen I received my summons to attend the queen.

"She was only with her wardrobe-woman, and accepted most graciously a little murmuring congratulation upon the day, which I ventured to whisper while she looked another way. Fortunately for me, she is always quick in conceiving what is meant, and never wastes time in demanding what is said. She told meshe had bespoke Miss Planta to attend at the grand toilette at St. James's, as she saw my strength still diminished by my late illness. Indeed, it still is, though in all other respects I am perfectly well.

" The queen wore a very beautiful dress, of a new manufacture, of worked muslin, thin, fine, and clear as the Chambery gauze. I attended her from the Blue Closet, in which she dresses, through the rooms that lead to the breakfast apartment. In one of these, while she stopped for her hair-dresser to finish her head-dress, the king joined her. She spoke to him in German, and he kissed her hand. The three elder princesses came in soon after; they all went up, with congratulatory smiles and curtseys to their royal father, who kissed them very affectionately; they then, as usual every morning, kissed the queen's hand. The door was thrown open to the breakfast-room, which is a noble apartment, fitted up with some of Vandyke's best works; and the instant the king, who led the way, entered, I was surprised by a sudden sound of music, and found that a band of musicians were stationed there to welcome him. The princesses followed, but Princess Elizabeth turned round to me to say she could hardly bear the sound. It was the first morning of her coming down to breakfast for many months, as she has had that repast in her own room ever since her dangerous illness. It overcame her, she said, more than the dressing, more than the early rising, more than the whole of the hurry and fatigue of all the rest of a public birthday. She loves the king most tenderly ; and there is something in receiving any person who is loved, by sudden music, that I can easily conceive to be very trying to the nerves.

" Princess Augusta came back to cheer and counsel her. She begged her to look out at the -window, to divert her thoughts, and said she would place her where the sound might be less affecting to her. A lively ' How d'ye do, Miss Burney ? I hope you are quite well now ?' from the sweet Princess Mary, who was entering the ante-room, made me turn from her two charming sisters. She passed on to the breakfast, soon followed by Princess Sophia, and then a train of their governesses, Miss Goldsworthy, Mademoiselle Mont- moulin, and Miss Gomme, all in full dress, with fans. We reciprocated little civilities, and I had then the pleasure to see little Princess Amelia, with Mrs. Cheveley, who brought up the rear. Never, in tale or fable, were there six sister princesses more lovely. As I had been extremely distressed upon the queen's birthday, in January, where to go or how to act, and could obtain no information from my coadjutrix, I now resolved to ask for directions from the queen herself; and she readily gave them, in a manner to make this gala-day far more comfortable to me than the last. She bade me dress as fast as I could, and go to St. James's by eleven o'clock; but first come into the room to her. Then followed my grand toilette. The hairdresser was waiting for me, and he went to work first, and I second, with all our might and main. When my adorning tasks were accomplished, I went to the Blue Closet. No one was there.

"The queen was seated at a glass, and the hairdresser was putting in her jewels, while a clergyman in his canonicals was standing near, and talking to her.

" I imagined him some bishop unknown to me, and

VOL. L O

13

SECTION 13

stopped; the queen looked round, and called out, ' Oh, it's Miss Burney ! come in, Miss Burney.' In I came, curtseying respectfully to a bow from the canonicals ; but I found not out, till he answered something said by the queen, that it was no other than Mr. Turbulent. Madame la Fite then presented herself at the door (which was open for air) of the ante-room. The queen bowed to her, and said she would see her presently : she retired, and her majesty, in a significant low voice, said to me, ' Do go to her, and keep her there a little !' I obeyed, and being now in no fright nor hurry, entered into conversation with her sociably and comfortably. I then went to St. James's. The queen was most brilliant in attire; and when she was arrayed, Mr. West was allowed to enter the dressing-room, in order to give his opinion of the disposition of her jewels, which indeed were arranged with great taste and effect. The three princesses, Princess Royal, Augusta, and Elizabeth, were all very splendidly decorated, and looked beautiful. They are indeed uncommonly handsome, each in their different way|the Princess Royal for figure, the Princess Augusta for countenance, and the Princess Elizabeth for face."

The unvarying courage shown by the king in many a dangerous crisis, when his life was attempted, or he was actually assaulted in the streets, was truly remarkable. In the year 1795, when revolutionary doctrines were openly preached in London, the Corresponding Society held vast meetings of 40,000 persons, at one of which invitations were thrown out to wait on his majesty as he went to the House of Lords. Gangs of ruffians accordingly swarmed on his carriage, throwingstones. These things seem inconceivable to us. Scarcely twenty years later the queen, grown old and feeble and near her death, was assailed in the streets in the same way. At one time the mob rushed on the carriage and strove to burst open the door, when he was rescued by Mr. Bedingfield, who rushed for the Life Guards. Lord Onslow, who was in the carriage with the king, gave this account of the scene in a private letter :

" Soon after two this day, his majesty, attended by the Earl of Westmoreland and myself, set out from St. James's in his state-coach, to open the session of parliament. The multitude of people in the Park was prodigious. A sullen silence, I observed to myself, prevailed through the whole, very few individuals excepted. No hats, or at least very few, were pulled off; little or no huzzaing, and frequently a cry of ' Give us bread !'I' No war !' and once or twice, ' No king!' with hissing and groaning. My grandson Cranley, who was upon the king's guard, had told me, just before we set out from St. James's, that the Park was full of people, who seemed discontented and tumultuous, and that he apprehended insult would be offered to the king. Nothing material however happened, till we got to the narrowest part of the street called St. Margaret's, between the two Palace-, yards, when, the moment we had passed the Office of Ordnance, and were just opposite the parlour window of the house adjoining it, a small ball, either of lead or marble, passed through the window glass on the king's right hand, and perforated it, leaving a small hole, the bigness of the top of my little finger (which I instantly put through it, to mark the size), and passed throughthe coach out of the other door, the glass of which was down. "VVe all instantly exclaimed, 'This is a shot!' The king shewed, and I am persuaded felt, no alarm ; much less did he fear, to which indeed he is insensible. We proceeded to the House of Lords, when, on getting out of the coach, I first, and the king immediately afterwards, said to the Lord Chancellor, who was in waiting at the bottom of the stairs robed, ' My Lord, we have been shot at;' and then, perfectly free from the smallest agitation, read his speech with peculiar correctness, and even less hesitation than usual. At his unrobing afterwards, when the event got more known (I have told it to the Duke of York's ear as I passed him and the throne, and to others who stood near us), it was, as might be supposed, the only topic of conversation, in which the king joined with much less agitation than anybody else. And afterwards, on getting into the coach, the first words he said were, ' Well, my Lords, one person is *proposing* this, and another is *supposing* that, forgetting that there is One above us all, who *disposes* of everything, and on whom alone we depend.' The magnanimity, piety, and good sense of this struck me most forcibly, and I shall never forget the words."

After such scenes the king would courageously go to the theatre to show himself in public, and would invariably hurry off to his family to tell the adventure in a gay, unconcerned manner, so that they should think as lightly of it as possible. The king being anxious to reward Mr. Bedingfield, sent him to Mr. Dundas with a request for some appointment. " On the gentleman being asked by Mr. Dundas what he could do for him, he answered, with characteristic humour,' The best thing, sir, you can do for me, is to make me a Scotchman;' a witty but unfortunate allusion, which so much offended Mr. Dundas, that he dismissed the gentleman as he came. The king repeatedly inquired of Mr. Duudas what he had done for the brave gentleman, and always receiving for answer, that no vacant situation had turned up, his majesty said at length very tartly, 'Then, sir, you must make a situation for him.' In fact, the minister did as desired, and a new office was created in favour of the king's deliverer, with a salary of $650 per annum."

The behaviour of the king on the attempt of Margaret Nicholson on his life was no less admirable for its unaffected courage.

"Mrs. Goldsworthy had taken every possible precaution so to tell the matter to the Princess Elizabeth as least to alarm her; lest it might occasion a return of her spasms; but, fortunately, she cried so exceedingly that it was hoped the vent of her tears would save her from those terrible convulsions. No information arrived here of the matter before his majesty's return, at the usual hour in the afternoon, from the leve.e. The Spanish minister had hurried off instantly to Windsor, and was in waiting, at Lady Charlotte Finch's, to be ready to assure her majesty of the king's safety, in case any report anticipated his return. The queen had the two eldest princesses, the Duchess of Ancaster, and Lady Charlotte Bertie with her when the king came in. He hastened up to her, with a countenance of striking vivacity, and said, ' Here I am Ilsafe and welllas you see !lbut I have very narrowly escaped being stabbed !' His own conscious safety, and the pleasure he felt inthus personally showing it to the queen, made him not aware of the effect of so abrupt a communication. The queen was seized with a consternation that at first almost stupefied her, and, after a most painful silence, the first words she could articulate were, in looking round at the duchess and Lady Charlotte, who had both burst into tearsl' I envy you !lI can't cry !'

"The two princesses were for a little while in the same state; but the tears of the duchess proved infectious, and they then wept even with violence.

"The king, with the gayest good humour, did his utmost to comfort them; and then gave a relation of the affair, with a calmness and unconcern that, had any one but himself been his hero, would have been regarded as totally unfeeling. You may have heard it wrong ; I will concisely tell it right. His carriage had just stopped at the garden-door at St. James's, and he had just alighted from it, when a decently-dressed woman, who had been waiting for him some time, approached him with a petition. It was rolled up, and had the usual superscription : ' For the King's Most Excellent Majesty.' She presented it with her right hand; and, at the same moment that the king bent forward to take it, she drew irom it, with her left hand, a knife, with which she aimed straight at his heart! The fortunate awkwardness of taking the instrument with the left hand made her design perceived before it could be executed; the king started back, scarce believing the testimony of his own eyes; and the woman made a second thrust, which just touched his waistcoat before he had time to prevent her; and at that moment one " the attendants, seeing her horrible intent, wrenchedthe knife from her hand. ' Has she cut my waistcoat ? ' cried he in telling itl' Look ! for I have had no time to examine.' Thank heaven, however, the poor wretch had not gone quite so far. ' Though nothing,' added the king, in giving his relation, 'could have been sooner done, for there was nothing for her to go through but a thin linen and fat.' While the guards and his own people now surrounded the king, the assassin was seized by the populace, who were tearing her away, no doubt to fall the instant sacrifice of her murtherous purpose, when the king, the only calm and moderate person then present, called aloud to the mob : ' The poor creature is mad ! Do not hurt her ! She has not hurt me!'

" He then came forward, and showed himself to all the people, declaring he was perfectly safe and unhurt; and then gave positive orders that the woman should be taken care of, and went into the palace, and had his leve'c.

" There is something in the whole of his behaviour upon this occasion that strikes me as proof indisputable of a true and noble courage : for in a moment so extraordinary|an attack, in this country, unheard of before |to settle so instantly that it was the effect of insanity, to feel no apprehension of private plot or latent conspiracy|to stay out, fearlessly, among his people, and so benevolently to see himself to the safety of one who had raised her arm against his life|these little traits, all impulsive, and therefore to be trusted, have given me an impression of respect and reverence that I can never forget, and never think of but with fresh admiration.

" Nor did he rest here ; notwithstanding the excess of terror for his safety, and doubt of further mischief, with which all his family and all his household were seized, he still maintained the most cheerful composure, and insisted upon walking on the terrace, with no other attendant than his single equerry. The poor queen went with him, pale and silent|the princesses followed, scarce yet commanding their tears. In the evening, just as usual, the king had his concert; but it was an evening of grief and horror to his family ; nothing was listened to, scarce a word was spoken ; the princesses wept continually; the queen, still more deeply struck, could only, from time to time, hold out her hand to the king, and say ' I have you yet!'

" The affection for the king felt by all his household has been at once pleasant and affecting to me to observe: there has not been a dry eye in either of the lodges, on the recital of his danger, and not a face but his own that has not worn marks of care ever since."

Being fairly established, she noted in her wonderful and always entertaining diary, the capital characters she encountered. Here, indeed, is the merit of her work, in contrast to the many records of Courts kept by the French, where they record incidents and conversations, but have not nearly the same feeling for character: witness that capital figure, La Giffardiere, the gallant French clergyman, who is worthy of a comedy.

" Monday, August 7th, 1786.

"This has been the first cheerful day since the memorable and alarming attack of the 2nd of August.

14

SECTION 14

It was the birthday of the little Princess Amelia ; and the fondness of the whole family for that lovely child, and her own infantine enjoyment of the honours paid her, have revived the spirits of the whole house. The manner of keeping the birthdays here is very simple. All the royal family are new-dressed; solat least so they appearlare all their attendants. The dinners and desserts are unusually sumptuous; and some of the principal officers of state, and a few of the ladies of the Court, come to Windsor to make their compliments ; and at night there is a finer concert, by an addition from town of the musicians belonging to the queen's band. If the weather is fine, all the family walk upon the terrace, which is crowded with people of distinction, who take that mode of showing respect, to avoid the trouble and fatigue of attending at the following drawing-room.

" Another method, too, which is taken to express joy and attachment upon these occasions, is by going to the eight o'clock prayers at the Royal Chapel. The congregation all assemble, after the service, in the opening at the foot of the great stairs which the royal family descend from their gallery; and there those who have any pretensions to notice scarce ever fail to meet with it. " To-day, the staircase drawing-room, as it is named by Major Price, was very much crowded ; and it was a sweet sight to me, from my windows, to see that the royal grouplrespectfully followed by many people of distinction, who came on the occasion, and, at a still greater distance, encircled by humbler, but not less loyal congratulators|had their chief attention upon my dear, aged, venerable Mrs. Delany, who was brought in bythe king and queen, to partake with them the birthday breakfast.

" It was really a mighty procession. The little princess, just turned of three years old, in a robe-coat covered with fine muslin, a dressed close cap, white gloves, and a fan, walked on alone and first, highly delighted in the parade, and turning from side to side to see everybody as she passed: for all terracers stand up against the walls to make a clear passage for the royal family the moment they come in sight. Then followed the king and queen, no less delighted themselves with the joy of their little darling. The Princess Royal, leaning on Lady Elizabeth Waldegrave, followed at a little distance. This princess, the second female in the kingdom, shows, I think, more marked respect and humility towards the king and queen than any of the family. Next the Princess Augusta, holding by the Duchess of Ancaster; and next the Princess Elizabeth, holding by Lady Charlotte Bertie. Office here takes place of rank, which occasioned Lady Elizabeth Waldegrave, as lady of her bedchamber, to walk with the Princess Royal. Then followed the Princess Mary with Miss Goldsworthy, and the Princess Sophia with Mademoiselle Monmoulin and Miss Planta; then General Bude' and the Duke of Montagu; and, lastly, Major Price, who, as equerry, always brings up the rear, while at a distance from the group, and keeps off all crowd from the royal family.

" On sight of Mrs. Delany the king instantly stopped to speak to her. The queen, of course, and the little princess, and all the rest, stood still in their ranks. They talked a good while with the sweet old lady,during which time the king once or twice addressed himself to me. I caught the queen's eye, and saw in it a little surprise, but by no means any displeasure, to see me one of the party. The little princess went up to Mrs. Delany, of whom she is very fond, and behaved like an angel to her; she then, with a look of inquiry and recollection, slowly, of her own accord, came behind Mrs. Delany to look at me. ' I am afraid,' said I in a whisper, and stooping down, ' your royal highness does not remember me ? '

" What think you was her answer ? An arch little smile and a nearer approach, with her lips pouted out to kiss me. I could not resist so innocent an invitation ; but the moment I had accepted it, I was half afraid it might seem, in so public a place, an improper liberty; however, there was no help for it. She then took my fan, and having looked at it on both sides, gravely returned it me, saying, ' Oh, a brown fan !'

" The king and queen then bid her curtsey to Mrs. Delany, which she did most gracefully, and they all moved on; each of the princesses speaking to Mrs. Delany as they passed, and condescending to curtsey to her companion."

This charming and brilliantly-touched scene might furnish a good subject for a painter like Marcus Stone or Mr. Frith. It is full of warmth and heart, and the whole ceremonial was, no doubt, drawn from the German Courts. It certainly lends to Windsor and Weymouth a pleasingly simple and pastoral air.

15

SECTION 15

CHAPTER V.

VISITS TO NUNEHAM.

In nothing is the excellence, the simple domestic taste, of the royal family better shown than in its relations with the Harcourts of Nuneham, who for a long course of years enjoyed the warmest friendship not only of the king and queen but of their children. There is something particularly attractive and engaging in the enthusiastic regard thus exhibited; and which, it may be presumed, is not exhibited to the same extent in the common relations of the Court and its officials. Mr. Edward Harcourt of Nuneham has for some years been furnishing from his family records substantial evidence of these agreeable and interesting revelations, filling many volumes. He has allowed me to make use of these papers, which will have the further purpose of dissipating that conventional and established idea of Queen Charlotte's harsh disposition best summarised in Mr. Massey's history:

" The queen (Charlotte) had none of those en- earing qualities of her sex, which often maintainharmony and happiness in a family. Bred up in the rigid formality of a petty German Court, her manners were cold and punctilious; her understanding was dull, her temper jealous and petulant.

"It is not surprising, therefore, that the younger members of the family longed for the day when they should be emancipated from the sober state and grim decorum of the palace. The princes rushed into the brilliant world of pleasure and excitement which awaited them with headlong impetuosity; but the less fortunate princesses were doomed to repine in their dreary captivity, longing for marriage, as the only event which could release them."

On which Mr. Harcourt observes justly, "that those who may happen to peruse the following extracts, selected from a large collection of Queen Charlotte's letters, will find in them abundant internal evidence that those historians who have saddled upon the queen the responsibility of being the cause of disorders in the conduct of her children, have done so with very slender knowledge of the facts of the case."

Elizabeth Lady Harcourt was a lady of the bedchamber to her majesty, while her husband, George Simon (Lord Harcourt), was in his majesty's service. They were regarded affectionately as friends rather than attendants, and the royal family ever took delight in writing to them, and, above all, in enjoyment of their society both at Court and at Nuneham. These visits took place frequently, and seem to have been considered as perfect galas by the whole of the interesting family. The king enjoyed nothing so much as goii to the houses of a few friends whom he

Mr. Weld's, at Lulworth, and Lord Petre's|who were both ardent Roman Catholics.

Such royal visits were, however, very different from those of our time; and if conducted on the same principle would have had no charm for the excellent and simple " Farmer George" and his family. Now such honours entail a vast expense for the subject, and the occasion usually requires the complete refitting and refurnishing of the family, with a great exhibition of State display, and a certain advertisement. With King George it was the pleasant excursion to a country house, with a few attendants, often with only the notice of a post; the whole giving pleasure to both host and guests, and causing little trouble or inconvenience. The queen, asking her friend to a birthday "in a quiet way," would leave it entirely to her own choice whether she would come on Wednesday or Thursday, " assuring my dear Lady Harcourt sincerely that she can never come too soon for me." Or, as in 1784, she would announce to her on the Wednesday that she was "particularly happy in the King's Commands of acquainting you that we propose Storming your Castle at Newneham, on *Saturday,* the 18th of this month, if perfectly convenient to you & Lord Harcourt; though we shall be a large party, pray don't be alarmed, for we are all *good Friends* & *well wishers* to the Owners of the Castle, but none more Sincerely so than my dear Lady Harcourt's very affectionate friend."

In the following year, when planning another visit, she would write: " and how happy I shall be to see the possessors of Nuneham again." This visit seems

16

SECTION 16

to leave a particularly pleasing impression on the whole family, and it will be interesting to give a little sketch of what took place, given by the amiable Princess Augusta, then seventeen years of age. There is a nature about it and a tone of enjoyment that is perfectly charming. A little morning visit had been originally proposed, the king and his family intending to return in the evening.

"The Journey to Nuneham, Sept., 1785.

" It being settled that We were to go to Nuneham, We set out from Windsor the 12 of this month at 7 in the morning. The King and Mamma went first in their Chaise; my two Sisters (Pss. Royal and Elizabeth) Lady Elizabeth Waldegrave and myself in a Coach followed them ; and my three youngest Brothers (Ernest, Augustus, and Adolphus), with Col. Manners and Mr Hayes, finished our Procession. We changed Horses a little beyond Henley (by-the-bye I must not forget that I eat a Sandwidge a little before eight, however, it was my Sisters' fault, for they order'd that some might be put in the Carriage), and a little past ten We arriv'd at Nuneham.

"We were met at the House door by Lord and *Dear Lady Harcourt,* and General Harcourt, who attended Papa and Mamma upstairs. We then went to Breakfast; a very good one indeed! and I think I was one of them who relished it the most, tho' I had eat a *Sandwidge before with the greatest appetite.* After Breakfast we walked in the

Garden, saw the Church and flower Garden; both total perfections in theirdifferent ways. At our return we saw M^{TM} Harcourt, who had been ill of fever.

" Whilst we were waiting for dinner in the Octagon Room (or my favorite), Lord Harcourt mentioned to the King that he had a Private Key of Christ Church Walk, and that he could see Oxford without the least trouble; and that if his Majesty would make Nuneham his Inn, it would make the owners of it very happy. Papa said, ' Why, Lord Harcourt, it's very tempting;' Mamma, my Brother, Sister, and myself (not by far the least delighted of the family) kept our wishful Eyes upon the King, who fixed his on Mamma; and upon Her saying, ' I will do as you please,' he said, ' Well, with all my Heart let us stay.'

"During all this Conversation I think our Countenances were so *curiously ridiculous,* and I don't doubt that our soliloquy's were as much so, that anybody must have laughed if they had looked on us without knowing why we looked ' so strange, so wondrous strange.' For my part, I know I could not refrain from saying, ' And 0 ye Ministers of Heaven protect me ! for I shall be in despair if we do not stay.' However, I was so Compleatly happy when I found we did not go back till the next day, that My Spirits rose mountains high in half a second.

"' Thanky, my Dr Lady Harcourt, God bless Lord Harcourt, heaven preserve you both ; You are the very best people in the Kingdom after Papa and Mamma:' these were the sayings for the rest of the day. ' Dear Augustus,' (said Ernest), 'think how amazing Good of Lord Harcourt; he has promised me that I shall sleep alone. I have seen my Room, it has a Yellow DamaskBed. I have got a toilette too, with fine Japan boxes on it. Beautiful lady Jersey has that Room when she is here. I suppose it is a great favour to let me have it; I fancy strangers in general are not allowed to sleep in it. . . .'

" ' Say what you please,' (says Augustus,) ' Lord Harcourt has given me a much better Room. I have got a fine view out of the window ; and what signifies a damask Bed when one has not a fine view. Besides, I am next Room to *Co Co;* and I shall knock against the Wall and keep her awake all night.' (Adolphus), 'I suppose you none of you have seen my Room, I have got a Tent Bed in it; I should have you dare speak against a Tent Bed. It puts me in mind already that when I am an Officer, and that I am incamp'd against an Enemy, I shall have One then.' ' Well,' crys Princess Royal, ' Mine is a Charming Room ; The Dear Duchess of Ancaster sleeps in it when she is here; I shall tell her of it when I see her. I am to take Care of Augusta to-night, She sleeps in my dressing Room.'

" ' Your dressing Room, Madam ! Your nonsense,' said I. ' I think it the best Room; for I can see into Dear Lady Harcourt's passage, and maybe I may see her in it to-morrow morning. Lord, how happy I am to get a little look of her whenever I can.'

"So we went on all day long; and I am sure we never shall hear the last of it, it was the most perfect thing that ever was known."

" How happy I am," had written the queen, " to see the possessors of Newneham ; and therefore, madam, you will not doubt my sincerity when I say that the

VOL. I. H

King never would choose anybody who more gladly did convey his intentions than your very affectionate friend, Charlotte."

On her majesty's return she wrote her thanks for " the Numberless Civilities we received during Our Stay at Newneham. Were I to say all I think upon that Subject, my Sincerity perhaps might be suspected, & therefore I will in a very few words only tell you, *that you did contrive to make us all feel happy,* which is a thing but seldom obtained."

A few days later came a more substantial recognition of their kindness, in the shape of promotion of her brother, Mr. Vernon. " The King," she said, " hopes you, dear lady Harcourt, will not Quarrel with Him for giving you a Neighbour at Christ Church by having appointed your Brother, Mr Vernon, a Canon of that Place. I congratulate, & rejoice with you on this event, & am with unalterable affection."

This divine shared in the favour extended to his family, and later became Archbishop of Canterbury.

The feeling of enjoyment had been so keen, that in the following year his majesty wished to repeat his visit, and wrote himself to propose it.

Lord Harcourt,

It would be want of justice to my feelings if, in writing to you, did I not first express my sensibility at the affectionate manner with which you received the account of my Providential escape on Wednesday. I desire both you and Lady Harcourt will not think of coming to St. James's, as the Queen & I propose, if not inconvenient to you, coming on Saturday to Newneham, agreeable to obliging hint before you left Town of wishing we could come this Summer. We mean to bring the three eldest Princesses with us, and stay a couple of days with you. This trouble your very hospitable conduct the last year has drawn upon you, from those who very sincerely regard both you and your excellent Countess.

George E.

THE QUEEN TO LADY HARCOURT.

The 6fch of August, 1786. My Dear Lady Harcourt,

It is His Majesty, not me, who is to give notice to Lord Harcourt, of the arrival of the Bande Joyeuse, and more joyeuse than ever after what has happened. God be praised for preserving the life of the best of Princes & of Men, and I will only add, may He live for ever, Amen. A Thousand thanks for your attention upon this Occasion; I do assure you it is not lost upon us, nor will it be forgotten.

I now come to a point upon which I beg you to answer Sincerely. The D. of Ancaster & Her Daughter are with us, and should it so happen that, as Lady Elizbeth Waldegrave not being here, the Dutchess should go with us, may lady Charlotte come? this is only amongst Ourselves, & I beg you will not take notice of it to them, as perhaps it may still be some other lady, for the Dutchess is not quite welL I also beg to know if my bringing Miss Planta & the Princesses Maid Servant will not be inconvenient; should it be indiscreet, Pray, my dear Madam, say Sincerely yes or no, & you will really oblige me.

I take this opportunity of inclosing a Specimen of my Summer's Work; may I flatter myself that you can find a place for it in your Packets, & that in- examining it closely, you will discover every knot *to* be the Tie of Friendship of your affectionate Friend,

Charlotte.

The young Princess Elizabeth wrote with the same delight after a later visit:

TO LADY HARCOUET.

Windsor, October 3rd, 1792.

.... Anything so disgusting as the breakfast at Woodgate's inn, on the way from Weymouth, I thank God I never saw before, and never wish to see again! bad butter, Tea, Coffee, bread, etc.; nothing to touch but boil'd eggs, which were so hard that I could not eat them. So I returned to the carriage just as I got out, starved. However, having wisely followed Sir Francis Wronghead's ways, & had a large Plumb Cake put up as *Stowage for the Stomach,* I rejoiced much at the thought of seizing this when I got back to the Coach; but the moment I had prepared myself in Battle array, with a knife in my hand to begin the massacre, they told me it was for Mama, so my knife returned innocent to my Pocket.

As I was not allow'd to eat, I determined, like a true woman, to talk. Lord Harcourt & you served as our constant topick; & we all agreed how sorry we were to have quitted you. When the conversation runs on the subject of those one truly loves, all unpleasant remembrances are at an end; so I forgot my hunger,.& you served me as a Breakfast. I was then, you perceive, satisfied, & got through Salisbury, Andover, & Overton vastly well, & very much contented to get to Hartford Bridge, where our diner quite made up for our Breakfast; for I never eat a better anywhere. The Bottle went round as on board our dear Juno; & the first toast was to all our friends we had quitted, and then to the Juno; so that none were forgot: in short, our journey went off as well as possible, & we arrived here at a quarter after six. But you may tell my good friend, Lord Harcourt, that we have not left the noise of Wind at Weymouth, for it has been louder here than I can express. However, I rely upon your dutiful Affection as a Wife, to tell his Lordship this with all proper precaution, for fear that it might hurt him to think that I did not find Windsor *Paradise.* The evening of our arrival a good Dish of Coffee set us up; and we were able to have the Cardigans, Harringtons, & Lord Cathcart, and set down, *come t V ordinaire,* to Cards. PBS Royal (God bless her) went to Bed, though she slept the best part of the time in the Coach, so did my younger Sisters; but Augusta and me, the two *Irons* of the Family, had each our party.
. . . Mama has ordered my younger Sisters to stay at home to-day, they cough so; but otherwise every body is well. We began going to Chaple this morning; it must be wholesome, it is so disagreeable. However, this is a life of trials, God knows it is, so I hope to be rewarded in the next. By-the-bye, I forgot to tell you that I had the unspeakable satisfaction of seeing Her Grace of B n,

The Grace that invited you to visit her when you

17

SECTION 17

began your journey. She was driving her sisters in the open chaise; & made me one of those bewitching Curtsis that have so often attracted the notice of your Lord. Her leg we saw at the back of her Phaeton; & I immediately rejoiced at having met Her, knowing what pleasure it would give Ld Harcourt, who I am always happy to please.
. . .

    Your Affectionate,
    Eliza.
    Windsor, July 7th, 1788.

It is out of my power, after the attention and cordiality I have met with when I visited the possessors of Nuneham, to pass by the gate of that beautiful place without calling to see them. This is therefore a friendly notice to Lord Harcourt, that on Saturday, the Queen and my three eldest daughters will, with me, thank him for some breakfast a little after ten, as by twelve we must continue our journey to Cheltenham. This will enable me to pay due *Respect* to the *Venerable Tapestry,* and just cast an eye on the more beautiful Flower Garden. I hope everything that is proper will be said in my name to the Excellent Countess, and that this season may be the time of Lady Vernon and her Daughter's visit at Nuneham.

    George R.

His majesty, always observant as to matters of etiquette, could be pleasantly sarcastic on the behaviour of certain of his subjects at his Court. He wrote from Cheltenham, July 14, 1788, "It may not be improper, as time is necessary to prepare a Wardrobe for anyWater-drinking Place, that Lord Harcourt should be apprized that on coming on Saturday to Cheltenham no one appeared with a cocked hat but the *modest* Lieut. - General Borough. This has obliged round hats aloue to be worn and the Plain coat; the other is kept for more public occurrences. On communicating this hint, the writer is desired to add that Lady Harcourt is desired, when she comes, to bring Liuncn gowns for the morning, as silk ones are instantly destroyed. This night is the Ball given by the Master of Ceremonies to the company. He thinks it will be very brilliant, and Lord Oxford is arrived, and he means to beg his Lordship to open the Ball; but if he cannot succeed, there is no doubt that Lieut.-General Borough, who dances every night, will make that conspicuous figure, to which the fame of having long been an admirer of the divine Cecilia gives him a just claim."

There is a pleasant gaiety, not to say humour, in these effusions. His majesty enjoyed the beauty of the place like his children, declaring on one occasion that they were " drunk with delight" after their visit.

Miss Burney's account of this visit and the expedition from Nuneham to Oxford is truly vivacious and even picturesque. There is a "cozy" tone over the whole which is very attractive; and, indeed, the whole forms a masterly and lifelike sketch. The figures stand out boldly, and the whole excites our warmest interest. " Their majesties," she says, " went to Nuneham to breakfast. Miss Planta and myself were not to follow till after an early dinner. Princess Elizabeth, in a whisper, after the rest left the rootn, advised me to go and lie down again as soon as they were gone. We setout at three o'clock, and took with us Mrs. Thielky, the queen's wardrobe-woman, and the comfort of my life in the absence of Mrs. Schwellenberg. We arrived at Nuneham at about six o'clock. The house is one of those straggling, half-new, half-old, half-comfortable, and half-forlorn mansions, that are begun in one generation and finished in another. It is very pleasantly situated, and commands, from some points of view, all the towers of Oxford. In going across the park to the entrance we saw not a creature. All were busy, either in attendance upon the royal guests, or in finding hiding-places from whence to peep at them."

Omitting much of Miss Burney's foolish affectations about the way she was treated and her coquetries to the equerries and everyone she met, we pass to one of the best passages in her work, the visit to Oxford. It will be seen what true dignity and perfectly natural enjoyment of the scene the royal party exhibited. " And now for the Oxford expedition. How many carriages there were, and how they were arranged, I observed not sufficiently to recollect; but the party consisted of their majesties, the Princesses Royal, Augusta, and Elizabeth, the Duchess of Ancaster, Lord and Lady Harcourt, Lady Charlotte Bertie, and the two Miss Vernons. These last ladies are daughters of the late Lord Vernon, and sisters of Lady Harcourt. General Harcourt, Colonel Fairly, and Major Price, and Mr. Hagget, with Miss Planta and myself, completed the group. Miss Planta and I, of course, as the only undignified persons, brought up the rear. We were in a chaise of Lord Harcourt's. The roads were lined with decently-dressed people, and the high street was so crowded wewere obliged to drive gently and carefully, to avoid trampling the people to death. Yet their behaviour was perfectly respectful and proper. Nothing could possibly be better conducted than the whole of this expedition.

" We all drove straight to the theatre, in procession. Here, in alighting from the carriages, there was some difficulty, on account of the pressure of the people to see the king and queen, and princesses : however, even then, it was still the genteelest and most decent crowd I ever saw.

"At the outward gate of the theatre, the vice- chancellor, Dr. Chapman, received their majesties. All the professors, doctors, etc. then in Oxford, arrayed in their professional robss, attended him. How I wished my dear father amongst them ! The vice-chancellor then conducted their majesties along the inner court to the door of the theatre, all the rest following; and there, waiting their arrival, stood the Duke and Duchess of Marlborough, the Marquis of Blandford, in a nobleman's Oxford robe, and Lady Caroline and Lady Elizabeth Spencer.

" After they had all paid their duties, a regular procession followed, which I should have thought very pretty, and much have liked to have seen, had I been a mere looker-on; but I was frequently at a loss what to do with myself. The theatre was filled with company, all well-dressed, and arranged in rows around it. The area below them was entirely empty, so that there was not the least confusion. The chancellor's chair, at the head of about a dozen steps, was prepared for the king; and just below him, to his left, a form for the queen and the princesses.

" The king walked foremost from the area, conducted by the University's vice-chancellor. The queen, followed by her own vice-chamberlain. The Princess Royal followed, led by the king's aide-de-camp, General Harcourt; and Princess Augusta, leaning on Major Price. Princess Elizabeth walked alone, no other servant of the king being present, and no rank authorising such a conduct without office.

" We were no sooner arranged, and the door of the theatre shut, than the king, his head covered, sat down ; the queen did the same, and then the three princesses. All the rest, throughout the theatre, stood. The vice- chancellor then made a low obeisance to the king, and producing a written paper, began the Address of the University, to thank his majesty for this second visit, and to congratulate him and the nation on his late escape from assassination. He read it in an audible and distinct voice; and in its conclusion, an address was suddenly made to the queen, expressive of much concern for her late distress, and the highest and most profound veneration for her amiable and exalted character. An address, to me so unexpected, on a subject so recent and of so near concern, in presence of the person preserved, his wife, and his children, was infinitely touching. The queen could scarcely bear it, though she had already, I doubt not, heard it at Nuneham, as these addresses must be first read in private, to have the answers prepared. Nevertheless, this public tribute of loyalty to the king, and of respect to herself, went gratefully to her heart, and filled her eyes with tears|which she would not, however, encourage, but, smiling through them, dispersed them with her fan, with which she was repeatedly obligedto stop their course down her cheeks." (The reader will note what a charming picture of natural feeling is here.)

"The princesses, less guarded, the moment their father's danger was mentioned, wept with but little control; and no wonder, for I question if there was one dry eye in the theatre. The tribute, so just, so honourable, so elegant, paid to the exalted character of the queen, affected everybody with joy for her escape from affliction, and with delight at the reward and the avowal of her virtues.

"When the address was ended, the king took a paper from Lord Harcourt, and read his answer. The king reads admirably|with ease, feeling, and force, and without any hesitation. His voice is particularly full and fine. I was very m,uch surprised by its effect. When he had done he took off his hat, and bowed to the chancellor and professors, and delivered the answer to Lord Harcourt, who, walking backwards, descended the stairs, and presented it to the vice-chancellor. All this ceremony was so perfectly new to me, that I rejoiced extremely in not missing it. Indeed I would not have given up the pleasure of seeing the queen on this occasion for any sort of sight that could have been exhibited to me.

"Next followed music|a good organ, very well played, anthem-ed and voluntary-ed us for some time. After this the vice-chancellors and professors begged for the honour of kissing the king's hand. Lord Harcourt was again the backward messenger. And here followed a great mark of goodness in the king. He saw that nothing less than a thoroughbred old courtier, such as Lord Harcourt, could walk backwards down these|steps before himself and in sight of so full a hall of spectators; and he therefore dispensed with being approached to his seat, and walked down himself into the area, where the vice-chancellor kissed his hand, and was imitated by every professor and doctor in the room.

" Notwithstanding this considerate good-nature in his majesty, the sight, at times, was very ridiculous. Some of the worthy collegiates, unused to such ceremonies and unaccustomed to such a presence, the moment they had kissed the king's hand, turned their backs to him, and walked away as in any common room; others, attempting to do better, did still worse, by tottering and stumbling, and falling foul of those behind them; some, ashamed to kneel, took the king's hand straight up to their mouths; others, equally off their guard, plumped down on both knees, and could hardly get up again ; *and many, in their confusion, fairly arose by pulling his majesty's hand to raise them.*

"As the king spoke to every one, upon Lord Harcourt's presenting them, this ceremonial took up a good deal of time ; but it was too new and diverting to appear long. It was vacation time; there were therefore none of the students present.

" When the whole was over we left the theatre in the same form we had entered.

" I cannot now go on with our progress regularly, for I do not remember it; I will only, therefore, in general, say that I was quite delighted with the City, and so entertained and so pleased with such noble buildings as it presented to me, that I felt, as I have told you, a consciousness to pleasure revived in me|which had long lain nearly dormant. We went to all the colleges in the same order that we came to the theatre. At Christ Church College, where we arrived at about three o'clock, in a large hall there was a cold collation prepared for their majesties and the princesses. It was at the upper end of the hall. I could not see of what it consisted, though it would have been very-agreeable, after so much standing and sauntering, to have given my opinion of it in an experimental way. Their majesties and the princesses sat down to this table|as well satisfied, I believe, as any of their subjects so to do. The Duchess of Ancaster and Lady Harcourt stood behind the chairs of the queen and the Princess Royal. There were no other ladies of sufficient rank to officiate for Princesses Augusta and Elizabeth. Lord Harcourt stood behind the king's chair; and the vice-chancellor, and the head master of Christ Church, with salvers in their hands, stood near the table, and ready to hand to the three noble waiters whatever was wanted : while the other reverend doctors and learned professors stood aloof, equally ready to present to the chancellor and the master whatever they were to forward. "We, meanwhile, untitled attendants, stood at the other end of the room, forming a semicircle, and all strictly facing the royal collationers. We consisted of the Miss Vernons, thrown out here as much as their humble guests|Colonel Fairly, Major Price, General Harcourt, and|though I know not why |Lady Charlotte Bertie ; with all the inferior professors in their gowns, and some, too much frightened to advance, of the upper degrees. These, with Miss Planta, Mr. Hagget, and myself, formed this attendant semi-

circle. The time of this collation was spent very pleasantly|to me, at least, to whom the novelty of the scene rendered it entertaining. It was agreed that we must all be absolutely famished unless we could partake of some refreshment, as we had breakfasted early, and had no chance of dining before six or seven o'clock. A whisper was soon buzzed through the semicircle, of the deplorable state of our appetite apprehensions; and presently it reached the ears of some of the worthy doctors. Immediately a new whisper was circulated, which made its progress with great vivacity, to offer us whatever we would wish, and to beg us to name what we chose. Tea, coffee, and chocolate, were whispered back.

"The method of producing, and the means of swallowing them, were much more difficult to settle than the choice of what was acceptable. Major Price and Colonel Fairly, however, seeing a very large table close to the wainscot behind us, desired our refreshments might be privately conveyed there, behind the semicircle, and that, while all the group backed very near it, one at a time might feed, screened by all the rest from observation.

" This plan had speedy success, and the very good doctors soon, by sly degrees and with watchful caution, covered the whole table with tea, coffee, chocolate cakes, and bread-and-butter.

"The further plan, however, of one at a time feasting and the rest fasting and standing sentinels, was not equally approved ; there was too much eagerness to seize the present moment, and too much fear of a sudden retreat, to give patience for so slow a proceeding. We could do no more, therefore, than stand in a double row, with one to screen one throughout the troop; and, in this manner, we were all very plentifully and very pleasantly served. The Duchess of Ancaster and Lady Harcourt, as soon as the first serving attendance was over, were dismissed from the royal chairs, and most happy to join our group, and partake of our repast. The duchess, extremely fatigued with standing, drew a small body of troops before her, that she might take a few minutes' rest on a form by one of the doors; and Lady Charlotte Bertie did the same, to relieve an ankle which she had unfortunately sprained.

"' Poor Miss Burney !' cried the good-natured duchess, ' I wish she could sit down, for she is unused to this work She does not know yet what it is to stand for five hours following, as we do.'

" The beautiful window of Sir Joshua Reynolds and Mr. Jervis, in New College, would alone have recovered me, had my fatigue been infinitely more serious.

" In one of the colleges I stayed so long in an old chapel, lingering over antique monuments, that all the party were vanished before I missed them, except doctors and professors; for we had a train of those everywhere; and I was then a little surprised by the approach of one of them, saying, 'You seem inclined to abide with us, Miss Burney ? 'land then another, in an accent of facetious gallantry, cried, ' No, no ; don't let us shut up Miss Burney among the old tombs!l No, no!'

" After this many of the good doctors occasionallyspoke to me, when there happened to be opportunity. How often did I wish my dear father amongst them ! They considered me as a doctor's daughter, and were all most excessively courteouslhanding, and pointing, and showing me about as much as possible.

" In another college (we saw so many, and in such quick succession, that I recollect not any by name, though all by situation) I saw a performance of courtly etiquette, by Lady Charlotte Bertie, that seemed to me as difficult as any feat I ever beheld, even at Astley's or Hughes's. It was in an extremely large, long, spacious apartment. The king always led the way out, as well as in, upon all entrances and exits : but here, for some reason that I know not, the queen was handed out first; and the princesses, and the aide-de-camp, and equerry followed. The king was very earnest in conversation with some professor; the attendants hesitated whether to wait or follow the queen ; but presently the Duchess of Ancaster, being near the door, slipped out, and Lady Harcourt after her. The Miss Vernons, who were but a few steps from them, went next. But Lady Charlotte, by chance, happened to be very high up the room, and near to the king. Had I been in her position, I had surely waited till his majesty went first; but that would not, I saw, upon this occasion, have been etiquette. She therefore faced the king and began a march backwardslher ankle already sprained, and to walk forward, and even leaning upon an arm, was painful to her: nevertheless, back she went, perfectly upright, without one stumble, without ever looking once behind to see what she might encounter; and with as graceful a motion, and as easy an air, as I ever saw anybody entera long room, she retreated, I am sure, full twenty yards backwards oat of one."

But for the guests, nothing was more enjoyable, however inconvenient it may have been to their hosts. It was well they did thus enjoy themselves, as the time was now nearly at hand when the season of disastrous troubles and anxieties was to set in, and there was literally to be no more happiness for any of the party.

18

SECTION 18

CHAPTER VI.
 WEYMOUTH.
 The little visits to Weymouth and other places after the king's recovery in 1789, seem more interesting than many a professional tour. It is pleasant to journey along with the royal party. Burney writes :
 " Thursday, June 25th.
 " This morning I was called before five o'clock, though various packages and business had kept me up till near three. The day was rainy, but the road was beautiful; Windsor Great Park, in particular, is charming. The crowds increased as we advanced, and at Winchester the town was *one head. I* saw Dr. Warton, but could not stop the carriage. The king was everywhere received with acclamation. His popularity is greater than ever. Compassion for his late sufferings seems to have endeared him now to all conditions of men.
 "At Romsey, on the steps of the Town Hall, an orchestra was formed, and a band of musicians, in common brown coarse cloth and red neckcloths, andeven in carters' loose gowns, made a chorus of ' God save the King,' in which the countless multitude joined. The New Forest is all beauty, and when we approached Lyndhurst the crowds wore as picturesque an appearance as the landscapes; they were all in decent attire,

and, the great space giving them full room, the cool beauty of the verdure between the groups took away all idea of inconvenience, and made their live gaiety a scene to joy beholders. Carriages of all sorts lined the road-side: chariots, chaises, landaus, carts, waggons, whiskies, gigs, phaetonslmixed and intermixed, filled within and surrounded without by faces all glee and delight. Such was the scenery for miles before we reached Lyndhurst. The old law of the forest, that his majesty must be presented with two milk-white greyhounds, peculiarly decorated, upon his entrance into the New Forest, gathered together multitudes to see the show. A party, also, of foresters, habited in green, and each with a bugle-horn, met his majesty at the same time. Arrived at Lyndhurst, we drove to the Duke of Gloucester's. The royal family were just before us, but the two colonels came and handed us through the crowd.

" The house, intended for a mere hunting-seat, was built by Charles II., and seems quite unimproved and unrepaired from its first foundation. It is the king's, but lent to the Duke of Gloucester. It is a straggling, inconvenient old house, but delightfully situated, in a villagellooking, indeed, at present, like a populous town, from the amazing concourse of people that have crowded into it. The bowmen and archers and bugle- horns are to attend the king while he stays here, in all his rides. The Duke of Gloucester was ready to receivethe royal family, who are all in the highest spirits and delight . I have a small old bedchamber, but a large and commodious parlour, in which the gentlemen join Miss Planta and me to breakfast and to drink tea. They dine at the royal table. We are to remain here some days.

" During the king's dinner, which was in a parlour looking into the garden, he permitted the people to come to the window; and their delight and rapture in seeing their monarch at table, with the evident hungry feeling it occasioned, made a contrast of admiration and deprivation truly comic. They crowded, however, so excessively, that this can be permitted them no more. They broke down all the paling, and much of the hedges, and some of the windows, and all by eagerness and multitude, for they were perfectly civil and well-behaved.

" They all walked out, about and around the village, in the evening, and the delighted mob accompanied them. The moment they stepped out of the house, the people, with one voice, struck up ' God save the King!' I assure you I cried like a child twenty times in the day, at the honest and rapturous effusions of such artless and disinterested loyalty. These good villagers continued singing this royal song during the whole walk, without any intermission, except to shout ' huzza!' at the end of every stanza. They returned so hoarse, that I longed to give them all some lemonade.

" We continued at Lyndhurst five days: and the tranquillity of the life, and the beauty of the country would have made it very regaling to me indeed, but for the fatigue of having no maid, yet being always in readiness to play the part of an attendant myself.

" On the Sunday we all went to the parish church ; and after the service, instead of a psalm, imagine our surprise to hear the whole congregation join in ' God save the King !' Misplaced as this was in a church, its intent was so kind, loyal, and affectionate, that I believe there was not a dry eye amongst either singers or hearers. This day we quitted Lyndhurst; not without regret, for so private is its situation, I could stroll about in its beautiful neighbourhood quite alone.

" The journey to Weymouth was one scene of festivity and rejoicing. The people were everywhere collected, and everywhere delighted. We passed through Salisbury, where a magnificent arch was erected, of festoons of flowers, for the king's carriage to pass under, and mottoed with ' The King restored.'

"At every gentleman's seat which we passed, the owners and their families stood at the gate, and their guests or neighbours were in carriages all round. At Dorchester the crowd seemed still increased. The city had so antique an air, I longed to investigate its old buildings. The houses have the most ancient appearance of any that are inhabited that I have happened to see : and inhabited they were indeed ! every window- sash was removed, for face above face to peep out, and every old balcony and all the leads of the houses seemed turned into booths for fairs. It seems, also, the most populous town I have seen; I judge not by the concourse of the young and middle-aged|those we saw everywhere alike, as they may gather together from all quarters|but from the amazing quantity of indigenous residers|old women and young children. There seemed families of ten or twelve of the latter in every house, and the old women were so numerous that they gave the whole scene the air of a rural masquerade. Girls, with chaplets, beautiful young creatures, strewed the entrance of various villages with flowers.

" Gloucester House, which we now inhabit, at Wey- mouth, is situated in front of the sea, and the sands of the bay before it are perfectly smooth and soft.

" I have here a very good parlour, but dull, from its aspect. Nothing but the sea at Weymouth affords any life or spirit. My bedroom is in the attics. Nothing like living at a Court for exaltation. Yet even with this gratification, which extends to Miss Planta, the house will only hold the females of the party. The two adjoining houses are added, for the gentlemen, and the pages, and some other of the suite, cooks, etc., but the footmen are obliged to lodge still farther off. The bay is very beautiful, after its kind; a peninsula shuts out Portland Island and the broad ocean. The king, and queen, and princesses, and their suite, walked out in the evening; an immense crowd attended them |sailors, bargemen, mechanics, countrymen; and all united in so vociferous a volley of ' God save the King,' that the noise was stunning.

" At near ten o'clock Lord Courtown came into my parlour, as it is called, and said the town was all illuminated, and invited Miss Planta and me to a walk upon the sands. Their majesties were come in to supper. We took a stroll under his escort, and found it singularly beautiful, the night being very fine, and several boats and small vessels lighted up, and in motion upon the sea. The illumination extended through Melcomb Regis and Weymouth. Gloucester Row, in which we live, is properly in Melcomb Regis, but the two towns join each other, and are often confounded.

" The preparations of festive loyalty were universal Not a child could we meet that had not a bandeau round its head, cap, or hat, of 'God save the King;' all the bargemen wore it in cockades, and even the bathing-women had it in large coarse girdles round their waists. It is printed in golden letters upon most of the bathing-machines, and in various scrolls and devices it adorns every shop and almost every house in the two towns.

" The king bathes, and with great success; a machine follows the royal one into the sea, filled with fiddlers, who play 'God save the King,' as his majesty takes his plunge!

" I am delighted with the soft air and soft footing upon the sands, and stroll up and down them morning, noon, and night."

"The bathing-machines" (Miss Burney wrote to her *padre*) " make it their motto over all their windows ; and those bathers that belong to the royal dippers wear it in bandeaux on their bonnets, to go into the sea; and have it again, in large letters, round their waists, to encounter the waves. Flannel dresses, tucked up, and no shoes nor stockings, with bandeaux and girdles, have a most singular appearance ; and when first I surveyed these loyal nymphs, it was with some difficulty I kept my features in order. Nor is this all. Think but ofthe surprise of his majesty, when, the first time of his bathing, he had no sooner popped his royal head under water than a band of music, concealed in a neighbouring machine, struck up ' God save great George our King.'

"One thing, however, was a little unlucky; when the mayor and burgesses came with the address, they requested leave to kiss hands. This was graciously accorded ; but, the mayor advancing in a common way, *to take the queen's hand,* as he might that of any lady mayoress, Colonel Gwynn, who stood by, whispered, ' You must kneel, sir!' He found, however, that he took no notice of this hint, but kissed the queen's hand erect. As he passed him, on his way back, the colonel said, ' You should have knelt, sir!' ' Sir," answered the poor mayor, ' I cannot.' ' Everybody does, sir.' ' Sir|I have a wooden leg !'

" Poor man! 'twas such a surprise! and such an excuse as no one could dispute."

It was when taking this little excursion, or *villeg- giatura,* at this place, that the royal family certainly appeared to most advantage. Their simple relish of a holiday was pleasant to note, and the highest personages of the kingdom showed more delight in a sail in their yacht, or an excursion to see a cathedral, than a citizen would have found in escaping from business.

One of the earliest trips to Weymouth was in 1789, after the king's convalescence, when a change of scene and touring was prescribed.

In order to complete his majesty's recovery, and to remove him from a too close attendance to thoseforms of state to which he was obliged to conform at Windsor, this trip to Weymouth was determined on. ;

"Accordingly, on the 25th of June, at a little after seven o'clock in the morning, their majesties and the Princess Royal, Princess Augusta, and Princess Elizabeth, set out for the Duke of Gloucester's Lodge at Lyndhurst. They were accompanied by Ladies Elizabeth and Caroline Waldegrave, Lord Courtown, General De Bade, Colonels Golds worthy and Gwynn, Misses Burney, Planta, etc. At three o'clock the royal tourists arrived at Lyndhurst, in Hampshire, near which is the manor of Langley, held as a royalty by the feudal tenure of presenting to the king, whenever he shall come within the limits of the New Forest, a brace of white greyhounds, with silver collars, coupled together with a gold chain, and led by a silken string. The lord of the manor, at that period, was Sir Charles Mills, Bart., an elderly clergyman, who, knowing that his majesty intended to stop at his house in the forest, and which had been for years occupied by the late Duke of Gloucester, took care to be prepared for this ceremony, and was in due attendance. Colonel Hayward, as principal bowman of the forest, was in waiting to receive his majesty, attended by all the keepers, in green uniform, laced with gold and ornamented with ribands, inscribed ' God save the

King.' They accordingly met the royal party about four miles from Lyndhurst, and rode with them to the entrance of the king's house, round which was an innumerable crowd, upwards of three miles in extent. On alighting, his royal highness the Duke of Gloucester received theirmajesties, whilst the loyal salutations of the assembled people rent the air.

"After dinner their majesties looked out of the windows, to admire the enchanting prospect, and were instantly hailed by a succession of national songs, in the choruses of which the queen and princesses joined with the utmost good-humour and affability. In the evening, the king, accompanied by her majesty and the princesses, walked round the village, mixing in the simplest manner with the peasantry, and affably noticing all ranks of persons that came in their way during the progress of the ramble.

"On the arrival of the royal travellers at Southampton on the 26th, the king and Duke of Gloucester being on horseback, they proceeded through the town to the audit-house amidst the huzzas of the people, the firing of cannon, the ringing of bells, and other demonstrations of joy. The procession through the town moved very slowly, and many carriages and gentlemen on horseback attended. The royal visitors continued in the audit-house about an hour, and went from thence on foot, accompanied by the corporation in their robes, to the quay and platform, at which place they took their leave, and rode round the beach. They then went up East Street, and stopped about half-an-hour at Colonel Hey wood's, before they set off on their return to Lyndhurst.

"In the evening the whole party walked to an eminence in the forest, called the Duke of Bolton's seat, in order to enjoy the very extensive prospect that may be seen from it. In this route they were attended by a very numerous but respectful body of the tradespeople, who were saved from a complete wetting by his majesty's skill in the weather, for, on asking the name of a distant object, and being told it was Portsdown Hill, the king instantly turning round, and looking at a black cloud, said facetiously, ' And pray, colonel, what prospect is that?|I fancy if we don't get home we shall soon know.' In a moment all was hurry to return, and they were just in time to escape from a summer deluge. The evening was spent in domestic amusements, and in witnessing the sleight- of-hand tricks of the then celebrated Jones, whom his majesty instantly recollected, after an interval of twenty years. On the 27th the king was occupied in the morning in reading despatches from the Duke of Leeds' office.

" Sunday, the 28th, was spent in exercises of devotion, the royal family walking to the church without ostentation, and freely mixing in the assembled crowd. The text chosen by the clergyman, the Rev. Willis Compton on this occasion, was from Colossians iii. 25 : ' Set your affections on things above, and not on things on earth,' after which there was the very novel scene of the whole congregation singing ' God save the King,' accompanied by instrumental music. In the evening the royal party walked through the town, amidst the blessings and salutations of the people, who were now assembled from all parts of the country in the most astonishing multitudes.

" Exactly at four o'clock on the 30th, their majesties, with the royal suite, arrived at Gloucester House. At the turnpike they were met by the corporation, and on their entrance into the town the cannon at PortlandCastle were fired, and immediately answered by the king's ships in the road. The time of his majesty was chiefly occupied at Weymouth, in receiving the formal addresses of the corporation, or the visits of the nobility and gentry of the vicinity, and partly on horseback, rambling over the hills and downs, or walking on the esplanade amidst respectfully joyous groups of his loyal subjects. The Sabbath Day was always passed in the offices of religion, the royal family walking to church without parade or ceremony, the service of the day always ending with ' God save the King.'

"The *Magnificent,* of 74, commanded by Captain Onslow, afterwards Sir Richard Onslow, and the *Southampton* frigate, being appointed to attend upon his majesty during his stay at Weymouth, the latter vessel was chosen by his majesty for his marine excursions, they being considered to be highly beneficial to the complete restoration of his health.

"During the attendance of the men-of-war, the condescending behaviour of the royal party could not fail to make a deep impression on the feelings of the honest seamen ; his majesty often conversed with the humblest sailor in the ship, and he seemed particularly to enjoy their coarse and eccentric manners. So little did their majesties pay in general any attention to present comfort, that on one occasion the whole party returned from their marine trip with a complete ducking, for, although it blew at the time a strong gale with a heavy sea, and the rain was descending in torrents, their majesties would not allow the awning to be spread, but seemed actually to enjoy the scene, and landed in the highest spirits, and laughing at each other's wet jackets.

" During one of these marine trips, his majesty was conversing with Captain Douglas, of the *Southampton,* when the lieutenant of the watch, agreeable to nautical custom, informed the captain, whilst conversing with his majesty, that it was twelve o'clock. ' Make it so, sir, ' replied the captain, meaning thereby to order the bell to be rung for the close of the nautical day, and the commencement of a new one. His majesty appeared much struck with this, and in a very pointed manner said to the captain : ' You, sir, possess more power than I do, I cannot make it what time I please.'

"One morning his majesty was both amused and delighted with a demonstration of simple-hearted loyalty, by the appearance before Gloucester House of two waggons loaded with the peasantry, principally females, who stopped before the house bare-headed, though exposed to a heavy rain, singing ' God save the King,' the close of which was accompanied by three loud huzzas, which were listened to by the royal visitants, who, in the most condescending manner, exhibited themselves to the honest party.

" In one of the king's excursions, during the hay- harvest, in the neighbourhood of Weymouth, he passed a field where only one woman was at work. His majesty asked her where the rest of her companions were. The woman answered, they were gone to see the king. ' And why did you not go with them ?' rejoined his majesty. ' The fools,' replied the woman, ' that are gone to town, will lose a day's work by it, and that is more than I can afford to do. I have five children to work for.' ' Well then,' said his majesty, putting some money into her hands, ' you may tell your companions who aregone to see the king, that the king came to see you.'

" The theatre was now become such a favourite resort of royalty, that the manager found himself enabled, by crowded houses, to engage the first Thespian performers;

accordingly Mrs. Siddons and Quick were both on his list, and added to the attraction of the scene. On the 3rd of August, the whole of the royal party went on board the *Southampton,* and proceeded to Lulworth- cove, from whence they visited Lulworth Castle, the seat of Mr. Weld, brother to Mrs. Fitzherbert, and a Eoman Catholic, where they were received by that gentleman at the vestibule of the venerable castle, eight of his children dressed in uniform being placed on the steps leading up to it."

The queen and princesses were very fond of seabathing, and also sailing about in the yacht, so that excepting during very boisterous or rainy weather they daily indulged in one or even both of those diversions. The royal family were called from their beds every morning at five o'clock, in order that they might be out by six. It will be readily imagined that such early hours at Gloucester House produced equally early movements throughout the population of Weymouth, and the shops were opened very regularly at half-past five o'clock, for by six the streets were thronged with all the fashionables at Court, and also by those who were anxious to be thought so. The great attraction was to see the queen and princesses walking from Gloucester House to their bathing-machines, or to cheer them on their embarkation with the king and a select party, on board of the royal yacht. These water excursionsoccurred generally three or four days in every week. Colonel Landmann, who was much about the Court, and on the Duke of Cumberland's staff, who then commanded in the district, in 1804, describes Weymouth during the time of the invasion panic, when every port was a scene of bustle, martello towers were erecting, and a squadron of some five or six frigates were at anchor in the Weymouth Roads for the protection of the king and royal family.

The German colonel Landmann relates an incident which befell him in Weymouth when the queen had grown old:

"Although I had not been hitherto," he says, "in the constant habit of being out at six o'clock, yet here I immediately fell into a practice so general, and out I went accordingly, with all the fashionables of Weymouth. Thus, on the second morning, after a whole night of heavy rain, I sallied forth to walk on the Esplanade, in the hope of seeing the queen and princesses on their way to bathe. In proceeding along a cross street, my steps were for a few moments arrested to look into the window of a caricature shop, where amongst those prints were several of the royal family, but particularly some of the king, and others of the queen (Charlotte). I had not been standing there many minutes, intermixed with several other persons, when I heard from behind me a voice repeating, ' The queen, the queen.' At this moment, the various clocks beginning to strike six, reminded me that unless I hastened forward I should be too late to see the royal ladies proceeding to their bathing-machines, I immediately began to move on, still, nevertheless, keeping my eyes fixed upon the window in search of the queen. I hadnot, however, taken two steps in that way, without looking before me, when I felt that I had come in contact with a female, whom, to save her and myself from falling, I encircled with my arms; and at the same moment, having observed that the person whom I had so embraced was a little old woman, with a small, black silk bonnet, exactly similar to those now commonly worn by poor and aged females, and the remainder of her person was covered by a short, plain, scarlet cloth cloak, I exclaimed, ' Hallo, old lady, I very nearly had you down.' In an instant I felt her push me from her with energy and indignation, and I was seized by a great number of persons, who grasped me tightly by the arms and shoulders, whilst a tall, stout fellow, in a scarlet livery, stood close before my face, sharply striking the pavement with the heavy ferrule of a long, golden-headed cane, his eyes flashing fire, and loudly repeating, ' The queen-|the queen|the queen, sir !'

" ' Where ?|where ?|where ?' I loudly retorted, greatly perplexed and even irritated, as I anxiously cast an inquisitive look about me, amongst the thirty or forty persons by whom I was surrounded.'

"' I am the queen!' sharply exclaimed the old lady.

" On this discovery I did not totally lose my presence of mind ; for without the delay of a moment I fell on one knee, and seizing the hem of the queen's dress, was about to apply it to my lips, after the German fashion, stammering out at the same time the best apology I was able to put together on so short a notice ; when the queen, although I believe much offended, and certainly not without cause, softened her irritated features, andsaid, as she held out to me the back of her right hand :

" ' No, no, no, you may kiss my hant. We forgiff; you must pee more careful; fery rute|fery rute, inteet; we forgiff; there, you may go.'

" As I withdrew, the mob, which had now greatly augmented, loudly cheered; but I had not gone on many yards before the running footman stopped me to demand my card. I never afterwards heard any allusion to this affair, and I certainly was not disposed to mention it to anyone at Weymouth.

"As the king invariably dined at three o'clock, in order that he might be on the Esplanade at six, in readiness to receive the salutes of the officers as they marched past when mounting picquet, the Duke of Cumberland, and all the military and civil officers immediately connected with the Court, also dined at the same hour.

" To avoid being on the parade too soon, or too late, a servant was stationed at the door of the house of the duke, whose special duty it was to rush to the dining-room and announce the appearance of the king on the Esplanade."

Being invited to enjoy a sail with the royal family, the colonel met the king on the pier, who, becoming interested in the engineering works then being prosecuted, questioned him with much affability :

"' You belong to the engineers, what are you doing here ?' and quickly said: ' Ay, ay, I know, I know, you are come about the martello towers;' and immediately said : ' They are capital things those martello towers|eh ?' and in so saying his majesty passed his

VOL. L K

19

SECTION 19

arm into mine, adding: ' I want to talk to you about those towers|come;' and immediately walked off along the Esplanade as fast as he could step out, drawing me quite tight towards him with his left arm. In this way we proceeded to the port, at the furthest extremity of the Esplanade, during which time the king never ceased talking about the towers, and appeared to be perfectly conversant with the merits of martello towers, particularly in regard of the one erected on Martello Point, in Corsica, which had with its solitary one gun caused so much damage to one of our ships of war; and whence the name Martello as applied to similar towers built in England had been derived. The king frequently observed: ' Those martello towers are capital things, we must have some here.' From the commencement to the termination of this walk I had no trouble in framing any replies to his majesty's questions, for he most obligingly answered them all himself.

" Having arrived near the wharf where the royal yacht lay, the king letting go my arm said : ' Well, well, I want to talk to you a great deal more|yes, yes, a great deal more, about those towers ; yes, yes| oh yes|that's true, you will be on board of the yacht to-morrow|that will do, that will do, there will be plenty of time to-morrow, plenty of time.' After this the king turned round, and, looking towards the numerous *cortege,* they hastened up to his majesty; for so long as he had continued to hold me by the arm, and was observed to be in active conversation with me, none had dared to approach nearer than some ten to twenty yards; and I now was not sorry to be at liberty to replace my hat on my head.

"In an instant the yacht shot off to sea with streamers flying, the royal standard hoisted at the main, the band playing ' God save the King,' the people huzzaing, the cannon on the shore thundering, to which the frigates responded, the whole re-echoed by the distant cliffs of Portland. Presently all this loyal uproar ceased, the crowd on the wharf dispersed, the smoke of the cannon was blown away, and nothing disturbed the sudden stillness which thus prevailed.

"During half-an-hour after our embarkation the queen and princesses remained below, but they passed nearly the whole of the day promenading on deck, excepting to partake of refreshments. After walking the deck during about an hour with Lady Charlotte Wilmot, with whom I had some very interesting conversation on various scientific subjects, I was accosted by one of the princesses who lead me to walk with her, supporting herself on my arm, as the vessel was pitching a good deal in consequence of having extended our distance beyond the shelter afforded by Portland. Her royal highness was exceedingly inquisitive, seeking for information, but very adroitly concealing this, and left me delighted with her amiability and condescension, which greatly surpassed all I had previously heard attributed to her.

"The royal family, at an early hour, quitted the deck, and dined alone, which did not occupy an hour; and none but their particular attendants were admitted to the same cabin. Refreshments for the remainder of the company were provided in a separate apartment; but they were required to hurry that repast in order that they might be ready to receive the king, queen.and princesses, on their returning to the deck. At about four o'clock the yacht was directing its course homewards, then distant full ten miles.

" I took one of the numerous spy-glasses provided for the use of the visitors, and went forward, thence to admire the picturesque cliffs ; whilst there, I was sharply slapped on the shoulder, and at the same moment heard the well-known voice of the king close to my elbow. As I turned, and dropped my hat, his majesty exclaimed :

" ' Well, what are you looking after ? Ay, ay|I know, I know|you are right|tins is the best place whence to select the fittest position for the martello towers|is it not ? eh, eh|is it not ? Yes, yes|I know, I know.'

"Upon this the king grasped my arm above the elbow, and drew me away aft to the quarter-deck, where we commenced walking up and down with great rapidity.

" In this way, during a considerable space of time, the king did the whole of the honours of the conversation, relieving me almost entirely from any perplexity as to the answers I ought to give, and of the opinions it would be prudent for me to express. The subject being, as I thought, quite exhausted, I expected to be dismissed|that is, I anticipated that the king was about to let go the fast hold he had taken of my arm, when the officer on [the look-out at the foretopmast- head announced a strange sail in the offing, and immediately afterwards declared there were five sail of vessels all standing towards us, with every inch of canvas they could spread.

" We were at this time running under topsails, and|taking it very leisurely, so that these vessels gained upon us very fast, and we soon made them out to be large armed ships: ' Probably,' observed the captain, 'men-of-war.'

" Upon this the king expressed a desire to put about, -and meet them ; but the captain on this occasion did not manifest the same degree of zeal in complying with the king's wishes, as I had noticed in other cases, when his majesty had directed the course of the yacht to be altered. This tardiness on the part of his captain was, however, soon explained by his observation, that ' he did not like the looks of those fellows;' and, moreover, he added, they had not yet made their numbers, in reply to the signal of the commodore, much nearer to them than ourselves.

" The king, instantly catching at this, said : " 'Well, well, what do you make them out to be?| eh, eh ?'

" The captain replied : ' They might be some of the Channel fleet, or, perhaps, some ships that were returning from chasing the Brest fleet, which, it was rumoured, had slipped out, passing our blockading squadron, during one of the late gales; or'|the captain looking very serious|' it might be some of the enemy's ships ; although,' he added, 'not very likely to be the case.'

" The king, on hearing this latter possibility, grasped my arm with redoubled force, and keeping his opera- glass up to his eye, during a whole minute at least, anxiously endeavouring to ascertain the truth, at length, with extraordinary energy, declared that he should like, above all things in this world, to fight Bony in single combat|which his majesty repeated several times ; then started off, still holding me by the arm, and drawing me away, walked with all haste he could master; occasionally halting for a couple of seconds, and fixing his looks on the strange sails, again he exclaimed, in an undertone :

" ' I should like to fight Bony single-handed ;' then, stamping his foot, darted away, taking five or six turns more, when the glass was, as before, raised, and fixed upon the ships in the offing, when at each turn, and sometimes oftener, the king repeated :

" ' I should like to fight Bony single-handed, I'm sure I should ; I should give him a good thrashing, I'm sure I should|I'm sure of it!'

" In the midst of this, the ships were discovered to be East Indiamen running towards the land, probably to take a fresh departure. At this discovery, the king was evidently disappointed; he relaxed the tight hold he had taken of my arm, and in the next moment I was set at liberty; the king had seized upon the captain, and walked the deck with him at a very slow pace.

" Having returned to the landing-place, the company on board fell back to the right and left, forming a wide avenue for the royal family to pass on to the wharf, the gentlemen with their hats off' and bowing low, the ladies in attendance saluting in the usual manner; whilst Colonel Campbell, a tall, serious, severe-looking man, his head uncovered, led the way, the king following close upon his heels, in a most condescending manner returning the salutations, with his hat in his hand, which he did not replace until he had proceeded many yards on the shore.

" Before quitting the yacht, on passing me as I stood with those forming the avenue, the king stopped short, and, pausing a moment, looking me full in the face, as one requiring time to reflect, he hastily said : ' Well, -well, to-morrow we shall consult on the spot about the martello towers for Portland. You must arrange with Garth about that|yes, yes|with Garth ; but you will be there, you understand|you understand; eh, eh, eh ?' The king passed on to the shore, followed by the queen and princesses, who were all met on the wharf by a large assemblage of well-dressed persons, cheering, waving handkerchiefs, and expressing their joy at their safe return.

" It was by that time nearly six o'clock; the king, therefore, left the royal ladies to return to Gloucester House, whilst he proceeded to the Esplanade, in order to receive the salutes of the picquet. I followed, and arrived just in time to take my place with the Duke of Cumberland's staff.

" I must here remark, that George III. was notorious for invariably taking more notice of the drum-major's salutes, who marched at the head of the band, than of any other person. In the course of a few minutes, the First Somerset regiment of Militia, whose tour of duty it was to mount the picquet, advanced in ordinary time, formed in open column as usual, and as soon as the drum-major came up, and began to flourish his dazzling silver, balloon-headed cane, with the large tassels, and had transferred the same to his left hand, and placed his right hand over the front of his hat, the king immediately seized his own hat by the forelock, and swinging it out with his right to the fullest extent he could reach, he dropped his arm close down to his side, and preserved that posture until the drum-major had gone past, and commenced to return the cane to its former position, upon which his majesty replaced his hat on his head."

At the early hour of six o'clock the following morning the royal party set sail; and the colonel gives the following lively sketch of the day :

" In accordance with his usual practice, the king now turned towards his staff and *cortege*, ready to hear anything amusing, or in any way worthy of being related to him, when Lieutenant-General Garth, a little man with good features, but whose face was much disfigured by a considerable purple mark on the skin, extending over part of his forehead and one eye, stepped forward, and after exchanging a few words with the king, which I did not hear distinctly, remarked that the sash his majesty had on was an exceedingly handsome one; upon which the king, with his left hand, taking up the ends that were hanging down, observed : ' Yes, yes ; this is a very handsome sash|very handsome|very handsome ; quite new : Charlotte makes all my sashes| all my sashes; she always makes them.' The sash was a very full-sized one, composed entirely of crimson netted silk, and quite fit for the purpose for which sashes were originally intended, that is, to carry off the wounded from the field of battle; for when spread out it would have measured a yard and a half in width, and at least three yards in length.

" The king had taken off one of his military white gloves, and in dropping the ends of his sash, he also at the same time dropped the glove, upon which, not only General Garth, but several others nearest to the king, scrambled for the glove on the ground, in order to mark their zeal and attention to his majesty; but the king, desirous of recovering his fallen glove without having to thank any one for it, or perhaps wishing to display his activity, also attempted to seize it, in which he succeeded. On rising, the king's cane slipped from his hold, and again the king was the successful candidate for the prize. Now the sensation which the scrambling for the glove and then for the stick had created amongst the vast concourse of spectators was increased to an uncontrollable degree by the falling off of the king's hat, for the capture of which an increased number of competitors presented themselves, whose ambition to serve his majesty greatly retarded its restitution.

" Colonel Campbell, at length, had the good fortune to rescue this from the hands of two members of the king's household, who were struggling with each other for victory; whilst the king, holding out his hands for his property, his face, in consequence of his stooping, as red as his coat, exclaimed: ' Never mind about the honour of the thing, never mind, never mind ; give me my hat, give me my hat; there, there,' as the king received his hat, ' thank youǀthank you all alikeǀyou all picked it upǀyes, yesǀall, all, allǀyou all picked it up.'

"The king, during the latter part of this contest, laughed most heartily, in which the whole of the *cortege* surrounding his majesty immediately joined, throwing off all restraint."

The queen herself supplies some little touches; but she found the place sometimes rather too " bustling."

20

SECTION 20

THE QUEEN TO LADY HABCOUBT.

Weymouth, 27th Sept., 1795. MY DEAR LADY HARCOURT,

You must be so good as to satisfy yourself with a few lines only. For indeed I am but a little at home, & almost constantly at sea, from 11 in the Mng till 11 at Night, where we pass our time in Singing, Dancing, Playing at Cards, & Working. The Stanhopes, & Onslows, Lrda Sudley & Chesterfield, & ldy Gertrude Villers, are our additional & pleasant Company. Yr Letter is arrived. I have no personal dislike to Miss Gambier, But the Prince of Wales, when here, interested Himself for Miss Seymour Coleman, & I am determined to oblige him; a little douceur from me to him is my inclination always; but at present j'aime encore mieux a la faire.

We are to be at Windsor on the 3rd of the next month ; & I understand to have a Circle on the 8th ; & after that I hope to have the Company of L"1 Harcourt & you ; & I long to assure you how sincerely I am

Yr affectionate Friend,

Charlotte.

" I did not write, my dear Friend, for various reasons, after all that has happened since we parted; but I thought much of you; I have been much alone. ... 1 am of oppinion that the quieter one keeps at present, the more prudent it must be; & by seeing but a few people, one has less Temptation to talk. The Chesterfields & Stanhopes come every night at 8, to make up our party; andthe rest of the Day is spent in walking, working, reading, & Drawing, & Music. All this will prove to you that our life is not very merry; & consequently nothing passes to make my letter either pleasant or agreeable, which I always wish to be when I write to you. There is, however, one thing which will make you laugh; & that is, that I take a very nice little *Trott* every Morning round my Grounds upon a pretty little Bourique, which is a Galanterie of the Dowager lady Spencer, & furnishes great amusement to myself, Princesses, Servants, & labourers. It sleeps in the Fields at night; it is taken up early in the morning to prevent its swelling itself by drinking too much water; & after a little ride, is fed with a piece of bread."

She also describes her " little garden-chaise," in which she was driven about the grounds.

THE SAME TO THE SAME.

Weymouth, the 2nd Sept., 1798.

My dearest lady Harcourt will be glad to hear of our safe arrival at Weymouth. ... I hope now to be a little quiet; for of late I have led a life perfectly unknown to me in England. One week really passed in going three times to a Review, to three Dinners, & three Balls; & the fourth day was breakfast at St. Leonards, which was called *a God Bless you,* to which the king also went.

.... I have still many things I could say, but Prudence imposes *Silence*; & that *little dear wordsilence* has so often stood my Friend in Necessity that I make it my constant Companion, which I hope will

not offend you.

Charlotte.

THE SAME TO THE SAME.

Weymouth, 25th July, 1800.

Thanks to a boisterous, blustering Day, we Females are at home to enjoy a little quiet; & what is more, to reflect a little, which, by the by, never will do harm to any body, & is without doubt most Beneficial to our Sex. For as our Minds are easier led away by Fashion, amusements, & trifles, so do we also require more time to recollect & to reflect. The first use I shall make of my power of commanding what I can call my own time, disposes me to write a few lines to an absent Friend. . . .

We have had some very pleasant parties both at Sea & Land. . . .

The Chancellor is at times in the most agreable spirits possible; but as things & Men are not always the same, so His Lordship is found very different in the Evening to what He was in the Morning; but His Niece, Miss Erskin, is & continues the same agreable, Sensible Girl at all times. . . .

Our Sailing Parties have gone on very quietly & pleasantly as far as relates to ourselves. The last time we were out, an unforeseen accident happened to poor Mr Sturt, who, thank God, was very Providentially saved; an account of which you will probably have seen in the papers; & tho' I do not intend to enterinto particulars about Him, knowing your feelings too well upon such horrible accidents, I think it my duty to state that the intimation of it in the papers of his being Drunk is perfectly false; & that it is Wonderfull that a Man after fighting *for full Jive hours* in the Eace of

Portland, against Winds & Waves, thinking every moment to be His last, & losing his Strength, should have retained his senses so well, as to remember where he had laid his valuable Watch, & to go back & fetch it. He assured the king in my presence, that the moment of greatest horror to him was when he saw the boats come off to save him; & the fear that they should not be able, by the violence of the Sea, to come up to Him. He is well, but greatly bruised, & sailed home on Tuesday last.

In our sailing parties many ludicrous events have happened, which I should wish to mention in order to make my letter entertaining; but as this cannot be done without naming People who should be nameless, I think it more prudent not to expose them; but when we meet, it will I hope render our Conversation more Chearfull. . . .

Symptoms of the king's old illness of 1789 having now once more shown themselves, it was determined by the physicians that he should " drink the waters ;" a step that materially, as it was believed, contributed to his malady.

This stay at Lord Fauconberg's seatllent to his majesty, and where much inconvenience was suffered, as it was a small houselis agreeably set out by Miss Burney, who went with the party.

" So now for yesterday, Saturday, July 12, 1788.

" We were all up at five o'clock; and the noise and confusion reigning through the house, and resounding all around it, from the quantities of people stirring, boxes nailing, horses neighing, and dogs barking, was tremendous. I must now tell you the party: Their majesties, the Princesses Royal, Augusta, and Elizabeth, Lady Weymouth, Mr. Fairly, Colonel Gwynn, Miss Planta, and a person you have sometimes met. Pages for king, queen, and princesses, wardrobe-women for ditto, and footmen for alL A smaller party for a royal excursion cannot well be imagined. How we shall all manage Heaven knows. Miss Planta and myself are allowed no maid; the house would not hold one.

"At Henley-on-Thames, at an inn beautifully situated, we stopped to breakfast, and at Oxford to take a sort of half dinner. The crowd gathered together upon the road, waiting for the king and queen to pass, was immense, and almost unbroken from Oxford to Cheltenham. Every town and village within twenty miles seemed to have been deserted, to supply all the pathways with groups of anxious spectators; yet, though so numerous, so quiet were they, and so new to the practices of a hackneyed mob, that their curiosity never induced them to venture within some yards of the royal carriage, and their satisfaction never broke forth into tumult and acclamation.

" All the towns through which we passed were filled with people, as closely fastened one to another as they appear in the pit of a playhouse. Every town seemed all face; and all the way upon the road we rarely proceeded five miles without encountering a band of mosthorrid fiddlers, scraping 'God save the King' with all their might, out of tune, out of time, and all in the rain; for, most unfortunately, there were continual showers falling all the day.

" The country, for the most part, that we traversed was extremely pretty; and, as we advanced nearer to our place of destination, it became quite beautiful.

" When we arrived at Cheltenham, which is almost all one street, extremely long, clean, and well paved, we had to turn out of the public way about a quarter of a mile to proceed to Fauconberg Hall, which my Lord Fauconberg has lent for the king's use during his stay at this place. It is, indeed, situated on a most sweet spot, surrounded with lofty hills beautifully variegated, and bounded, for the principal object, with the hills of Malvern, which, here barren, and there cultivated, here all chalk, and there all verdure, reminded me of Box Hill.

"When we had mounted the gradual ascent on which the house stands, the crowd all around it was as one head ! As soon as we got up the steps we encountered the king. He inquired most graciously concerning our journey; and Lady Weymouth came downstairs to summon me to the queen, who was in excellent spirits, and said she would show me her room. *'This,* ma'am !' cried I, as I entered it, 'is *this* little room for your majesty ?' 'Oh stay,' cried she, laughing, ' till you see your own before you call it little!' Soon after, she sent me upstairs for that purpose, and then, to be sure, I began to think less diminutively of that I had just quitted. Mine, with one window, had just space to crowd in a bed, a chest of drawers, and three small chairs.

"The prospect, however, from the window is extremely pretty, and all is new and clean. So I doubt not being very comfortable, as I am *senza Cerbera*l though having no maid is a real evil to one so little her own mistress as myself. I little wanted the fagging of my own clothes and dressing to add to my daily fatigues. I began a little unpacking and was called to dinner.

"We settled to have our tea upstairs. But then a difficulty arose as to where ? We had each equally small bedrooms and no dressing-room ; but, at length, we fixed on the passage, near a window looking over Malvern hills and much beautiful country.

"The royal family had all been upon the walks. I have agreed with myself not to go thither till they have gone through the newsmongers' drawing up of them and their troop. I had rather avoid all mention ; and after a few days I may walk there as if not belonging to them, as I am not of place or rank to follow in their train.

" But let me give you, now, an account of the house and accommodations.

" On the ground-floor there is one large and very pleasant room, which is made the dining-parlour. The king and royal family also breakfast in it, by themselves, except the lady-in-waiting, Lady Weymouth. They sup there also, in the same manner. The gentlemen only dine with them, I find. They are to breakfast with us, to drink tea where they will, and to supl where they can; and I rather fancy, from what I have yet seen, it will be commonly with good Duke Humphrey.

" A small but very neat dressing-room for his majesty is on the other side of the hall, and my little parlour is the third and only other room on the ground-floor: so you will not think our monarch, his consort, and offspring take up too much of the land called their own!

" Over this eating-parlour, on the first floor, is the queen's drawing-room, in which she is obliged to dress and to undress, for she has no toilette apartment! Who, after that, can repine at any inconvenience here for the household ?

" Here, after breakfast, she sits with her daughters and her lady, and Lady Courtown, who, with her lord, is lodged in the town of Cheltenham. And here they drink tea and live till supper-time.

" Over the king's dressing-room is his bedroom, and over my store-room is the bedroom of the Princess Royal.

"And here ends the first floor. The second is divided and sub-divided into bedrooms, which are thus occupied: Princess Augusta and Princess Elizabeth sleep in two beds in the largest room. Lady Weymouth occupies that next in size. Miss Planta and myself have two little rooms, built over the king's bedroom, and Mrs. Sandys and Miss Macentomb, and Lady Weymouth's maid, have the rest."

This mineral course had been recommended by Sir George Baker, and Cheltenham was the place fixed upon for his majesty's visit. His majesty was accompanied by the queen and the three princesses, and the whole party were now established, having set off from Windsor and arrived at the end of their journey in the afternoon,

VOL. I L

21

SECTION 21

Their table was kept in the plainest manner; it has, however, been stated that the abstemiousness of the king was, at this time, so great, that he never drank more than a single glass of wine; it is, however, incorrect. The etiquette of the royal table *en famille* was, that bottles of every kind of wine usually called for were placed upon the sideboard, and although his majesty did not sit to drink after dinner, he generally, whilst at table, drank from four to six glasses. His favourite wine was claretlthe queen's burgundy. The remainder of the wine was the perquisite of the table- decker. In respect to his dinner his majesty generally ate heartily, but of the plainest food, preferring butchers' meat to poultry or made dishes. He never supped but *pro forma.*

" His majesty's time at Cheltenham was occupied in drinking the waters, and in making excursions to all the places worthy notice in Gloucestershire and Worcestershire ; in which he was everywhere hailed with the most loyal acclamations. Amongst other visits was one to Hartelbury Castle, the episcopal palace of Bishop Hurd, whither he was also accompanied by the Duke of York, who had arrived at Cheltenham on the preceding day. The royal party, attended by a small suite, set off at such an early hour as to travel the distance (thirty-three miles) in time for breakfast at half-past eleven ; previous to sitting down to which, in the library, they examined that ancient residence with great precision and curiosity. After breakfast they walked into the gardens and took several turns on the terraces, especially the green terrace in the chapel garden, as minutely detailed by the worthy prelate inhis own memoir, where they showed themselves to an immense crowd of people who flocked in from the vicinity; and, standing on the rising grounds of the park, saw and were seen to great advantage.

" The king in his walks at Cheltenham, accompanied by the queen and the princesses, was constantly attended by crowds of people. His majesty pleasantly observed to the queen: ' We must walk about for two or three days to please these good people, and then we may walk about to please ourselves.' His manners were unaffected and condescending to everyone. He walked about unattended by any pomp, without a single guard ; more secure in the hearts of his faithful subjects than in all the parade attendant on foreign princes. His majesty would not allow any soldiers to do duty or reside within ten miles of the Royal Spa. The band of Lord Harrington's regiment only were permitted to attend his majesty.

"The first morning the king was at Worcester he went down the street *incog.* He was soon recognised, and when he came upon the bridge he turned round to the people and said : ' This, I suppose, is Worcester new bridge.' ' Yes, please your majesty,' said a cobbler. ' Then,' said he, ' my boys, let's have a huzza!' His majesty set the example, and a fine shout there was. Afterwards they continued huzzaing all the way to the palace.

" The second morning the king was out at half after five. He went to Colonel Digby's and Colonel Gwynn's lodgings. The maid-servant was cleaning the door. The girl threw down her mop and ran away to the bell. The king stopped her and desired her to show

him where *the felloivs* slept. The girl obeyed, and his majesty went himself and called them up. The colonels leaped out of their beds as if surprised in camp by an enemy, but the king was off and they were obliged to run over the town to find him.

"Before his majesty left the city he ordered the following donations : To the charity, $200 ; the corporation, $100, to be distributed among the poor citizens; to the infirmary, $50; to the workmen at the china manufactory, $20, and an order for a set of china, value $100, to be presented to the queen.

" He took his leave very affectionately of the bishop, the mayor, recorder, and corporation, and expressed the highest satisfaction at his reception, and with the dutiful and respectful manner in which they had conducted themselves. On his visit to Guildhall on Friday, he was extremely affable and agreeable. After viewing everything worthy attention he was shown into the grand parlour, where some excellent viands, wines, fruit, etc., were placed. The mayor being previously informed that his majesty never touched wine in the morning, humbly intreated him to take a jelly. The king replied : ' I never did yet take wine in the morning, but upon this interesting and pleasing occasion I will venture upon a glass.' The mayor filled a glass of rich old mountain, and his majesty drank 'Prosperity and happiness to the corporation and citizens of Worcester.' This being made known to the multitude without there was a thundering shout. The king then asked if there was anything he could confer upon the city, or upon anyindividual of the corporation. The recorder gave his humble thanks, and said that they had only to supplicate that he would condescend to sit for his picture. The royal reply was: ' Certainly, Mr. Mayor and gentlemen, I cannot refuse you that slender favour ; but I could wish to confer something more substantial.' Upon his return to the palace he walked through the streets, as he came, with only one attendant, 'besides the lord in waiting. The crowd pressing each other to make a respectable space for him to walk at ease, and forming a phalanx on each side to prevent any rude intruder, if there had been one, from breaking in upon the passage.

"An attempt was made to move the spirit in the Quakers of Worcester to address his majesty. About a dozen of the more curious among them got leave to step into the courtyard when his majesty's coach left the palace, but they stood unmoved, with their hats on their heads. The king saw that they were Quakers, and, taking off his hat, bowed to them. They, in return, moved their hands, and the eldest of them said : ' Fare thee well, friend George !' The king and queen laughed heartily.

" Shortly after his majesty had left Worcester, he forwarded, by a noble lord residing in that neighbourhood, the sum of $300, not only for the relief of debtors, but that such of the criminals whose conduct since commitment was meritorious, should share the gift.

" But perhaps the most remarkable incident attending this royal visit has still to be related. The only person who, by his majesty's desire, accompanied him,as conductor through the town, was the great-grandson of the Protector, Cromwell. The king appeared to converse with him with great affability and condescension. The singularity of the circumstance attracted general notice."

I pass over all the dreadful details of his malady, described with such dramatic power by Miss Burney, and with great minuteness by Lady Harcourt in her diary given in Mr. Harcourt's privately printed volumes.

On his recovery from his illness a new progress through various counties, with visits to some cheering scenes, was prescribed, with a view to distract his thoughts and enliven him after the dreadful trial through which he had passed. Nothing more pleasing, or even pastoral, can be conceived than the description of this simple tour, or the display of genuine delight exhibited by the honest rustics who greeted him.

The venerable Charles Knight, who had been brought up at Windsor, used to recall the familiar figure of the king as he appeared in the existing days of expected invasion.

"The king, in this summer of excitement, was constantly to be seen in the cocked-hat and jack-boots of the Blues, in which regiment he had a troop of his own. He inspected the volunteers, who were drawn up under the wall of the Round Tower. He invited their officers to be present at the Sunday evening performances of sacred music. He walked upon the Terrace|' every inch a king'|and would call, with a stentorian voice, for the band to play ' Britons, strike home !'"

Again, after setting out for Weymouth :

" My father writes to me, at the end of August, that he is busy, for the royal family are going to Weymouth. Every year did the king thus visit his favourite watering-place. This journey, actually exceeding a hundred miles, wonderful to relate, was accomplished in one long summer's day. At an early hour the royal carriages, and their escort of light dragoons, are clattering through the streets of Windsor. Away they dash, along turnpike roads, and sometimes through rough lanes. The people of the towns are out to gaze and shout. Villagers hear the rumour that the king, so rarely seen, is coming; and the thrasher ever and anon looks forth from his barn-door, whilst his wife sits at the cottage-porch spinning in the sun. In these excursions to the coast, ' Farmer George' would see many rural sights with which he was familiar. He might see five horses dragging a heavy plough over light land.

" Weymouth is reached without any fuss. The next morning the king is on the Esplanade, before breakfast has been thought of at the genteel hotels and boarding-houses; and the fishermen, who have just come in with the produce of their night's labour, are rather puzzled to believe that the tall gentleman can be the king, who asks the price of a turbot and does not wait for an answer.

"In the April of 1805 I went home for a week, that I might behold the grand ceremony of the installation of Knights of the Garter. St. George's Day was on a Tuesday. On the Monday, Windsor was in a tumult of excitement far greater than in the experience of the oldest inhabitant. The road from London

22

SECTION 22

presented the view of an almost endless succession of carriages. Hounslow could not meet the demand for change of horses. The inns of our town could not find standing for the carriages, so they blocked up the streets. Ladies in coal-scuttle bonnets, and gentlemen in monstrous Hessian boots, filled our narrow pavements. The bells rang; the Foot Guards were inspected in the park; beds were occupied by the wealthy at extravagant prices, whilst the curious pedestrian paid half-a-guinea to stretch his limbs on a tap-room settle. At eight o'clock on the morning of the 23rd of April, the kiag presented, at the grand entrance to the Castle, a pair of silver kettle-drums to his favourite regiment, now called the Royal Horse Guards Blue. The drums were lifted upon a gray horse bestrid by a black man ; the old walls resounded with 'God save the King,' and 'Britons, strike home!'" A glimpse at the interior of the little Windsor Theatre, of which his majesty was a patron, is also given by Mr. Knight. "From my eighth year upwards, I could always obtain a free admission to that smallest of playhouses, the Theatre Royal of Windsor, where majesty oft was delighted to recreate itself with hearty laughs at the comic stars of sixty years since. Tragedy was not to the king's taste. Was there ever such stuff as great part of Shakespeare ? only one must not say so! But what think you ? What ? Is there not sad stuff ? What ? The publicity of which I have spoken was, in the Windsor Theatre, carried to its extremest limit. That honoured playhouse no longer exists. The High Street exhibits a dissenting chapel on its site, whose

frontage may give some notion of the dimensions of that cosy apartment, with its two tier of boxes, its gallery, and its slips. It was not an exclusive theatre. Three shillings gave the entrance to the boxes, two shillings to the pit, and one shilling to the gallery. One side of the lower tier of boxes was occupied by the Court. The king and queen sat in capacious armchairs, with satin playbills spread before them. The orchestra, which would hold half-a-dozen fiddlers, and the pit, where some dozen persons might be closely packed on each bench, separated the royal circle from the genteel parties in the opposite tier of boxes. With the plebeians in the pit the royal family might have shaken hands; and when they left, there was always a scramble for their satin bills, which would be afterwards duly framed and glazed as spoils of peace. As the king laughed and cried : ' Bravo, Quick !' or ' Bravo, Suett!'|for he had rejoiced in their well-known mirth-provoking faces many a time before|the pit and gallery clapped and roared in loyal sympathy: the boxes were too genteel for such emotional feelings. As the king, queen, and princesses retired at the end of the third act, to sip their coffee, the pot of Windsor ale, called queen's ale, circulated in the gallery. At eleven o'clock the curtain dropped. The fiddles struck up ' God save the King;' their majesties bowed around as the house clapped; and the gouty manager, Mr. Thornton, leading the way to the entrance (carrying wax-lights and walking backwards, with the well practised steps of a Lord Chamberlain), the flambeaux of three or four carriages gleamed through the dimly-lighted streets, and royalty was quickly at rest."

Here is another scene at the play at Weymouth :

"The loyalty and obedient respect of the people here to their king are in a truly primitive style. The whole royal party went to see Lulworth Castle, intending to be back to dinner, and go to the play at night, which their majesties had ordered, with Mrs. Siddons to play Lady Townly. Dinner-time, however, came and passed, and they arrived not. They went by sea, and the wind proved contrary; and about seven o'clock a hobby groom was despatched hither by land, with intelligence that they had only reached Lulworth Castle at five o'clock. They meant to be certainly back by eight; but sent their commands that the farce might bo performed first, and the play wait them.

" The manager repeated this to the audience|already waiting and wearied; but a loud applause testified their agreeability to whatever could be proposed. The farce, however, was much sooner over than the passage from Lulworth Castle. It was ten o'clock when they landed ! And all this time the audience|spectators rather| quietly waited !

" They landed just by the theatre, and went to the house of Lady Pembroke, who is now here in attendance upon the queen : and there they sent home for the king's page, with a wig, etc.; and the queen's wardrobe-woman, with similar decorations ; and a message to Miss Planta and me, that we might go at once to the theatre. We obeyed; and soon after they appeared, and were received with the most violent gusts of joy and huzzas, even from the galleries over their heads, whose patience had not the reward of seeing them at last. Is not this a charminf trait of provincial popularity ?"

This is the glimpse we shall have of the amiable monarch. Very soon the clouds of hopeless and incurable insanity were to descend on and shut him out from all domestic enjoyment.

Having thus given a very complete and, I hope, interesting view of the private life of the royal family, I will now pass on to a more particular account of the royal dukes and princesses who were members of this large family.

23

SECTION 23

CHAPTER I.

  THE STORY OF CAROLINE MATILDA.

  Excellent king, father, and husband, careful in all his duties, as was George III., no one was ever so afflicted with troubles and misfortunes in his family. The fate of his sister, Caroline Matilda, was itself a sore trial, as well as a romance. The behaviour of his eldest son helped to unsettle his reason, and that of his other sons caused much anxiety and disappointment. His daughter-in-law was associated with perpetual scandal and disgrace ; his grandchild, her daughter, the hope of the country, was cut off in the bloom of her youth, while with her perished the infant. His own favourite child, the Princess Amelia, was snatched from him also at an early age. The Duke of Brunswick, his kinsman, fighting fell; his eldest daughter was overwhelmed with misfortune and humiliation at the hands of Bonaparte. Another child was sacrificed to a gross German prince, described as " a man with a snout," " a monster of a man," etc. ; while, finally, he himself became blind, a lunatic, and died in that condition. So sad a career, and so weary a life|harassed from the beginning with|mortification, the loss of territory, resistance to what he believed were unrighteous claims, make his attempting to maintain cheerfulness and enjoy domestic happiness with his family as meritorious as it was more difficult. The fate of his sister, the queen of Denmark, is in truth singularly romantic, and has furnished a subject for the opera and the play. Sir N. Wraxall, who had the advantage of being on the spot at various seasons, gives a dramatic sketch of the crisis when the supposed favourite Struensee was seized.

" It was at length resolved to seize on the queen Matilda, and the principal persons attached to her, at the close of a masked ball, which was to be given in the royal palace upon the 15th of January, 1772. Count Rantzau undertook the commission of persuading the king to sign the order for the purpose, and of putting it afterwards into execution. On the afternoon of the 15th of January, only a few hours before the ball was to begin, Rantzau wrote to the minister, desiring to see him at his own apartments upon business of the utmost importance. Struensee intended to have gone thither; but being detained by a variety of affairs till it grew late, he went straight to the ball, and thereby lost the fairest occasion of extricating himself from destruction.

"Roller Banner was the animating soul of the enterprize, to whose coolness, presence of mind, and intrepidity its success must be principally attributed. During the whole night, while at the ball, he maintained the utmost serenity of deportment, and played at the same game of cards with Monsieur Berger, whom he immediately afterwards arrested. Two circumstanceswhich took place in the course of the evening excited remark, and ought to have awakened suspicion. The king, queen, and their attendants, entered the ball-room before ten o'clock; but Prince Frederic, contrary to his usual custom, and in some measure contrary to the respect due from him towards their majesties, did not arrive till more than an hour later. His countenance was flushed, and his disordered looks betrayed the agitation of his mind. As soon as he came, the queen advancing towards him said : ' Vous venez d'arriver bien tard, mon frere : Qu'avez yous ?'l' C'est que j'ai eu des affaires, madame,' replied he. ' Il me semble,' answered she gaily, ' que vous auriez mieux fait de penser a vos plaisirs qu'a vos affaires, pendant une soire'e de bal.' The prince made little or no reply, and the conversation ended. As Struensee was conscious of his own unpopularity, and dreaded some commotion among the people, he had surrounded the ball-room with guards, on whose fidelity he knew or believed he could rely. But the officer who commanded them, having been gained by the opposite part)', changed the soldiers.

" Between twelve and one o'clock the king quitted the room and retired. The queen continued there to a later hour, and supped with a large party in her own box, to which Prince Frederic was not admitted nor invited. After dancing the greater part of the night with Struensee, her majesty and he both withdrew nearly at the same time, about three o'clock. The company soon followed, and the two last persons who remained in the ball-room, were Brandt and the Countess d'Ostein.

" The moment for action was now arrived. Rantzau,

VOL. I. M

without loss of time, entered the bed-chamber of the king, awoke him, and acquainted him that there existed a conspiracy against his person and dignity, at the head of which were his wife, Struensee, and various of their associates. He then besought his majesty to consult his own security, by instantly signing an order for their arrest, which Rantzau tendered him, using every argument to enforce his solicitations. But Christian, though feeble in mind, and taken by surprise, hesitated, and refused to affix his name to the paper. The Queen Dowager and Prince Frederic were therefore called in to his bedside; and by means of expostulations, supported by exaggerated or false representations of the danger which he incurred from delay, they at length procured his reluctant consent. He signed the order, which was immediately carried into execution.

" Koller Banner repairing to Struensee's chamber, forced open the door, and seized him in his bed. He was asleep when this event took place; for which he was so totally unprepared that, having no clothes near the bedside except his masquerade dress, he was necessitated to put on the domino breeches which he had worn at the ball, from the want of any others. The weather being extremely cold, he was permitted to wrap himself in his fur cloak, and they then conveyed him in a coach to the citadel.

" But the most dangerous and important act of the enterprise still remained to perform; that of arresting the queen Matilda. Horace, in his Journals, states that the English Court were long before well aware of the behaviour of the queen. After retiring from the ball, she continued some time in her own room. Struensee'schamber being situated directly under the queen's, the noise made by Koller Banner in seizing his person was indistinctly heard by her majesty. She by no means however attributed it to the real cause. On the contrary, imagining that the disturbance was occasioned by the company which, as she knew, was to meet in the apartment of Madame d'Ostein, and which party, she concluded, had been transferred to Struensee's, she ordered one of her women to go down, and to request them to be less intemperate in their mirth, as they would otherwise prevent her from taking any repose. The woman did not return ; the noise ceased ; and the queen having soon retired to rest, fell into a profound sleep.

" It was about five o'clock in the morning when she was awakened by a Danish female attendant, who always lay in the adjoining room. Holding a candle in one hand, she held out a paper to the queen in the other, which, with marks of agitation, she requested her majesty to peruse. It contained a request, rather than an order, couched in very concise but very respectful terms, stating that ' the king of Denmark, for reasons of a private nature, wished her to remove to one of the royal palaces in the country for a few days.' Conscious that, if she could only gain access to the king, she could in a moment overturn the plans of her enemies, the queen sprang out of bed, and without waiting to put on anything except a petticoat and shoes, she rushed into the antechamber. There the first object which she met was Count Rantzau, seated quietly in a chair. Recollecting then her dishevelled state, she cried out: 'Eloignez vous, Monsieur le Comte, pour l'amour deDieu, car je ne suis pas presentable.' She immediately ran back into her chamber and hastily threw on some clothes, assisted by her women.

" On attempting a second time to leave her room, she found that Rantzau had withdrawn himself, but had stationed an officer in the doorway, who opposed her further passage. Rendered almost frantic by this insult, added to her distress, she seized him by the hair, demanding to see Count Struensee or the king. ' Madam, ' said he, ' I only do my duty, and obey my orders. There is no Count Struensee now, nor can your majesty see the king.' Having pushed him aside, she advanced to the door of the antechamber, where two soldiers had crossed their firelocks in order to stop her progress. The queen commanded them to let her pass, and added promises of reward if they obeyed. Both the soldiers fell on their knees, and one of them said in Danish: ' It is a sad duty, but we must perform it. Our heads are answerable if we allow your majesty to pass.' As no one, however, dared to lay hands upon the queen, she stepped over the muskets which were crossed, and ran half wild along the corridor to the king's apartment . She even forced her way into it by violence ; but her enemies, aware that she might try to gain admittance, and justly apprehensive of her influence over him, had taken the precaution of removing him betimes to another part of the palace.

"Exhausted by the agitation of her mind, and by such exertions of body, the queen attempted no further resistance. She returned to her own chamber, where she was aided to dress herself, and informed that she must instantly quit Copenhagen. Rantzau had the insolence to say to her, alluding to his gouty feet: ' Vous voyez,madame, que mes pieds me manquent; mais mes bras sont libres, et j'en offrirai un a votre majest, pour l'aider a monter en voiture.' She was then put into a coach, which waited for her at the door near the chapel of the palace. Two ladies, a maid-servant, the little princess her daughter, whom she suckled, and a major in the Danish service, got into the carriage with her. They took the road to Cronsbourg, a distance of about twenty-four miles, which, as they drove at a great rate, they soon reached, and in which fortress the queen was confined.

"All Europe knows the tragical catastrophe of Brandt and Struensee; the former of whom suffered for his political and private connection with the minister, while the latter was the favourite of Caroline Matilda."

The story of the ill-fated queen is pretty familiar in its general outlines, but there are many interesting details about her later history which connect her directly with the English Court. It was in 1772 that the revolution against the king, or rather against Struensee and the queen, took place; and when they were put on their trial, only for the spirited attitude of the English minister, and the angry "growlings" of the English people, who showed they would not suffer the English princess to be ill-treated, she would probably have shared the fate of Struensee, or at least have suffered one of those mysterious " natural" deaths in prison, which was then the fashionable mode of removing inconvenient personages. When it was learned that a fleet was about to sail for Copenhagen the regency showed themselves prompt in surrendering the queen, promised to repay her dowry, and allow her an annuity.

24

SECTION 24

The squadron left England on May 22nd, and arrived at Elsinore on the 27th.

The queen wrote her brother a letter asserting her innocence, and asking to be allowed to return to England. By October she had reached Celle, or Zell, which was to be henceforward her place of honourable imprisonment.

Sir R. M. Keith, who had been sent to report, thus wrote to the ministers atiome from Zell, Nov. 2, 1772 :

" My Lord,

" I arrived here on the 31st October, late in the evening, and the next day had the honour of delivering the king's letter to her Danish majesty, whom I found in perfect health, and without any remains of pain from her late accident. In two very long audiences, which her majesty was pleased to grant me, I endeavoured to execute, with the utmost punctuality, his majesty's command, and shall now lay before your lordship all the lights those audiences afforded me, relative to the queen's wishes and intentions. I cannot enter upon that subject without previously assuring your lordship that the queen received those repeated proofs of his majesty's fraternal affection and friendship, which my orders contained, with the warmest expressions of gratitude and sensibility; and that nothing could be more frank or explicit than her answers to a great number of questions, which she permitted me to ask upon any subject that arose.

" In regard to Denmark, the queen declares that, in the present situation of the Court, she has not a wish for any correspondence or connection there, beyond wha-timmediately concerns the welfare and education of her children. That she has never written a single letter to Denmark since she left it, or received one thence. That the only person belonging to that kingdom from whom she hears lives in Holstein, and is not connected with the Court.

" The queen having expressed great anxiety with respect to the false impressions which may be instilled into the minds of her children, particularly regarding herself, I thought it my duty to say that such impressions, however cruelly intended, could not, at the tender age of her majesty's children, nor for some years to come, take so deep a root as not to be entirely effaced by more candid instructions, and the dictates of filial duty, when reason and reflection shall break in upon their minds. The queen seemed willing to lay hold of that hope, yet could not help bursting into tears, when she mentioned the danger of losing the affections of her children.

" Her majesty talked to me of several late incidents at the Court of Denmark, but without appearing to take much concern in them. She mentioned, with a smile, some of the paltry things which had been sent as a part of her baggage from Denmark, adding, that this new instance of their meanness had not surprised her. But the Princess of Brunswick, who happened to be present when the baggage was opened, expressed her indignation at the treatment in such strong terms, that she (the queen) could not help taking notice of it in her letters to the king. She let me understand that a small collection of English books would be very agreeable to her, leaving the choice of them entirely to his majesty."

It is curious to see what a practical tone this official letter imports into the business, after the romantic scenes which have just been described.

In this confinement she was to spend nearly three years; but it was alleviated by a certain state and some amusement, chiefly dramatic performances; tragedies, however, being strictly forbidden, as likely to .work on her rather morbid disposition.

It came to pass that in the year 1774 Mr. Wraxall, afterwards Sir Nathaniel, the energetic traveller and gossip, was on his travels|which he has recounted ill an entertaining way|when he came by Strelitz, and there passed two days, at a country palace of the Duke of Mecklenburg-Strelitz, detained by his hospitality.

" Adolphus Frederic IV.," he says, " eldest of the four brothers of George III.'s queen, was then about six-and-thirty years of age; unmarried, slender in figure, of an adust complexion, agreeable in his manners; receiving English gentlemen, who occasionally, though rarely, visited his summer retreat, with peculiar attention. I had the honour to dine twice with the duke during my short stay in his territories. At table, surrounded by his little Court, composed of young and agreeable individuals of both sexes, he amused me by recounting some particulars of the English who had from time to time been his guests. The Earl and Countess of Effingham were among the number. ' They were always seated,' he said, ' opposite each other at dinner; and no sooner was the dessert placed before us than my lord, ordering his lady to open her mouth, threw *dragees* (sugar-plums) into it across the table with surprising dexterity.' On quitting Strelitz Idirected my course to Zell, impelled by a desire to see and to pay my respects to the young queen of Denmark. I experienced from her majesty the most gracious reception. She was not, indeed, a captive at Zell; but could by no means be regarded as a free agent. Her own sister, the hereditary Princess of Brunswick, acted by directions of George III. as a spy on her conduct; usually coming over to Zell every Wednesday, and returning to Brunswick on the ensuing Saturday. I know the fact from the queen's own mouth. There was in the aspect of the castle of Zell, its towers, moat, drawbridge, long galleries, and Gothic features, all the scenery realising the descriptions of fortresses where imprisoned princesses were detained in bondage. It was the age of those exhibitions when I travelled in Germany. At Stettin, while dining with the Prince of Anhalt-Dessau, a few days before I arrived at Zell, I had seen the Princess Royal of Prussia, Elizabeth Christina of Brunswic-Wolfenbuttel, first wife of the late king, Frederic William II., who was there confined for her gallantries. Robert, Duke of Ancaster, then Marquis of Lindsey, a young nobleman of extraordinary eccentricity of character, and capable of undertaking any enterprise, however desperate or dangerous, was so touched with her misfortunes and imprisonment that in 1777 he planned her liberation. And he would certainly have attempted it, if the design had not been discovered and prevented. The Princess of Tour and Taxis, Augusta Elizabeth, was about the same time immured, during many years, in a castle of Wirtemberg, by her brother, the reigning duke of that country.

" Often, as I was placed opposite to the queenCaroline Matilda at table, Sophia of Zell, consort of George I., from whom she lineally descended, recurred to my recollection. Both expired under a dark cloud ; and both now repose, side by side, in the great church of Zell, without any monument to commemorate their existence."

In his Private Journal Mr. Wraxall gives this lively sketch of the queen :

" Her majesty and the princess kept me in constant talk before and after dinner. Her majesty related to me Mr. Morris's affair with Miss Calvert. She was very gay, and seemed in no way a prey to melancholy. She was very fat, for so young a woman. She asked me my age. I told her. ' You are, then,' said she, ' exactly as old as I am; we were born in the same year.' Her features are pretty, and her teeth very small, even, and white. She resembles his majesty (George III.) infinitely in face : but the princess said, not so strongly as she. I don't think so, and told her royal highness so. Her majesty appealed to one of her maids of honour, who agreed in opinion with me. The queen was dressed in a Barre' coloured gown, or at least an orange-red, so very nearly resembling it that I could not distinguish the difference. I asked her how many languages she spoke. ' Five,' she said, 'Danish, English, French, German, and Italian.' The princess is much thinner in face, but not a great deal less in her person: she wants the queen of Denmark's teeth, but has a very good complexion. She asked me about the Duchess of Glo'ster, if I had seen her, if I knew her. 'She is a very fine woman,' she

added, ' even now.' Mrs. C was mentioned. ' She

was a prodigious favourite,' I remarked, ' of the Duke ofYork.' She replied, with a smile: ' For a moment/ She did me the honour to ask me to take Brunswick in my way next summer, or whenever I visited Germany again. She said she should have mistaken me for a Frenchman. 'You don't take that for a compliment, do you ?' the queen observed. ' Indeed, no ! I am too proud of my country.'"

He then describes how, at Hamburg, he met a sort of Danish exile, named Texier, who told him many interesting facts about the queen, and finally asked him would he act as a means of communication with her, as there was a plan on foot for restoring her to her throne. Wraxall, who delighted in intrigue, eagerly accepted the offer, and was furnished with credentials in the shape of an impression in wax of a seal. He returned to Zell.

" Having written to the Baron de Seckendorf, one of the queen's chamberlains, I acquainted him I had been charged by Mr. Mathias with a letter for her majesty. I received soon afterwards an invitation to dine at Court on the same day. No sooner had I accomplished this first object, than I drew up a letter to the queen. One very embarrassing circumstance yet remained. The etiquette of the Court of Zell was, that all strangers who had the honour of being admitted to the royal table were received by her majesty in her drawing-room, a short time before dinner. In this circle, with the eyes of so many individuals directed towards me, among whom, as I knew, would be the Princess of Brunswic, I must of necessity present my letter.

" After drawing up my letter, I wrote on a sheet of paper, so placed that she must of necessity cast her eye upon it, before she could peruse any other of the enclosure, these, or nearly these words. 'As the contents of the present letter regard your majesty's highest and dearest interests ; and as the slightest indication or suspicion of its nature might prove fatal to its object; it is earnestly entreated that your majesty will be pleased to reserve the perusal till you are alone. It is particularly incumbent to conceal it from her royal highness the Princess of Brunswic, who will be present at its reception.'

" When I had finished all my preparations, I repaired in a sedan-chair to the castle, at half-past one, as the queen sate down at two to table. The company, consisting of ten or more persons of both sexes, were already met; and in a few minutes, her majesty, accompanied by her sister, entered the apartment. She advanced with a quick step towards me, and holding out her hand, ' I am glad to see you here again,' said she ; ' I understand that you have a letter for me from Mr. Mathias.' ' I have, madam,' answered I, ' which he wished me to deliver to your majesty. I believe it regards the company of comedians who are preparing to arrive here.' At the same time I presented it, and the queen instantly withdrew to one of the windows, a few paces distant, in order to peruse it. The Princess of Brunswic then accosted me, asking a variety of questions relative to Hamburg. I contrived to answer them, though my attention was internally directed towards the queen ; who, after reading the lines prefixed, hastily put the letter into her pocket. She then rejoined us|for I was standing out of the circle, engaged in conversation with her sister|and attempted to mix in the discourse. But her face had

25

SECTION 25

become of a scarlet colour, and she manifested so much discomposure, that I felt no little uneasiness lest it should excite remark. Fortunately, at that moment dinner was announced, and we followed the two princesses into the eating-room. I was placed opposite to them. During the repast her majesty soon recovered her gaiety and presence of mind, keeping me in continual conversation, as did the princess. But no sooner was the dessert served, than the former, pushing back her chair, drew out my letter; and holding it in her lap read it from beginning to end ; raising her head from time to time, uttering a few words, and then resuming her occupation. I returned to the inn, and waited till I should hear from the queen."

The chamberlain soon came to him with news that her majesty was ready to throw herself into the scheme, and gave a sort of commission to treat with the conspirators at Hamburg. On this, our indefatigable English plotter set off once more. Bulow then informed him it was necessary to secure the adhesion of the King of England.

" We trust that the queen will despatch you as her agent to England, and will support with all her exertions the application to her brother. Without that co-operation we shall want our best guarantee for the permanence of our success. Our means are fully adequate to produce the change in the government, and to place the queen Caroline Matilda at its head. Besides our numerous and powerful friends in Copenhagen, we have the Viceroy of Norway in our interests, and the two governors of Gluckstadt and Rendsburg."

On this, Wraxall returned again to Zell. "Arrivingin the middle of the night, on the 24th of October, I gave a French name to the sentinel at the gate, describing myself as a merchant. Then proceeding ound the walls, I drove, not, as before, to the great inn in the principal street of the place, but to an obscure public-house, situate in the suburb of Hanover, denominated the 'Sand Krug.' The Baron de Seckendorf having gone on the preceding day to Hanover, I despatched an express to hasten his return. I learned, however, with no small satisfaction, that the Princess of Brunswic was not at Zell, and before I awoke on the ensuing morning, Seckendorf presented himself at my bedside. I delivered him the letter. Scarcely four hours afterwards Seckendorf came again to me. ' The queen,' said he, ' having thoroughly weighed the contents of your despatch, is determined to see you without delay. Her sister's absence favours her design. Go instantly to the Jardin Francais, not distant from hence. In the centre stands a small pavilion. Her majesty, attended only by one lady, who is wholly devoted to her interests, will be there in a very short time. You may then converse unreservedly upon every point.' I followed his directions, and had not been more than ten minutes in the pavilion, when I saw the royal coach drive up to the garden-gate. The queen alighting, sent it away, together with her domestics. She then entered on business, having first assured me that she could rely on the fidelity of her attendant." She promised him letters for the English foreign secretary and the Hanoverian minister. Mr. Wraxall set off once more, having had an interview with Bulow, who, according to the law of melodrama, came " wrapped up in a cloakon a common post waggon," remaining till one in the morning.

"It was not till the 15th of November that I arrived in London. Next morning, having repaired to Lord Suffolk's residence in Downing Street, his private secretary acquainted me that his lordship being then confined by a severe fit of the gout, unless my business admitted of communication through a third person I must defer it till the secretary of state should be able to grant me an interview. I therefore proceeded immediately to the Baron de Lichtenstein's lodgings in Chidleigh Court, Pall Mall. He received me with great cordiality. ' The queen of Denmark,' said he, ' has written to me, and refers me in her letter entirely to you for information upon every point; but the king has been pleased to communicate to me her majesty's despatch to himself, which renders me master of the whole affair. It is one of no slight importance, and will require mature consideration. Meanwhile I will inform his majesty of your arrival. As he permits me to form one of his small evening circle, I enjoy the means of laying before him many matters and of receiving his orders. Be assured of my zeal in every particular which can affect the honour or the interests of the queen Matilda.' At our next meeting, which took place a few days afterwards, he delivered me the king's commands. ' His majesty,' said Lichtenstein, ' having considered the nature and delicacy of the mission entrusted to you, enjoins you not to return to Lord Suffolk. The business must be managed and negotiated exclusively through me.'

"Towards the middle of January, 1775, the affair,however, assumed a more auspicious aspect; and on the 3rd of the following month the baron delivered to me, in

Chidleigh Court, a paper containing?/' articles. They were drawn up in French, by tho king's permission, and with his sanction.

" By the *first* his majesty declared that the attempt to restore the queen had his approbation, only annexing to it a stipulation that no act of severity should be exercised. By the *second* his majesty promised that as soon as the revolution was effected his minister at Copenhagen should declare that it had been done with his co-operation. By the *third* he guaranteed the repayment of such sums as should be expended in procuring the queen's return. By the *fourth* he engaged that when the revolution should be completed, he would maintain it, if requisite, by the forces of Great Britain.

" This paper the Baron de Lichtenstein signed, and having enclosed it in a cover, sealed the pacquet with his coat of arms. I was then directed to carry it, first to the queen at Zell, who would instantly recognise his signature and seal."

I pass over Mr. WraxalTs many journeys between London, Hamburg, and Zell, under circumstances of great hardship; as also his many secret meetings with the conspirators. They were most eager to obtain an engagement from the king of England that he would declare his approval of their proceedings at a proper time.

"After passing and repassing between London and Zell, and Hamburg, with more midnight interviews with the queen, and after writing to the Baron de Bulow, and acquainting him with all the particulars ofmy interview with the queen, I began my journey to England. I was forty-eight hours on my passage, and got to London on the 5th of that month, 1 775.

"My earliest visit was paid .to Chidleigh Court, Pall Mall; but the Baron de Lichten-stein had already quitted England, on his way to Hanover. Monsieur Hinuber, charge' d'affaires d'Hanover, on whom I waited at his residence in Jermyn Street, informed me that he had received the king's commands to enclose whatever pacquets I might bring in a box; to seal it up, and to carry it immediately to him. Lichtenstein, in the letter which he left to direct my conduct, had expressly prepared me. ' I must,' said he, ' warn you not to be surprised if you do not receive from him (George III.) an answer. It will be addressed to me at Hanover. Reasons with which you are well acquaintedlnamely, that he will give nothing under his hand touching this affairlallow of no other line of conduct.'

" Being thus situated I waited till the 21st of April, when Hinuber having informed me that he had not received any orders from his majesty respecting me, I wrote to the queen, to Scckendorf, and to Bulow. On Friday, the 19th of May, as I was entering my lodgings in Jermyn Street, my servant, who daily expected me to set out again for Germany, asked me whether I had heard ' that the queen was dead ?' Conceiving him to mean our own queen, I replied in the negative ; but he soon undeceived me by explaining that he spoke of Caroline Matilda. The intelligence was fully confirmed to me a few minutes afterwards; with the additional information that the king her brother having received the account by a messenger from Zell, while he was on voi. i. N horseback, bad manifested strong marks of concern, and returned instantly to the queen's house. It was not till the 25th of May that the post brought me a letter from Seckendorf, conveying the lamentable particulars of the same event. He subjoined a fact of no ordinary interest: that his majesty had returned an answer to his sister's letter brought over by me. It was sent by the Hanoverian courier, under cover to

Lichtenstein, as that nobleman warned me would happen. He forwarded it without delay to her majesty; but she being then at the last extremity it was never opened, and Lichtenstein transmitted it, with the seal unbroken, back to George III. Its contents have ever remained unknown."

The unfortunate lady, however, died of fever on May 11, 1775, at eleven o'clock at night, being only twenty- three years of age. On her deathbed she declared solemnly to Roques, a pastor who attended her, that before God she was innocent of the charges laid against her. A more touching proof was the letter written on her dying bed to her brother, whose authenticity is vouched for by Sir Lascelles Wraxall, to whom a copy was given by the Duchess of Augustenburg, and who procured it from the late king of Hanover.

Sire,

In the most solemn hour of my life, I turn to you, my royal brother, to express my heart's thanks for all the kindness you have shown me during my whole life, and especially in my misfortune.

But I die innocent‖I write this with a trembling hand, and feeling death imminent‖I am innocent ! Oh that it might please the Almighty to convince the

26

SECTION 26

world, after my death, that I did not deserve any of the frightful accusations by which the calumnies of my enemies stained my character, wounded my heart, traduced my honour, and trampled on my dignity!

Sire ! believe your dying sister, a queen, and even more, a Christian, who would gaze with terror on the other world if her last confession were a falsehood. I die willingly : for the unhappy bless the tomb.

But more than all else, and even than death, it pains me that not one of all those whom I loved in life is standing by my dying bed, to grant me a last consolation by a pressure of the hand, or a glance of compassion, and to close my eyes in death.

Still I am not alone: God, the sole witness of my innocence, is looking down on my bed of agony, which causes me such sufferings. My guardian angel is hovering over me, and will soon guide me to the spot where I shall be able to pray /or my friends, and also for my persecutors.

Farewell, then, my royal brother! May Heaven bless you, my husband|my children|England|Denmark|and the whole world ! Permit my corpse to rest in the grave of my ancestors, and now the last unspeakably long farewell from your unfortunate
Caroline Matilda.

Mrs. Trench thus describes the prison of the unhappy queen:

" The apartment once inhabited by Matilda is a suite of five rooms, terminating in her bed-chamber. They are all hung with tapestry, and her bed is ofgreen damask. Though unsuitable to a youthful queen, they are yet spacious, convenient, and have a certain air of dignity. Her mattrass and quilt, the one of white, the other of dark-green satin, have been preserved untouched since her death. I also went to see the church, which is ornamented with painting and sculpture. A nervous person would have been startled at seeing in the floor of the chancel a large open space, discovering a flight of steps leading down to a vault, and on each side a man in black with a lighted taper. I was soon given to understand that the burying-place was here the chief object of curiosity. The coffin of the queen of Denmark is the most ornamented, and not far from it stood that of Dorothea, wife of George I."

Wraxall concludes his narrative as follows : " After her decease, Bulow and Seckendorf joined in making to the Baron de Lichtenstein the most pressing solicitations in my behalf. They entreated of him to recommend me to his Britannic majesty, for remuneration or employment. But no reply was given. I made likewise myself two applications in the course of those years to the king, which were delivered to him by persons of rank or of consideration, who had means of access to his private hours. I may now name them : they were Viscount Barrington and Dr. William Hunter. He still observed, nevertheless, the same silence; and the whole transaction had long ceased to occupy my thoughts, when, in the last days of February, 1781, nearly six years subsequent to the demise of Caroline Matilda, it most unexpectedly revived. In 1780 I came into parliament; and some months afterwards, as I wasseated nearly behind Lord North in the House of Commons, only a few members being present, and no important business in agitation, he suddenly turned round to me. Speaking in a low tone of voice, so as not to be overheard : ' Mr. Wraxall,' said he, ' I have received his majesty's commands to see and talk to you. He informs me that you rendered very important services to the late queen of Denmark, of which he has related to me the particulars. He is desirous of acknowledging them. We must have some conversation together on the subject. Can you come to me to Bushy Park, dine, and pass the day ?' I waited on him there, in June, 1781, and was received by him in his cabinet alone. Having most patiently heard my account of the enterprise in which I engaged for the queen Matilda's restoration, he asked me what remuneration I demanded ? I answered, one thousand guineas, as a compensation for the expense which I had incurred in her majesty's service, and an employment. He assured me that I should have both. Robinson, then secretary to the treasury, paid me the money soon afterwards." Such was this curious and interesting adventure.

27

SECTION 27

CHAPTER II.
   The Duke Of Cumberland And His Marriage.
"princess Olive."

   In the year 1771, when the royal children were still in the schoolroom, an event took place which was the cause of considerable trouble, confusion, and much family bickering. There was then in London Lord Carhampton, formerly better known as Colonel Simon Luttrell, an Irishman of the combative sort, and of wild habits, who had been put forward to fight the battle with Mr. Wilkes. His family seat was at Luttrell's Town, now known as Woodlands, close to Dublin, a finely wooded and not unpicturesque demesne; while traditions still cling to the walls of the mansion of the old earl's revels and fierceness of temper.
   Sir Nathaniel Wraxall, who appears to have known the father of this gentleman, describes him in his old age as active, and of a pleasing figure and a high spirit, possessing a mind cast in a very original mould, though uncultivated, and an indefatigable votary of pleasure. He relates a pleasant trait of him, which shows thegentlemanly good-humour which distinguished the man of pleasure of those days, "In 1812, during the Regency, when lying in an apparently hopeless state, at his house in Bruton Street,

Berkeley Square, where he laboured under a dangerous internal malady, intelligence of his decease was prematurely carried to Carlton House. The regent, who was at table when the report arrived, lending rather too precipitate credit to the information, immediately gave away his regiment, the carabineers, to one of the company, a general officer; who lost not a moment in kissing his royal highness's hand on the appointment. No sooner had the report reached Lord Carhampton, than he instantly despatched a friend to Pall Mall, empowered to deliver a message for the prince. In it he most respectfully protested, that far from being a dead man, he hoped to surmount his present disease; and therefore humbly entreated him to dispose of any other regiment in the service, except the carabineers. Lord Carhampton humorously added, that his royal highness might rest assured he would give special directions to his attendants not to lose a moment, after it could be ascertained that he was really dead, in conveying the news to Carlton House."

One of this nobleman's daughters, Lady Anne, had married Mr. Christopher Horton, of Catton Hall, Derby, but had been left a widow. She is thus described : "A young widow of twenty-four, extremely pretty, with bewitching languishing eyes, which she could animate to enchantment if she pleased; and her coquetry was so active, so varied, and yet so habitual, that it was difficult not to see through it, and yet as difficult to resist it. She danced divinely." The Duke of Cumberland,the king's brother, was attracted by this lady, and in this year actually married her. He was considered a very weak man; and, as Wraxall says of him, " limited as his faculties were, his manner rendered them apparently meaner than they would otherwise have been esteemed "|a remark that shows the writer to have possessed considerable power of observing character.

" This lady," the same writer says, " like every member of her family, by no means wanted talents ; but they were more specious than solid|better calculated for show than for use, for captivating admiration than for exciting esteem. Her personal charms, allowance being made for the injury which they had sustained from time|for in 1786 she was no longer young|fully justified the duke's passion. No woman of her time performed the honours of her own drawing-room with more affability, ease, and dignity. The king held her in great alienation, because he believed that she lent herself to facilitate or to gratify the Prince of Wales's inclinations on some points beyond the limits of propriety|Carlton and Cumberland Houses communicating behind by the gardens." Of this there can be no doubt; the duke and his wife taking a scandalous pleasure in indoctrinating the heir-apparent into gambling and other vices, and urging him into rebellion against his father. There was also another member of the Luttrell family who lived with them when they returned to Cumberland House from abroad|Lady Elizabeth Luttrell|who is thus described. " She inherited no portion of the duchess's beauty, elegance, or prudence. Coarse and destitute of

See the Author's " Life of George IV." i. 28.

28

SECTION 28

softuess in her manners, wanting principle, and devoured by a rage for play, she finally closed her life in a manner the most humiliating as well as tragical. The Luttrells," the writer adds, "had succeeded, under George III., to the character for eccentricity enjoyed by the Herveys during the two preceding reigns."

Sir R. Heron, in his Notes, describes the fate of this lady. After saying that " she played high and cheated much, and was called the ' Princess Elizabeth,'" he tells that on the death of her sister the duchess she was thrown into jail. There she gave a hairdresser $50 to marry her, and thus assume her debts, on which she obtained her discharge. She then went to Germany, where, "being convicted of picking pockets at Augsburg, she was sentenced and condemned to clean the streets," chained to a wheelbarrow. She then poisoned herself. A strange unexpected finale for the sister-in-law of a king's brother !

Associated with this prince is the strange story of one who claimed to be of the royal family by a secret marriage, a claim that was maintained through a couple of generations. Not until the year 1866 was the matter brought to a distinct issue by public trial in a court of law, and put to rest. This was the case of the notorious Mrs. Serres, calling herself " Princess Olive," and whose daughter, Mrs. Ryves, supported her claim in our own time. This imposture, for such it was, is almost ludicrous in the impudence of its assertions and the reckless carelessness of the details of the fabrication. Mrs. Serres|" Princess Olive "|claimed to be the daughter of Prince Henry Frederick, Duke of Cumberland, brother of king George III., and Olive Wilmot.

Olive Serres was born in April 3rd, 1772, and her mother was married to the duke " at the house of Lord Archer, in Grosvenor Square, the marriage being celebrated by Dr. Wilmot, father of Olive Wilmot." At the trial, Mr. J. W. Smith set out Mrs. Ryves' case, first giving an account of Dr. Wilmot, the celebrant of the marriage, who was a doctor of divinity of Oxford, and professed to have married "Prince Poniatowski's sister." Mrs. Ryves brought the action herself, and was duly examined in support of her claims, producing a vast number of documents, certificates, etc. Here are the most important:

" The marriage of the underwritten parties was duly solemnised according to the rites and ceremonies of the Church of England, at Thomas Lord Archer's house, London, March 4th, 1767, by myself. J. Wilmot.

" Henry Frederick.
" Olive Wilmot.

"Present at the marriage of these parties,
"brooke. (Lord Warwick.)
"J. Addis.
" Attested before

" J. Dunning.
" Chatham."

But the duke, after four years, deserted this lady and married Mrs. Horton.

Olive, Princess of Cumberland, was born on April 3rd, 1772, and was privately baptised as Olive Wilmot on the same day at the house of the mother. The king,it seems, was anxious to save his brother from the dangerous consequences of the bigamous marriage with Mrs. Horton, so he had this cautionary certificate prepared:

"April 4th, 1774. " G.R.

"Whereas it is our royal will that Olive, our niece, be baptised Olive Wilmot, to operate during our
royal pleasure.

" To Lord Chatham."

Dr. Wilmot required all the steps in this mystery to be certified by the king under his hand. The truth was, he had the king in his power, for was it not he that had married his majesty to the fair Quakeress, Hannah Lightfoot ? At the back of the certificate first given was to be read:

" This is to solemnly certify that I lawfully married George Prince of Wales to Princess Hannah, his first consort, April 17th, 1759, and that two princes and a princess were the issue of such marriage. London, April 2nd, 176-.|J. Wilmot."

This was also attested by "Chatham " and " J. Dunning." Further certificates were produced, one of which was to declare that Lord Chatham was bound to pay the princess five hundred pounds a year. By the other paper his majesty gave yet more valuable recognition of the relationship.

" George R.

" We are hereby pleased to create Olive ofCumberland Duchess of Lancaster, and to grant our royal authority for Olive, our said niece, to bear and use the title and arms of Lancaster, should she be in existence at the time of our royal demise.

" Given at our palace of St. James, May 17, 1773.

" Chatham.

"J. Dunning."

Next was shown a testamentary instrument from his majesty, bequeathing her fifteen thousand pounds. Certificates of the marriage of Hannah Lightfoot and the king were also produced, signed George Guelph and Hannah Lightfoot, the witnesses being William Pitt and Anne Taylor. There was also a will of the fair Quakeress herself, signed " Hannah Regina," witnessed by William Pitt.

Dr .Wilmot, the husband of Princess Poniatowski, died in 1807, and all his papers passed into the hands of Lord Warwick. Mrs. Serres was ignorant of her illustrious birth until!815, when Lord Warwick being seriously ill thought it right to reveal it to her, and also to the Duke of Kent. These papers, as regards their abundance, were convincing enough. There were forty-three signatures of Dr. Wilmot, twelve of George III., eighteen of the Duke of Kent, etc.

Various awkward certificates were produced from the custody of the regular official, such as the baptismal one of Princess Olive as the daughter of Robert and Anne Wilmot. But this was explained as being done by direction of the king.

" I solemnly certify that I privately was married tothe Princess of Poland, the sister of the king of Poland. But an unhappy family difference induced us to keep our union secret. One dear child blessed myself, who married the Duke of Cumberland, 4 March, 1767, and died in the prime of life of a broken heart, 5 December, 1774, in France."

" As a testimony that my daughter was not at all unworthy of her royal consort, the Duke of Cumberland, Lord Warwick solemnly declares that he returned privately from the Continent to offer her marriage, but, seeing how greatly she was attached to the Duke of Cumberland, he witnessed her union with his royal highness."

" George R.

" We declare the birth of Olive, the infant of the Duke of Cumberland, by Olive his duchess, to be legitimate, who is condemned to privacy by the act of bigamy committed by her royal father.

" Warwick, Chatham,

" J. WILMOT, J. DUXNING."

All this matter was gravely set forward, but the case quickly broke down. The signatures were found not to correspond with the handwriting of the parties supposed to have made them. Lord Brooke was proved to have been Lord Warwick when he signed as " Brooke," and the Chief Baron sarcastically pointed out that such patents or grants of the king's as were put forward would have been under the great seal, and hence it was *improbable* that Dunning would have attached hissignature to an irregular paper. It could scarcely indeed be considered with due gravity, and it was dismissed by the jury before it was concluded.

The amiable Duke of Kent, I have heard, always thought there was " something " in Mrs. Serres' story, and tried to get some attention paid to her claims. Not having any money of his own, he was said to have asked Eobert Owen to make her some advances, whilst he guaranteed.

29

SECTION 29

CHAPTER III.

THE DUKE OF GLOUCESTER AND HIS MARRIAGE.

Another of the royal brothers had also contracted marriage with a subject. On the arrival of the Duke of Gloucester from abroad, in May, 1772, he found that his brother, the Duke of Cumberland, had declared his marriage, and was in complete disgrace. A Marriage Act, virtually forbidding all such marriages, had been passed; while his own with Lady Waldegrave, though of course known to everyone, yet was now become a matter that could no longer be left concealed. To add to the embarrassment of the situation, the duchess, who had been married six years, now found herself near her confinement. Both these royal brothers, who had perpetrated these *mesalliances,* were at war, as well as their ladies|the " Cumberlands " circulating stories about the " Gloucesters," and giving out that the Duchess of Gloucester's impending accouchement was " a sham," got up to excite sympathy.

But this is anticipating. Two such important marriages were not likely to remain a secret, and the king, when he learned them, showed his displeasure in the most marked way. There was a signal difference, however, between the behaviour of the two brothers. The Duke of Cumberland and his wife openly set up against the Court, and, as it were, defied his majesty. It will be seen that the Duchess of Gloucester showed more amiability and tact. So angry was the king, that in February, 1772, he sent a message to the Houses, introducing the well-known Royal Marriage Act which indeed seemed to be called for by the number of clandestine marriages with subjects in which the numerous branches of the family were to indulge themselves. Of these, within a very few years, no less than six were believed to have taken placelviz. that of the Prince of Wales, the Duke of Sussex with Lady Augusta Murray, those of the Dukes of Gloucester and Cumberland, and the two princesses, daughters of the king, who it is almost established were secretly married.

Mr. Horace Walpole's brother, Sir E. Walpole, had four illegitimate daughters, their mother being a Mrs. Clements, of Durham. These were all married to persons of position ; one when a young and beautiful girl being united to Lord Waldegrave, who in the common phrase was old enough to be her father. She became the mother of the three daughters who are grouped in one of Reynolds' most celebrated pictures. Even when she was a child she showed her impetuosity and ambition, and used to say " she would be a lady." Her father would tell her that was impossible, " for she was a beggar." " Then," she would answer, " I will be a lady- beggar."

Mr. Horace Walpole had been holding himself in reserve, being naturally fearful of compromising himselfat Court; and though persuaded the marriage had taken place, affected to know nothing of it. However, one day in May, 1772, Sir Edward sent his brother her formal acknowledgment in a letter, which the attached father calls " one of the sweetest samples of sense, language, and goodness of heart I ever saw." Nor will the reader think the praise excessive.

St. Leonards, 19 May, 1772. My DEAR AND EVER HONOURED SIR,

" You cannot easily imagine how much every past affliction has been increased to me by my not being at liberty to make you quite easy. The duty to a husband being superior to that we owe a father I hope will plead my pardon, and that instead of blaming my past reserve, you will think it commendable. When the Duke of Gloucester married me (which was in September, 1766), I promised him, upon no consideration in the world to own it, *even to you,* without his permission, which permission I never had till yesterday, when he arrived here in much better health and looksl better than ever I saw himlyet, as you may suppose, much hurt at all that passed in his absence; so much so that I have had great difficulty to prevail on him to let things as much as possible remain as they are. To secure my character, without injuring his, is the utmost of my wishes, and I daresay that you and all my relations will agree with me that I shall be much happier to be called Lady Waldegrave and respected as Duchess of Gloucester than to feel myself the cause of his leading such a life as his brother the Duke of Cumberland does, in order for me to be called your royal highness.

VOL. I. 0

I am prepared for the sort of abuse the newspapers will be full of. Very few people will believe that a woman will refuse to be called princess if it is in her power.

" *To have ike power is my pride,* and not using it in some measure pays the debt I owe the duke for the honour he has done me. All that I wish of my relations is that they will show the world that they are satisfied with my conduct, yet *seem* to disguise the reason. If ever I am unfortunate enough to be called Duchess of Gloucester there is an end of *almost* all the comforts which I now enjoy, which, if things go on as they are now, *are many."*

To this remarkable lady Mr. Walpole gives the highest praise for her good sense, sweetness, and wit. She was pious, charitable, and sincere. The effect of her letter on him was extraordinary. He declared that he was ready before to kiss her hand, now he could kiss her feet. He was filled with shame at his caution, and owned that he, a professional letter-writer, with all his long practice had never approached it in effect. As the next step towards declaring the marriage it was given out that the duke would hold a levee, as so many people had been eager to recognise them and show them respect. Numbers attended.

The Duke of Cumberland went boldly to the king to announce his marriage, and took this mode of doing so. He walked with him in the garden and gave him a letter. The king took it, saying he supposed that he need not read it now. "Yes, sir," said the duke, "you must read it directly." On doing so his majesty broke out into the most violent language, addressing his brother as " You fool! You blockhead !" and declaring that " this woman could be nothing and never should be anything." He then told him to go abroad. This led to an open breach.

" By the end of May the Duke of Gloucester fell ill, his wife was near her time; so, harassed with anxiety and the fear of disgrace, he sent a letter to the king warning him of the approaching event, and asking that the great officers of state might attend. No notice was taken. He wrote again with the same result. At last the king was induced to send a message to the effect that after the birth of a child he would send and have " your marriage, as well as the birth, inquired into, in order that both may be authenticated." This was the only part, he said, he could take with propriety, as he could not but disapprove the marriage. By her relations this was thought to be an inquisitorial proceeding, with a view to breaking it. The duke became unexpectedly equal to the occasion, and sent a firm and dignified reply, pressing that he might be allowed to authenticate the marriage at once, as the privy council might be disinclined to attend at the birth owing to the want of this authentication. This had its effect. The duke threatened that he would go to the House of Lords and tell his case and beseech despatch."

Accordingly on the 23rd May the archbishop, Terrick, waited on the duke to fix the method of proceeding. In the evening arrived the chancellor and two other lords, and were received by the duke and duchess, Bishop of Exeter, Dunning and Lee, two lawyers. The strange scene was opened by the chancellor presenting a declaration to the duke to sign. The duke indignantly refused, and sarcastically suggested it would be better for them to listen to what he had to tell. He then related that he had been married to Lady Waldegrave on September 6th, 1766, at her house in Pall Mall, by her own chaplain, Dr. Norton, who was now dead, " and there were no witnesses." The duke then said: " Your lordships remember that I was at the point of death at Florence. At that awful moment I called for Colonel Rainsford. I told him I was married. I then enjoined him on his duty to a dying master, as soon as he should have closed my eyes, to hasten to England, and repair to the king, and declare my marriage, and say that my last request was that his majesty would allow a small pittance to the widow of his favourite brother. My lords, Colonel Rainsford took notes of what I said; he has them in his pocket, and shall read them. And now, my lords, your lordships will not wonder that the last thoughts of a dying man turned on the woman he loved."

He then called on the Bishop of Exeter to state what he knew. That prelate said: " That when a marriage bill was brought in he thought it right to question Lady Waldegrave, then on a visit at his deanery. I went into her room, and telling her my reasons for inquiring, I asked whether she was married ? She burst into a flood of tears, and cried : ' I am ! I am married!' and then falling into a great agony, she wrung her hands and exclaimed : ' Good God! what have I done! I have betrayed the duke, and broken my promise to him !' "

After all, this certainly not very legal evidence wasduly registered and sworn to, the duke appealed to the three lords to lose no time: " Look," he said, " at the condition of the duchess." At a council held on the 26th, the matter was reported, and the king ordered the depositions to be entered on the books. The word " legal" was omitted, it was believed at the instigation of Lord Mansfield. Indeed, doubts were pretty general as to its legality, which reached the duke, who instantly posted off to the Archbishop of Canterbury very late at night. The Bishop of London, who was with him, was retiring, but the strange duke insisted that both should hear him, and enjoined them, by their functions, by their duty to their country, to go that moment to the king, and tell him that if he had still any doubts he would remove them. The two prelates pleaded that they would not intrude on his majesty at that hour. "Ye shall not lay your heads on your pillows till ye have seen him," was his reply. They had to go, and soon returned with a reply that, though satisfied, he would agree to the duke's being married over again if he chose it. At last, the king agreed to make no further difficulties, and to accept the marriage. His consent was given on May 27th, only just in time, for two days later the duchess was confined, and delivered in presence of the great officers of state, and with all formalities.

The Duke of Gloucester was fond of travelling, and made several tours to the Continent, of which a rough MS. journal has been preserved, kept by his equerry, Colonel Rainsford. This is but of a meagre order as, indeed, the officer honestly confesses in a note on the title. " This was lent," he says, "to the duke's chaplain,Dr. Duval, who considered it too *inexpressive,* not taking into account the hurry I was in."

A few notes from these progresses will be found interesting:

He set off, attended by four officers, at six o'clock in the morning, and reached Harwich by two in the afternoon, and at once embarked. They did not reach Helvet till June 9th. They were entertained by the Prince of Orange, and saluted with cannon on every pretence wherever they went. They were shown the fortifications, reviews, etc. At a ball, the colonel " was surprised to see the Dutch ladies and gentlemen dance the English country dances with as much exactness and as regular a step as is done in England, in particular the Princess of Orange." At the different Dutch towns, The Hague, Harlaam, etc., they proved themselves indefatigable sightseers, reviewed troops, inspected fortifications, and saw everything that was to be seen. At Harlaam "they visited Mr. Oscheides, a famous printer and letter founder. This man furnishes types to great part of Europe."

As they approached the Hanoverian frontier (the Dutch furnished escorts all the way) a party of burghers, mounted and on foot, came out to escort them. By July they had reached Copenhagen. Outside this city " the misery and poverty of the houses and villages is scarce to be conceived|the cattle making the same appearance as the owners. Nothing here has the least mark of liberty and ease but the birds, everything else being solely at the king's disposal, and it is really proper," philosophises the colonel, " for an Englishman.to come here, and have a true idea of his own happiness and enjoyment of true liberty."

On July 22nd, being the queen's birthday, the duke received company in honour of his sister, and both the king and queen gave away two blue ribbons and three white ones, as the Orders of the country. In the evening a French opera was played at Court, and after supper a ball, in which there was some difficulty relative to the officers composing the duke's suite being permitted to sup at the king's table, who, on this evening supped with about one hundred of the first class, it being a day of ceremonial. After some warm representations from Mr. Gunning, the English envoy, they were invited.

" It is the custom here on these occasions to draw tickets to hand the ladies to supper."

On the evening of the following day "a carousal was exhibited about seven o'clock. It was indeed magnificent, and well performed. It consisted of two quadrilles, each of which was composed of eight persons. The king entered the lists through Pall Mall at the head of the first quadrille, dressed in blue and silver, like Mars, and preceded by a detachment of Horse Guards, followed by 8 footmen. Then her majesty and the knights. On the other side was Count D'Andfeldt, governor of the town, at the head of the second quadrille, in white and silver. After twice making the tour of the lists, they ranged themselves on each side. The judges of the lists took their places under a canopy. They then charged their horses in order to run at the ring, and at the sound of trumpets theking and Count D'Andfeldt advanced." After various crossings, they rode at the rings which were to be carried off. " They now changed their exercise to a very extraordinary one : one man on each side advanced, and, taking a shield rode round the posts, shaking them at each other by way of defiance; and one galloping first covers his head with his shield, while the other pursues him and throws pasteboard balls at his head. Eight heads are now placed on posts of about four or five feet high at each end of the lists; when a knight advances from each side and runs with his spear at a head."

Setting off from Copenhagen they visited many towns, Coblentz, Lille, etc., still being shown fortifications, going to balls and banquets. On the last day of their travels, the indefatigable duke journeyed seventy-five miles, reaching Calais at midnight on September 1st, where he instantly embarked on the Dover packet, and reached London, having been absent only three months.

In the following year, 1770, in June, a fresh journey was undertaken, with the Princess of Wales, Lady Howe, and Lord Boston. They reached Calais after four hours' sail, which was called "an extraordinary passage." They passed to Brunswick, Pyrmont-Waldeck, now become interesting to English people from the recent alliance, and where, we were told, " 236,000 bottles were sent abroad every year, which at sixpence each, amounts to $5900." The royal party visited Vienna, when, on September 17th, "the duke was seized with a pain in his side, and was immediately blistered.

He had complained ever since his journey. He soon recovered." By October they had returned

30

SECTION 30

home, after a series of extraordinary fatigues. " The princess had never made the least complaint of the bad accommodation she often met with, but showed a cheerfulness of temper, the most complacent affability, and the most gracious behaviour to the duke's suite, and made the whole journey a most pleasant one, and took off the restraint that would otherwise have made it very unpleasant to those that attended her royal highness."

The Duke of Gloucester's health was seriously affected by these hurried journeys, and in August, 1771, he once more set out on his travels, accepting an invitation from the Grand Duke of Tuscany to visit him at Florence. Two frigates, the *Venus* and *Alarm,* were appointed to take him to Lisbon, Gibraltar, and other ports. He was to travel incognito as " Count of Connaught." He embarked from Portsmouth on the 13th of August. Of this journey some pleasant and interesting sketches are preserved by the colonel. On arriving at Lisbon the duke, though an invalid, was forced to discard his incognito and accept the honours which the rigid etiquette of the Court would impose on him. Thus the king, having ordered his barge to be manned to take him up the river, though the night was cold and the hour late, he felt himself constrained to go, and thus brought on a return of his asthma. When on other occasions he continued to maintain his incognito, he was actually not allowed to sit with their majesties at the

Royal Opera (maintained at a cost of $70,000 a-year), but was consigned to a side box, and his suite sent down into the pit. " When the king calls for any of his attendants to come to him, though of the first nobility, they fall upon their knees and remain so till he has done speaking.

At the concert the king happened to sneeze, on which the queen and princesses rose up and curtseyed; and as he continued sneezing two or three times, the curtseying was so often repeated, that the English suite could scarcely restrain their laughter." They reached Genoa by September 27, "where a very extraordinary event occurred. The Pretender was here also. He came in a felucca from Antibes this morning. This personage very naturally raised our curiosity to see him, and being lodged at the same hotel with General Harvey, he was easily seen, though he was here incognito, with a Captain Moore, of the French Service, and a Mr. Stonyeer, of a Yorkshire family, who were his only attendants. Himself was dressed in a green frock, laced with gold, a bob wig, and an English cocked hat; was tall in his person, but stooped very much, thin in the face, and red hair, and very much resembled the late General Wolfe, which discovered him to us." Two days later when the duke " was passing the corner of the street, his royal highness and the Pretender met suddenly, the latter immediately pulled off his hat with great civility, and gave place to the duke, which his royal highness returned with his usual polite manner. He was attended at this time by many English and Genevese gentlemen."

At Leghorn the duke was seized with a most serious illness, and for a time his life appeared to be in danger ; but he happily recovered.

After his marriage with Lady Waldegrave, the duke and duchess went to Italy together, when he was taken seriously ill; all through the course of which we find his attendants begging earnestly from the English representatives small portions of wine!" 6 bottles of claret and Burgundy, &c." The illness at Venice was indeed laid to the account of the " bad wine." It may be conceived there were many difficulties as to etiquette in the acknowledgment of the duchess. These were got over. It was, however, to be a disastrous wedding tour. The duke was always ill, and often the whole party, even the pages ! " You see," writes Pleydell, " we are but an invalid family." On October 18, while at Padua, "he was much worse, and really in great danger," but Mr. Pleydell begs for a little more wine!" G bottles of Burgundy and 6 of claret." He was attended by Dr. De la Rona, though he had a horror of the Italian physicians. "The duchess looks very ill from her constant attendance on the duke." By October 25 he was pronounced out of danger, though " both in bed," and " nothing but wine and peppermint were wanted."

With this may be compared "Wnutall's Sketch, given in his Memoirs.

When they were going to Venice there was much difficulty in selecting a suitable palace. There travelled with them in this party Mr. and Mrs. Heywood, Mr. Spencer, and Mr. Pleydell, six women, six pages, and seven livery servants.

In June of the next year he again fell ill at Trent, where he became extremely emaciated. Dr. Jebb and Mr. Adair were sent out from England, and arrived there in eleven days, but so ill provided was the establishment that they were " glad to have anything, even a few potatoes."

By July 30 : " The distress of the duchess is more than I can describe. His royal highness passed a very bad night, in great pain, no sleep, weak beyond expression ; in short, in all human appearance the poor amiableduke can live but a very short time. This is the opinion of the doctors." In August he was so low that the physicians expected him to expire every moment. However, by October he got to Augsburg, and by October 26 had returned to London quite restored.

In Mr. Horace Walpole's account, given in his last *Journals,* the duke is made to take a highly chivalrous partlthat of the tender and loyal husband. This, of course, came of family prejudice, for the duke was accounted a foolish, unstable man, scarcely able to take any part. It was told how when his wife was sitting to Sir Joshua, he came in without noticing the painter, and on his wife whispering him to do so, he said : " So you always begin with the head, do you ? " So to Gibbon : "What, still scribble, scribble, scribble ?" Nor did his show of attachment for his beautiful wife endure, for in a few years we find him devoted to other1 attractions.

There was another house given up to social pleasure, at which the Duke of York, then a young man of twenty- six, was an *habitug,* the attraction being the Countess of Tyrconnel, Lord Delaval's youngest daughter. "My particular acquaintance," says Sir N. Wraxall, " feminine and delicate as her figure, very fair, with a profusion of light hair." And he goes on to tell us in his odd way : " Her husband, the Earl of Tyrconnel, might be said to contribute at this time, more than any nobleman about the Court, to the recreation of the reigning family : for while his wife formed the object of the homage of one prince of the blood, his sister had long presided in

" He has sucked the breasts of some healthy country women that were sent for from the mountains." This last resource, however, seems to have had little effect.

31

SECTION 31

the affections of another. Lady Almeria Carpenter, one of the most beautiful women of her time, but to whom Nature had been sparing of intellectual gifts, was the person that attracted the Duke of Gloucester, who soon forgot all he had gone through for his amiable wife."

The duchess, a high-spirited lady, was not inclined to accept this treatment, and by 1787 a separation had taken place. This again led to very strained relations between them, reaching even to painful disputes over the education of their daughter, Princess Sophia of Gloucester. The point arose in the selection of a governess, and we find the good king interfering, and giving his advice in the choice of a certain Miss Dee, of Taplow.

In 1803 he was seized with his last illness, and the queen thus wrote to her friend Lady Harcourt of the duke's approaching end:

"Weymonth, the 29th August, 1803.

" We are in hourly expectation of the news of the poor Duke of Gloucester's Death. His sufferings must have been dreadfully Painfull; but his good temper & chearfullness never have left him. I understand that He was not quite open with His Physicians, & that some Complaint He kept a Secret for three days, to which the Medicines which they administered at that time were almost fatal. How unfortunate to deceive oneself,

& much more when one wishes to deceive others. This the King is not to know; but the Physicians stand justifyed to the world. Vaughan's attention has been quite exemplary. What a change to his poor Family. Harcourt Papers, vi. 318.

" So far I was, when they came in & told me that Mr. Vincent was arrived from. London, & that all was over with the poor Duke ; & since that moment I have never had a quarter of an hour to myself. The dear King was so well prepared for the stroke, & every thing managed with so much delicacy, that I have the satisfaction to say that His Health has not suffered. . . .

" Prince William hath behaved uncommonly well. His letter to the King was short, but very expressive of what He felt, and Respectfull, & the dear King answered it very kindjy. The Dukes of York and Cambridge arrived this morning; the Duke of Kent was here ; & I understand the Prince of Wales is a coming on Monday. . . .

" The poor Duke has left a Will, & desires to be buried at Windsor; which is granted. He left the Dutchess sole Executrix ; but with a proviso to pay His Debts, which the World says arebut very few. Yesterday we put on Mourning, which enables the King to have some air; without which His Health does suffer; but we shall reckon the beginning of it from the 1st Septr. . . .

" I ever am your Sincere Friend,

" Charlotte."

In the year 1767 news arrived of the death of another of the king's brothers, Prince Edwardlan agreeable accomplished man, a good musician, whom the Rev. Mr. Sterne had heard performing on the " Bass."

" This prince," says one of the obituary accounts of

the time, " had always been remarkably popular, being of a more open and lively disposition than the king. He was, besides, less careful of his money; and, in his early days, when his week's allowance was all expended, he would have recourse to his brother George, who readily gave him whatever he wanted."

"I well remember," writes an old domestic of the family, " Prince Edward having been forbidden to enter his mother's doors, on account of some mischievous tricks he had played; and the grooms of the chambers and pages had positive orders not to admit him. Whilst Edward lay under this interdict, some of the great nobles dined with the princess. The Prince of Wales interceded very hard to have him restored to favour, and, if not permitted to dine at her table, that he might enter with the dessert; but all was in vain. The prince, hurt by his mother's refusal, was very glum all dinner-time ; but when they withdrew to the music room, lo, and behold, there sat master Edward, full dressed !!who rose and made a very low reverence, as his mother and sisters entered. ' Hey-day, sir,' says the princess, ' who has dared to disobey my commands, and permitted you to enter these doors ?' The prince replied, ' Don't be angry, my dear mother, nobody has disobeyed you; I have not been admitted within these doors, nor violated your orders ; for I came in through the middle window, by the help of the lamplighter's ladder: so I hope you will give me permission to remain.' The elder prince looked at his mother in a way that spoke more powerfully than words; the frolic was laughed at, and Edward obtained his pardon, at which no one was more pleased than his brother George, who was always ready, but notalways able, to help him out of the numerous scrapes into which he was continually falling.

" On the same authority, it is said, that after Prince Edward was fifteen, he was for ever scaling walls and getting down areas on daring adventures. Once he was locked up for six hours in the dairy at Kew, by a girl whom he plagued sadly, and who promised she would come to him at dusk, instead of which, she turned the key upon the frolicsome youth, who had no means of escape till his mother came home. During this restraint he amused himself with disarranging the economy of the dairy, under the pretext of endeavouring to make butter and cheese. When the princess was informed of this affair, she became very highly offended; the girl was immediately discharged, and the prince was severely reprimanded. But he displayed no sense of shame or sorrow, telling his mother that, being fond of rural studies, he had gone into the dairy merely to learn how to churn.

" Prince Edward, soon after the accession of his brother to the throne, was created Duke of York; but the volatility of his temper would not suffer him to fix his residence at Court. Travelling was his great delight, and his practice was to rise early every morning, when he set down in writing all the transactions and observations that had occurred during the preceding day. By this means he could, on turning to his diary, immediately ascertain where he had been, what he had noticed, and with .whom he had conversed at any particular time. After visiting most parts of the kingdom, he went through France, Germany, and Italy; receiving everywhere the honours due to his exalted rank, andgiving pleasure to all by the liberality of his conduct, the suavity of his manners, and the habitual cheerfulness of his temper."

There is an account of this prince in Mr. Cole's papers, a portion only of which has been printed. Of his character it thus speaks : " He was considered a very good-tempered and affable prince, but he was certainly a very trifling and insignificant one. His very appearance showed what he was ; added to a very indifferent person, being rather undersized, *baker-kneed,* as it is called, with large white eyes and whitish or light- coloured hair. He was of an amorous disposition. . . . I have been told that his private conversation was as weak and low as his person was contemptible."

In the month of September, 1767, the Duke of York, who was, as usual, travelling abroad, was seized with a fatal illness at Monaco, and died. This gay and interesting prince was not thirty years of age, and had made a favourable impression on everyone he encountered. The papers of the day contained the following account :

" On Sunday last Captain Wrottesley arrived here from Monaco with the melancholy account that his royal highness, Edward Augustus, Duke of York and Albany, died at that place on the 17th instant, about eleven o'clock in the morning, of a malignant fever, after a severe illness of fourteen days, to the great grief of their majesties and all the royal family. The body was opened and embalmed, and was ordered by Commodore Spry to be put on board his majesty's ship Montreal, Captain Cosby, to be brought to England.

" His royal highness had danced rather too much

VOL. I.

at the chateau of a person of fashion ; and this had not only fatigued him, but occasioned a very strong perspiration. As soon as the ball was finished the prince gave orders for his carriages to be got ready immediately to set off for Toulon, from whence he was distant some three or four leagues. The gentlemen of the train, Colonels

Morrison and St. John, and Captain Wrottesley, earnestly represented to his royal highness the necessity of his remaining where he was, if not to go to bed, yet till he was cool and had shifted himself. The prince declared there was no actual occasion for such caution ; that he would wrap himself up in his cloak, and that would be sufficient; he did so, and stepped into his carriage. This was on the 29th of August. The next day his royal highness complained of a slight chilliness and shivering; the indisposition, however, appeared so very trifling that he went at night to the comedy, but before it was over his royal highness found himself infinitely worse, and was obliged to withdraw. He was feverish, thirsty, and complained of an immoderate heat all over his body. By proper care, and drinking plentifully, the duke was greatly better in the morning, and therefore set forward for Monaco, the prince of which (who was personally acquainted with his royal highness in his former tour to Italy) was waiting there in expectation of the honour of a visit from him ; and the duke was the rather inclined to accelerate his journey thither, as in that prince's palace he might naturally look for an assistance and accommodation superior to what he could reasonably hope to meet with in common places.

"The weather happened to be uncommonly hot,

which not a little incommoded his royal highness. He nevertheless arrived at Monaco in good spirits, but feverish, and with a headache; the latter of which he imputed principally to the intense heat of the sun that whole day. The next day the duke was worse, and took to his bed entirely. In hopes of a recovery, and unwilling unnecessarily to alarm the king, his royal parent, and relations, the duke enjoined his attendants on no account to write concerning his illness to England. All possible advice and assistance were given, but to no purpose; the fever was unconquerable. His royal highness now saw the danger of his situation; and he saw it with a fortitude and resignation rarely to be met with where bloom of youth and dignity of station are united. Convinced that, without some unexpected turn in his distemper, he must die, his royal highness, with the utmost calmness and composure of mind, adjusted every step consequent on the fatal event himself. His royal highness ordered that Captain "Wrottesley should bring the news to England, and in what method it should be disclosed. The captain was first to wait on Mr. Le Grand, of Spring Gardens, and with him to go to Leicester House, and then to Gloucester House ; and having communicated the event to the dukes his brothers, to proceed to their majesties, submitting it to the king and queen in what manner and by whom it should be imparted to his royal parent. After his royal highness had settled this arrangement he seemed remarkably easy. He declared himself perfectly resigned to the Divine will; and he spoke of his dissolution with all the piety and resolution of a Christian and a man; acting up to those exalted characters to his latest breath.His royal highness, through the mercy of the Great Creator, was sensible to his latest breath; and the very morning of his death dictated a letter to their majesties, his illustrious parent, and the royal family ; desiring the writer to expedite it, as he had but a few moments to spare, and those to employ in still more momentous concerns.

" Before his royal highness died we are told that he ordered all the gentlemen of his retinue to his bedside, where he took a very affectionate leave of them ; and desired that, as he could not possibly live many hours longer, his blisters might be taken off, to give him a little ease in his last moments, which, it is said, was done accordingly.

"Among many other particulars related upon this melancholy occasion, the following seems also to be authenticated. His royal highness had not taken to his bed above three or four days before Colonel Morrison also found himself exceedingly ill. The duke insisted on the colonel's declining his attendance on him, and that he should keep his own chamber. The colonel humbly begged permission to continue in the performance of his duty. His royal highness was, nevertheless, still very pressing ; most amiably and benevolently urging : ' Morrison, thy life is of much consequence ; the preservation of it is of more importance than mine ; you have a family, be careful of your health for their sakes.' However, Colonel Morrison importuned so strongly, that the duke at length acquiesced.

" His royal highness was desirous of being attended by a Protestant clergyman, and expresses were sent to several sea-ports, distant as well as neighbouring, inhopes of meeting with some ships of Commodore Spry's squadron, on board of which might be a chaplain; but the search was fruitless.

" The morning his royal highness died, he called Mr. Murray, his first page, to his bed-side; he asked him some questions, gave him some particular directions and advice, and took a moving leave of him ; even in dying, his royal highness showed the most zealous affection for him ; ' Ah ! Murray,' said he, ' thou wilt lose thy master !' "

The duke's remains were interred in Westminster Abbey.

The Prince of Monaco showed the greatest feeling, putting all his Court, officers, servants, even the bells, in mourning ; and having cannon fired every half-hour till the duke's remains were put on board. A magnificent present of horses was sent to him from the Court of England in gratitude. It was curious that, like Goldsmith, and many more, he carried his devotion to "James's Powders" to the extent of imperilling his life.

" The person who conveyed the news to the princess dowager was Mr. Le Grand. His name was carried to her royal highness and he was ordered in. Mr. Le Grand began by saying that Captain Wrottesley was arrived (the captain of the vessel). He had no occasion to say more ; her royal highness, in the most piercing tone of agony stopped him short with : ' Mr. Wrottesley come ? There needs no more. I know the rest;' and immediately withdrew in the greatest anguish. Her royal highness is something better though still in much affliction."

By his will it was said he had left his house in Pall Mall, furniture, etc., to the Duke of Gloucester; his diamond star, George and Garter, to the Duke of Cumberland. The Duke of Gloucester was much affected, and declared that he " never could live in a house, every room of which would only serve to put him in daily remembrance of the loss."

It was curious that the king, in February, 1773, should have allowed the effects, curios, etc., of his mother to be disposed of by auction. This step was taken by order of her executors. She left no debts, but considerable savings, so the proceeding caused surprise. A French collection of silver medals of Louis XIV. and XV. fetched only eight pounds. A German Prayer- book, with various devices enamelled in gold, and embellished with diamonds and miniature paintings, was sold for twenty-six guineas.

In October, 1786, died the Princess Amelia, the king's aunt. She had sometime before been anxious to have a separate residence of her own, and the king had purchased for her Gunnersbury House, close to Acton, for which he was said to have paid the sum of 9000 guineas. About a fortnight previous to her death, she consulted her physician, Dr. Warren, asking him with the most firm composure, "how long he thought her existence might be prolonged." He replied, " that it was impossible strictly to tell: that her dissolution would probably take place within three or four days, but it was within the limit of possibility her life might be extended to a week." This decision she received with Christian fortitude. Her time from that moment

was employed in arranging her affairs, and providing for all who depended upon her. Her loss was little felt by the royal family of Great Britain, to none of whom did she leave the smallest legacy out of her large property; the bulk of which passed, by her bequest, to the Prince of Hesse Cassel, who was mean enough to refuse giving mourning to her domestics. The habits of the deceased princess were very peculiar. Every morning she regularly paid a visit to her stables, for the purpose of examining the state of the horses; and she never got into or out of her carriage at the front of the house, but always in the back yard. Her dress was such, that at first view she might have been taken for one o$ the masculine gender. She took snuff immoderately, and was no less addicted to cards. Her deportment, however, was exceedingly repulsive, even when engaged at her favourite amusement. One evening in the rooms at Bath, which fashionable place of resort she regularly visited, the princess addressed her partner in the technical language of the game: " We are eight, love." The other jocosely answered: " Yes, my dear;" on which she got up indignantly, threw the cards in his face, and retired. At another time, a general officer, who was standing by the table where the party were playing, perceiving the snuff-box of the princess standing open, incautiously took a pinch ; which, when her royal highness observed, she ordered the servant in waiting to throw the remainder of the contents into the fire. She was uncommonly attached to her brother, William Duke of Cumberland, whose clumsy statue, opposite to her windows in Cavendish Square, would sometimes engage her attention for

hours together. The princess was the patroness of the celebrated Father le Courayer, who had been obliged to leave France on account of the liberality of his opinions; and this venerable man, out of gratitude, bequeathed to her the whole of his manuscripts, which she gave to Dr. Bell for publication ; though, it must be confessed, they were little deserving of that distinction.

3ook the

THE PRINCESSES.

32

SECTION 32

CHAPTER I.

PRINCESS AMELIA AND HER SISTERS.

The interesting Princess Amelia, her affectionate nature, and the tragic incidents of her death, have endeared her memory to her contemporaries. The parting with her father, her solemn "remembrance" as she put a ring on his finger, certainly precipitated his final attack of madness. During her illness she wrote :

"As to myself I certainly proceed towards my recovery slowly and surely; wch is, I hope, more likely to be lasting than if it took place rapidly. The kindness I experience is very very great; *deeply* felt, but not easily expressed. Indeed, my dear I/ Harcourt, volumes would not contain all I *feel;* & when I had *used* all the words that the English Language contains, to express Gratitude & affection, it would neither do justice to my *feelings,* nor satisfy them. God knows my heart is gratefully devoted to my family. I possess the greatest of blessings, kind Parents & Sisters. But where one feels most, it makes one silent; & the generality of mankind will think me a *bnite,* I know.

" Allow me to wish you & Lord Harcourt the usual compliments of the season, a happy return of the New year; & I must add, I hope this time next year we shall find this country has happily weathered the storm which still threatens it. I am a little superstitious. The Sun *Shone* this morning ; a good omen ; & particularly as it now seldom happens.

" Our dear King, who is our Sheet Anchor, & whom we look up to next to heaven, is well. If he is preserved to us, I think we must do well. Providence has never forsaken him; & I hope I don't presume too much in putting my firm trust in *Him,* & relying on Him not to withdraw, in the hour of apparent *need,* that protection our dear Good father has so wonderfully experienced on many occasions.

"Adieu. Believe me ever, my dear I/ H., with kind remembrance to Ld H.,

" Yours very sincerely,

"amelia."

Again, she showed a thoughtful interest in a child, the daughter of her brother|Augusta d'Este, daughter of the Duke of Sussex, and Lady Augusta Murray, late Countess d'Ameland.

" My Dear LT Harcourt,

" You & I have had so many conversations upon the subject of a *little Girl,* that I should feel myself to blame did I not communicate to *you* the enclosed letter ; which will explain better than I can *all I* had to sayupon the subject. You must not own to Augustus I *now write,* or that you have received this letter; but I thought it would prepare you for what you *are* to *expect.*

" I have written to Augustus to advise his now writing to you. The idea he had concerning M^{TM}. Walker will not do in any way; as, besides living here, her health would not admit of her paying that attention to the child she must require. If you propose M^{TM}. Williams, don't you think for two years she had better keep the child with her entirely away from *all* her connections."

There is in existence, too, a charming letter of hers to some poor girl who had gone astray, full of sympathy, advice, and wholesome counsel.

Her amiable sister, the princess royal, happily described her:

" Poor dear Amelia has had a long and dreadful illness. She is a Sweet, amiable, Pious, good *little Soul,* Patient beyond all description; and has the greatest Resolution and Fortitude. She is a perfect Example ; I really am benefitted by Her goodness. I never saw so good a disposition, so thoughtfull and considerate to those about Her, so afraid to fatigue them by their sitting up with Her. I never saw any body more careful! to disguise Her sufferings for fear of vexing others; and truly it is most vexing to see Her so long in such a sad state of Health.

Miss Knight gives the following graphic picture of these last scenes :

" I come now to a most melancholy time. Dear Princess Amelia, who had derived no benefit from a lengthened visit to Weymouth, was removed to Windsor, and inhabited a lodge near the Castle. Day by day she sank more and more under her great sufferings. Though pale and emaciated, she still retained her beauty. She wished to live, but was thoroughly resigned when she found there was no hope of her remaining long upon earth. Her sentiments of piety were pure, enlightened, and fervent. I saw her a few days before her death, when, taking off her glove, she showed me her hand| it was perfectly transparent.

" She was particularly fond of music, but latterly could not bear the sound of a pianoforte even in another room. The Princess Augusta thereupon gave her a bird which sang very sweetly, and with a very soft note, and she took pleasure in listening to it. When the king saw his beloved daughter for the last time, she said to him : ' Remember me, but do not grieve for me.'

" I shall never forget the last evening of my seeing him. It was the anniversary of his accession. The whole family, except the Queen of Wurtemberg and dear Princess Amelia, were present when he entered the- room, the queen holding his arm. As he went round the circle as usual, it was easy to perceive the dreadful excitement in his countenance. As he could not distinguish persons, it was the custom to speak to him as- he approached, that he might recognise by the voice whom he was about to address. I forget what it was Isaid to him, but shall ever remember what he said to me : ' You are not uneasy, I am sure, about Amelia. You are not to be deceived, but you know that she is in no danger.' At the same time he squeezed my hand with such force that I could scarcely help crying out. The queen, however, dragged him away.

Previously Princess Boyal of England.

" Princess Amelia expired on the birthday of the Duke of Kent, who had had some dispute with the Duke of York, then commander-in-chief. I was told, however, by Lady Aylesbury, who was in waiting, and had dined quietly with the melancholy party of the royal family, that the Duke of York said to her, in a whisper :' Though this is a sad day, I must drink the health of poor Edward.'

" Two days afterwards Princess Augusta sent for me, and as I was sitting with her, one of her dressers entered the room with a birdcage in her hand, and her fingers in her eyes. ' Princess Amelia,' she said, ' gave orders before her death that this bird should be returned to your royal highness; but not on the day she died, nor the day after, that it might not afflict you too much in the first hours of your grief. But she wished you to know how much she was obliged to you for giving it to her, and what a comfort its sweet voice had been.

" Two ladies sat up with the corpse every night until the time of tho funeral. I was directed to perform this duty one night with Lady George Murray. We were in a room, adjoining that in which was the coffin, with the doors open. On the table was a book, which had been a favourite with Princess Amelia. It was Tilikeper's 'Thoughts on Religious Subjects,'and many of them had a pencil mark.

" The king recovered sufficiently to be told of her death, and he arranged everything relating to the ceremony of the funeral. One of the queen's ladies was to go as chief mourner, followed, of course, by others belonging to the princesses ; but, although I had no engagement of that kind, the king chose that I should have a place in the procession, knowing how sincerely I was attached to the princess. I also heard that, when lying on her death-bed, the two persons whom the princess most warmly recommended to her father, were Mrs. Williamslwho had been her nurse and was then attending herland myself. I was also named amongst the few persons to whom she desired that remembrances should be given. For the anthem the king had selected a passage from the sixteenth Psalm, which used to be often sung by the princess and her father."

The tragic incident of the dying young princess giving a ring to her father, with the declaration, " Ecmember me," is well known, but the details of what actually took place are not so familiar, and add interest to the affecting scene :

" She had given orders to the jeweller to prepare a ring for his majesty, which she wished to have immediately, as she now became sensible of her approaching dissolution. It was twelve o'clock before Mr. Rundell left her presence, and he undertook to be back from London before three o'clock the following day. One of Mr. Rundell's men knocked up a Frenchman (Lebarre) at two o'clock in the morning to do the principal part of the ring. The jeweller brought the ring to her royal highness at a quarter before three, so that there was

33

SECTION 33

plenty of time before the king went to visit the princess. On his majesty's approaching the bed of the princess he put out his hand to take hold of hers as was his daily custom, and her royal highness at that time put the ring on his finger, without saying anything, which agitated him very much. The inscription was her royal highness's name and the words ' Remember me.' A lock of her royal highness's hair was worked into the ring."

Mr. Charles Knight describes how, " after the death of Amelia the princess, I had the task of making a catalogue of her well-selected library. It seemed like a voice from the tomb when I recently lighted upon a touching prayer, which I had copied from a blank leaf of her Prayer Book. It will not now be considered a violation of confidence if I print it:

"Gracious God, support thy unworthy servant in this time of trial. Let not the least murmur escape my lips, nor any sentiment but of the deepest resignation enter my heart; let me make the use Thou intendest of that affliction Thou has laid upon me. It has convinced me of the vanity and emptiness of all things here; let it draw me to Thee as my support, and fill my heart with pious trust in Thee, and in the blessings of a redeeming Saviour, as the only consolations of a state of trial. Amen."

" Some lines have been circulated and admired as her composition:

Unthinking, idle, wild, and young,
I laughed, and danced, and talked, and sung.
VOL. I. Q

The truth is-, *as* was pointed out to me by Mr. Hawkcs- worth, they are to be found in a volume of poems written by a lady and admired and copied by the princess."

It is well known that there were strange stories in circulation as to the attachments of the princesses, who were kept under almost conventual restraint. Princess Amelia was believed to have told her father on her death-bed the secret of her irregular or illegal marriage to the late General Fitzroy.

Another princess was said to have wedded, in the same unlicensed fashion, an equerry who figured a good deal in Madame D'Arblay's memoirs, and the offspring of this union was after remarked for his strange likeness to the royal family. It was no doubt in connection with reports of this character that Princess Sophia wrote to her friend:

PRINCESS SOPHIA TO LADY HARCOURT. "MY VERY DEAR LADY HAR-COURT,

"... You will easily believe that our *private conversation* has often occurred to my mind ; how happy I now am that I had courage to begin it, for the excessive kindness of yr manner has, I assure you, greatly soothed my distressed and unhappy days & hours. Be assured, dearest I/ H., that I will do all in my power to prove I am not ungrateful for all your kind concern about me, by the prudence of my conduct; but you willallow, I am sure, that I require time to recover my Spirits, which have met with so severe a blow.

His second wife has assured a friend of the author's that the general had informed her that the story was true. This is further confirmed by her bequest to him of her jewels, and of the Regent'a behaviour to him.

" I have no doubt that I was originally to blame, therefore I must hear patiently the *reports,* however unjust they are, as I have partially myself to thank for them ; but, dearest I/ H., when I reflect of the difference of y behaviour & that of others, it shows me how *insincere* the generality of this world are, & how one ought to *value* & revere a *true friend,* which is most justly stiled *'the most precious Jewel in life.'* It is grievous to think what a little trifle will *slur a young woman's character for ever.* I do not complain, I submit patiently, & promise to strive to regain mine, which, however imprudent I have been, has I assure you been injured unjustly."

It will be interesting to see the Princess Royal, as she appeared in all the state and ceremonial of a Court ball on the royal birthday night. The ball was opened soon after nine by his royal highness the Prince of Wales, who danced the two first minuets with the Princess Royal and Lady Augusta Campbell; after which the Duke of Cumberland danced with the Ladies Salisbury and Aylesford.

" At the leve'e his majesty wore a rich suit of black velvet, decorated with a brilliant star and garter loop, her majesty, as usual, was plainly dressed, without her jewels, in a boue de Paris satin, trimmed with gold, crape, &c. The Princess Royal had a white and gold, with a green spot, the beautiful manufacture of England, superbly ornamented with a profusion of jewels. The Prince of Wales was dressed in a faint peach-colouredvelvetcoat and small-clothes, with a light-coloured satin waistcoat, the whole most splendidly embroidered with silver; the seams of the coat were likewise lined with an extensive embroidery, which rather disgusted the eye, and gave an idea of expense without conveying the least appearance of taste or elegance. His royal highness wore a white feather in his hat, which was adorned with three double strings of brilliants to each side, and a most beautiful button and tassel of the same sparkling composition."

On these occasions some such notification as the following was issued :

"Lord Chamberlain's Office, May 24, 1782.

" Such ladies as desire to dance minuets at the ball which is to be at St. James's on Tuesday, the 4th of June next, are requested to send their names and rank in writing to this office, on or before Saturday, the 1st of June, and to send for their tickets the Monday following, between the hours of ten in the morning and two in the afternoon.

" N.B.|No attendance will be given at this office on the day of the ball after two o'clock.

" To prevent the inconveniences which have arisen from the space before their majesties, which is allotted to minuet dancing, being exceedingly crowded, it is requested that those ladies only who mean to dance will send for dancers' tickets, and sit in those places, as the seats have been found too few to accommodate the dancers."

" The Princess Royal in going down the first country dance had the fringe of her petticoat by some meansentangled with her buckle, which occasioned the dance to stop for some little time. On recovering from this accident her royal highness appeared rather embarrassed ; but the involuntary blush which this circumstance called forth added to her native beauty. This incident, however, gave rise to the following piece of ingenious levity :

SONG.

Twas at the birth-night ball, sir,
God bless our gracious Queen,
Where people great and small, sir,
Are on a footing seen :

    As down the dance,
With heels from France,

    A royal couple flew,
Tho' well she tripped,
The lady slipped,

    Doodle, doodle, doo,
    The Princess lost her shoe;
    Her Highness hopp'd
    The fiddlers stopp'd,
    Not knowing what to do.
    Amaz'd at such a pause, sir,

The dancers to a man,
Eager to hear the cause, sir,
Around the Princess ran,
Lord Hertford too,
Like lightning flew,

And tho' unused to knuckle,
Laid down his wand,
And lent a hand

Her royal shoe to buckle.
Doodle, doodle, doo, &c.

" The queen retired a little before twelve, after which the country dances were resumed ; and, though some of the company withdrew, the room continued very full till two in the morning.

After Miss Burney had resigned ner place at Court la foolish frivolous step, which she must have afterwards repented oflshe enjoyed the privilege of coming to see the royal family, who all welcomed her with the most affectionate cordiality. There were a hundred little touches of thoughtfulness and unaffected kindnesses that bear testimony so effectively to their goodness, that the account of one of the visits may be introduced here, as it gives a series of sketches of all the members of the family, each presented under the most engaging and agreeable aspect. A picture of a more affectionate family circle could not be conceived.

" I went upstairs," she says, " to Miss Planta'a room, where, while I waited for her to be called, the charming Princess Mary passed by, attended by Mrs. Cheveley. She recollected me, and turned back, and came up to me with a fair hand graciously held out to me. 'How do you do, Madame d'Arblay !' she cried : ' I am vastly
clad to see you again; and how does your little boy
"do?'

" I gave her a little account of the rogue, and she proceeded to inquire about my new cottage, and its actual state. I entered into a long detail of its bare walls and unfurnished sides, and the gambols of the little man unencumbered by cares of fractures from useless ornaments, that amused her good-humoured interest in my affairs very much; and she did not leave me till Miss Planta came to usher me to Princess Augusta.

"That kind princess received me with a smile so- gay, and a look so pleased at my pleasure in again seeingher, that I quite regretted the etiquette that prevented a chaste embrace. She was sitting at her toilette, having her hair dressed. The royal family were all going at night to the play. She turned instantly from the glass to face me, and insisted upon my being seated immediately. She then wholly forgot her attire and ornaments and appearance, and consigned herself wholly to conversation, with that intelligent animation which marka her character. She inquired immediately how my little boy did, and then with great sweetness after his father, and after my father.

" She then gave me some account of the ceremony; and when I told her I had heard that her royal highness the bride had never looked so lovely, she confirmed the praise warmly, but laughingly added: " 'Twas the queen dressed her I You know what a figure she used to make of herself, with her odd manner of dressing herself; but mamma said, " Now really, Princess Royal, this one time is the last, and I cannot suffer you to make such a quiz of yourself; so I will really have you dressed properly." And indeed the queen was quite in the right, for everybody said she had never looked so well in her life.'

" The word *quiz,* you may depend, was never the queen's. I had very great comfort, however, in gathering, from all that passed on that subject, that the royal family are persuaded this estimable princess is happy.

" The Princess Elizabeth now entered, but she did not stay. She came to ask something of her sister relative to a little fete she was preparing, by way of a collation, in honour of the Princess Sophia, who wastwenty this day. She made kind inquiries after m)' health, etc., and, being mistress of the birthday-fete, hurried off, and I had not the pleasure of seeing her any more.

" I must be less minute, or I shall never have done.

" My charming Princess Augusta renewed the conversation.

"Admiral Duncan's noble victory became the theme, but it was interrupted by the appearance of the lovely Princess Amelia, now become a model of grace, beauty, and sweetness, in their bud. She gave me her hand with the softest expression of kindness, and almost immediately began questioning me concerning my little boy and with an air of interest the most captivating. But again Princess Augusta declined any interrupters : ' You shall have Madame d'Arblay all to yourself, my dear, soon,' she cried, laughingly; and, with a smile a little serious, the sweet Princess Amelia retreated.

" It would have been truly edifying to young ladies living in the great and public world to have assisted in my place at the toilette of this exquisite Princess Augusta. Her ease, amounting even to indifference, as to her ornaments and decoration, showed a mind so disengaged from vanity, so superior to mere personal appearance, that I could with difficulty forbear manifesting my admiration. She let the hair-dresser proceed upon her head without comment and without examination, just as if it was solely his affair; and when the man, Robinson, humbly begged to know what ornaments he was to prepare the hair for, she said, ' Oh, there are my feathers and jewels, and my gown is blue, so take what you think right.' And when he begged she wouldsay whether she would have any ribbons or other things mixed with the feathers and jewels, she said, ' You understand all that best, Mr. Robinson, I'm sure; there are the things, so take just what you please.' And after this she left him wholly to himself, never a moment interrupting her discourse or her attention with a single direction. I begged permission to return afterwards for my unfinished narrative, and then proceeded to the White Closet.

" The queen was alone, seated at a table, and working. Miss Planta opened the door and retired without entering. I felt a good deal affected by the sight of her majesty again, so graciously accorded to my request; but my first and instinctive feeling was nothing to what I experienced when, after my profoundly respectful reverence, I raised my eyes, and saw in hers a look of sensibility so expressive of regard, and so examining, so penetrating into mine, as to seem to convey, involuntarily, a regret I had quitted her. This, at least, was the idea that struck me, from the species of look which met me, and it touched me to the heart, and brought instantly, in defiance of all struggle, a flood of tears into my eyes. I was some minutes recovering; and when I then entreated her forgiveness, and cleared up, the voice with which she spoke, in hoping I was well, told me she had caught a little of my sensation, for it was by no means steady. Indeed, at that moment, I longed to kneel and beseech her pardon for the displeasure I had felt in her long resistance of my resignation ; for I think, now, it was from a real and truly honourable wish to attach me to her for ever.

" She looked ill, pale, and harassed. The king was but just returned from his abortive visit to the Nore, and the inquietude she had sustained during that short separation, circumstanced many ways alarmingly, had evidently shaken her. I saw with much, with deep concern, her sunk eyes and spirits ; I believe the sight of me raised not the latter.

" We spoke of poor Mrs. Schwellyland of her successor, Mile. Backmeisterland of mine, Mrs. Bremyere; and I could not but express my concern that her majesty had again been so unfortunate, for Mile. Jacobi had just retired to Germany, ill and dissatisfied with everything in England. The Princess Augusta had recounted to me the whole narrative of her retirement, and its circumstances. The queen told me that the king had very handsomely taken care of her. But such frequent retirements are heavy weights upon the royal bounty. I felt almost guilty when the subject was started; but not from any reproach, any allusionlnot a word was dropped that had not kindness and goodness for its basis and its superstructure at once.

" ' How is your little boy ?' was one of the earliest questions. ' Is he here ?' she added.

" ' Oh yes,' I answered, misunderstanding her, ' he is my shadow ; I go nowhere without him.'

" ' But *here, I* mean ?'

" ' Oh no ! ma'am, I did not dare presume '

" I stopped, for her look said it would be no presumption. And Miss Planta had already desired me to bring him to her next time; which I suspect was by higher order than her own suggestion.

" She permitted me to speak a good deal of the Princess of Wirtemberg, whom they still all call PrincessRoyal She told me she had worked her wedding garment, and entirely, and the real labour it had proved, from her steadiness to have no help, well knowing that three stitches done by any other would make it immediately said it was none of it by herself ' As the bride of a widower,' she continued, ' I know she ought to be in white and gold ; but as the Bang's eldest daughter she had a right to white and silver, which she preferred.'

" She then deigned to inquire very particularly about our new cottage, its size, its number of rooms, and its grounds. I told her honestly it was excessively comfortable, though unfinished and unfitted up, for that it had innumerable little contrivances and conveniences, just adapted to our particular use and taste, as M. d'Arblay had been its sole architect and surveyor. ' Then, I dare say,' she answered, 'it is very commodious, for there are no people understand enjoyable accommodations more than French gentlemen, when they have the arranging them themselves.'

" This was very kind, and encouraged me to talk a good deal of my partner in his various works and employments; and her manner of attention was even touchingly condescending, all circumstances considered. And she then related to me the works of two French priests, to whom she has herself been so good as to commit the fitting up of one of her apartments at Frogmore. And afterwards she gave me a description of what another French gentleman|elegantly and feelingly avoiding to say emigrant|had done in a room belonging to Mrs. Harcourt, at Sophia Farm, where he had the sole superintendence of it, and has made it beautiful.

"When she asked about our field, I told her we hoped in time to buy it, as Mr. Locke had the extreme kindness to consent to part with it to us, when it should suit our convenience to purchase instead of renting it. I thought I saw a look of peculiar satisfaction at this, that seemed to convey pleasure in the implication thence to be drawn, that England was our decided, not forced or eventual residence. And she led me on to many minute particulars of our situation and way of living, with a sweetness of interest I can never forget.

" She talked a good deal of the Duchess of York, who continues the first favourite of the whole royal family. She told me of her beautiful works, lamented her indifferent health, and expatiated upon her admirable distribution of her time and plan of life and charming qualities and character.

" Of her own royal daughters she permitted me also to talk, especially of my two peculiar idols. And she gave me a copious description of the new improvements still going on at Frogmore, with a detail of some surprises the king had given her, by orders and buildings erected in the gardens during her absence.

" A door was now opened from an inner apartment, where, I believe, was the grand collation for the Princess Sophia's birthday, and a tall thin young man appeared at it, peeping and staring, but not entering.

" ' How do you do, Ernest ?' cried the princess ; ' I hope you are well; only pray do shut the door.'

" He did not obey, nor move, either forwards or backwards, but kept peering and peeping. She called to him again, beseeching him to shut the door; but he was determined to first gratify his curiosity, and when.he had looked as long as he thought pleasant, he entered the apartment; but Princess Augusta, instead of receiving and welcoming him, only said, ' Good-bye, my dear Ernest; I shall see you again at the play.'

" He then marched on, finding himself so little desired, and only saying : ' No, you won't; I hate the play.'

" I had risen when I found it one of the princes, and with a motion of readiness to depart; but my dear princess would not let me.

" When we were alone again: ' Ernest,' she said, ' has a very good heart; only he speaks without taking time to think.'

" She then gave me an instance. The Orange family by some chance were all assembled with our royal family when the news of the great victory at sea arrived; or at least upon the same day. ' We were all,' said she,''distressed for them upon so trying an occasion; and at supper, we talked, of course, of every other subject; but Ernest, quite uneasy at the forbearance, said to me: ' You don't think I won't drink Admiral Duncan's health to-night ? " " Hush !" cried I. " That's very hard indeed!" said he, quite aloud. I saw the Princess of Orange looking at him, and was sure she had heard him ; I trod upon his foot and made him turn to her. She looked so disturbed, that he saw she had understood him, and he coloured very high. The Princess of Orange then said : " I hope my being here will be no restraint upon anybody; I know what must be the subject of everybody's thoughts, and I beg I may not prevent its being so of their discourse."

"Our next interruption, I think, was from a very gentle tap at the door, and a " May I come in ?' froma soft voice, while the lock was turned, and a youthful and very lovely female put in her head.

"The princess immediately rose and said: '0 yes,' and held out her two hands to her ; turning at the same to me, and saying, ' Princess Sophia.'

" I found it was the Duke of Gloucester's daughter. She is very fat, with very fine eyes, a bright, even dazzling bloom, fine teeth, a beautiful skin, and a look of extreme modesty and sweetness.

" She curtseyed to me so distinguishingly, that I was almost confused by her condescension, fearing she might imagine, from finding me seated with the Princess Augusta, and in such close conference, I was somebody.

"' You look so fine and so grand,' cried she, examining the princess's attire, which was very superb in silver and diamonds; ' that I am almost afraid to come near you!'

" Her own dress was perfectly simple, though remarkably elegant.

" ' Oh ! I hate myself when so fine!' cried Princess Augusta; ' I cannot bear it; but there is no help! the people at the play always expect it.'

" They then conversed a little while, both standing; and then Princess Augusta said: ' Give my love to the duke' (meaning of Gloucester), ' and I hope I shall see him by-and-by; and to William' (meaning the duke's son).

" And this, which was not a positive request that she would not prolong her visit, was understood; and the lovely cousin made her curtsey and retired.

"To me, again, she made another, so gravely low and civil, that I really blushed to receive it, from addedfear of being mistaken. I accompanied her to the door, and shut it for her; and the moment she was out of the room, and out of sight of the Princess Augusta, she turned round to me, and with a smile of extreme civility, and a voice very soft, said: ' I am so happy to see you!I have longed for it a great, great while Ifor I have read you with such delight and instruction, so often!'

" I was very much surprised indeed : I expressed my sense of her goodness as well as I could; and she curtseyed again, and glided away.

"' How infinitely gracious is all your royal highness's house to me!' cried I, as I returned to my charming princess, who again made me take my seat next her own, and renewed her discourse.

" I stayed on with this delightful princess till near four o'clock, when she descended to dinner. I then accompanied her to the head of the stairs, saying: ' I feel quite low that this is over! How I wish it might be repeated in half of a year instead of a year !'

"' I'm sure and so do I!' were the last kind words she condescendingly uttered.

" I then made a little visit to Miss Planta, who was extremely friendly, and asked me why I should wait another year before I came. I told her I had leave for an annual visit, and could not presume to encroach beyond such a permission. However, as she proposed my calling upon her, at least when I happened to be in town or at Chelsea, I begged her to take some opportunity to hint my admission, if possible, more frequently.

" In the evening I went to the play with James andMarianne. It was a new comedy called ' Cheap Living,' by Reynolds or Morton, and full of absurdities, but at times irresistibly comic.

"Very soon afterwards I had a letter from Miss Planta, saying she had mentioned to her majesty my regret of the long intervals of annual admissions ; and that her majesty had most graciously answered: ' She should be very glad to see me whenever I came to town.'"

We shall turn from this interesting royal circle and follow the careers of the princesses and their brothers in more detail.

34

SECTION 34

CHAPTER II.

PRINCESS CHARLOTTE.

In the year 1796, it was determined to contract an alliance for the Princess Charlotte, Princess Royal of England. In 1791, some offers were made by Prince Ferdinand of Wirtemberg, but he was not deemed acceptable; and in 1796, the Crown Prince of Wirtemberg came forward, and was received with favour. But when the project became known a series of extraordinary difficulties and obstacles arose, which it took a long time to surmount. Almost at once strange rumours reached England connected with the mysterious fate of his first wife, whose end was said to have associated with it some mystery. The garrulous Sir Nathaniel Wraxall, whose stories are entitled to more respect and credibility than they have hitherto received, gives a fair account of what he heard upon his travels :

"This princess, who was born towards the end of the year 1764, before she attained the age of sixteen, was married to the Prince of Wirtemberg. He was then about twenty-six years old, and might be considered as eventual presumptive heir to his uncle, the reigning

VOL. I. B

Duke of Wirtemberg, Charles Eugene, who had no issue. When I was at the Court of Brunswic, in the autumn of 1777, at which time the princess was near thirteen, I saw her more than once, in the apartments of her mother. She had a very fair complexion, light hair, pleasing features, and an interesting figure. . . .

" Early in the summer of 1798, a gentleman conversing with me on the subject of the first Princess of Wirtem- berg's death, assured me that he had seen and perused all the papers relative to her imprisonment and decease; which, at the desire of the prince himself, and by his authority, had been transmitted to George III.; who, after a full inspection of them, became perfectly convinced of his having had no part, direct or indirect, in that dark and melancholy transaction.

"Frederic William, reigning Duke of Wirtemberg, entered when young, as is well known, into the Prussian service. Old Frederic liked and distinguished him. Wishing to attach him to the House of Branden- burgh by permanent ties, and considering him as a man of promising abilities, the king himself set on foot, and finally concluded his marriage with the eldest daughter of his own favourite nephew and general, the Duke of Brunswic. This event took place in 1780. About five years afterwards Frederic, being disposed to form a second alliance with the family of Wirtemberg by marrying his great nephew, the present King of Prussia, as soon as his age would allow, with the Princess Elizabeth, sister to the prince, dispatched him to Peters- burgh for that purpose. His instructions were, to apply to his sister the grand duchess, for the exertion of her influence at the Court of Stutgard, in order to prevail on the duke to promise his niece to the heir of the Prussian Monarchy.

"When the Prince of Wirtemberg arrived in the capital of the Russian Empire, this Austrian alliance was already settled, or, at least, was too far advanced in its progress, to be overturned by his interference. After making therefore every effort in his power, through the grand duchess, to prevent its accomplishment, and finding these exertions fruitless, he returned to Potzdam. Whether Frederic suspected any duplicity or insincerity on his part, or, whether it was the result merely of disappointment, it is certain that he received the prince very coldly : and the Empress of Russia having soon afterwards invited him into her service, he quitted that of Prussia, and revisited Petersburgh.

" At the time that he entered the Russian service, he carried the princess his wife with him to Petersburgh, as well as the two sons and daughter which she had brought him. Being in the flower of her youth, endowed with many amiable qualities of mind and of deportment, she soon became a favourite of Catherine; in whose society and intimate confidence she occupied a distinguished place.

"... During his absence she conducted herself so imprudently, that when he returned after the conclusion of the campaign to Petersburgh, he found himself compelled to adopt some strong measures respecting her. Being placed in this painful situation, he wrote to her father, the Duke of Brunswic, informing him of his daughter's misconduct, and consulting him on the mode of action proper to be pursued under those circum- stances. It was agreed between them that she should be removed out of Russia, and the prince accordingly demanded Catherine's permission to quit her dominions, together with his wife and his family. The empress allowed him to retire, and to take with him his children; but she peremptorily refused to permit him to carry his consort back to

Germany, All remonstrance proving vain, the princess therefore remained behind, and he quitted Petersburgh, with his sons and daughter, to return to Wirtemberg.

" About a fortnight after his departure, the princess, without any reason assigned, was sent by order of Catherine to the Castle of Lhocle, about two hundred miles from Petersburgh ; but, in what part of that vast empire I am unable to assert. There, it seems, under close confinement, she remained about eighteen months : but all her German attendants, male and female, were withdrawn from her. At the end of that time, the prince received letters from the empress, informing him that his wife was dead of a hemorrhage. Similar information was conveyed by Catherine to the Duke of Brunswic, the unfortunate princess's father. No particulars were stated; nor, as far as appears, were any other circumstances ever known respecting her. Thus situated, the Duke of Brunswic acquiesced patiently in the calamity : but, during some years, he did not communicate to the duchess his wife the intelligence of her daughter's death. She, therefore, remaining in ignorance of the catastrophe, continued to believe that the princess was still confined at Lhode, or existing somewhere in the deserts of Russia. The duchess used even to speak of her as being alive in Siberia, and this fact will account for the universality of the report.

" If the account given me by Sir John Dick, relative to the supposed Princess Tarrakanoff, left many circumstances obscure and unexplained in the history of that female, it must be owned that, after considering this narrative, no less uncertainty still pervades the story of the Princess of Wirtemberg. It is natural to ask, why did Catherine cause the princess to be imprisoned ?

" When Miss Knight was on a visit to the Queen of Wirtemberg (the successor of this princess) she asked me about this delicate matter. The queen-dowager tells me her husband said that she was always imprudent; but that when she was in Russia with him the Empress Catherine gave her very bad advice, and had great power over her. One evening, instead of retiring with him and the grand-duke and duchess, as usual, she went out of the other door with Catherine. He never saw her again, but went off, and took away his children with him. The queen-dowager says she died in a Russian fortress ; but whether poisoned by order of the empress, or in child-bed, cannot be known.

" There are particulars which may lead us to hesitate in forming a decisive opinion on the subject. The death of the Princess of Wirtemberg at Lhode was announced and stated in all the German almanacks, printed by authority, to have take place on ' the 27th September, 1788.' Her husband remained a widower near eight years after that event. During so long a period of time he seems to have adopted no measures for repelling the calumnious reports circulated all over Europe; reports which, however false (and such I esteem them to have been), yet had made the most unfavourable impression, even in England. GeorgeIII. became indeed perfectly convinced of his innocence before he consented to the union of the prince with his eldest daughter. So far, indeed, was he from pushing forward the alliance, that I know from good authority, he offered the princess, after all the preliminaries were adjusted, and the marriage was fixed, to break it off, if she chose to decline it, taking on himself personally the whole responsibility of its failure. . . .

"Before I quit this subject I cannot help remarking that during the course of the eighteenth century the family of Brunswic, in its different branches, produced no less than five princesses, who exhibited in succession the most conspicuous examples of human infelicity. The first of them was Sophia of Brunswic Zell, married to George I. ; who, for her alleged, but unproved gallantries with Count Konigsmark, was confined during near forty years at the sequestered seat or Castle of Ahlden, in the electorate of Hanover, where she expired in 1726. Charlotte-Christina of Brunswic Blanckenberg, who espoused in 1711 the Czarowitz Alexis, only son of Peter the Great; a princess endowed by nature with almost every amiable and estimable quality of body and of mind, equally beautiful and virtuous, fell a victim in the flower of her youth to the ferocious treatment that she experienced from her husband. She died at Peters- burgh, in child-bed, at twenty-one years of age, in 1715 ; or, at least, she disappeared, for her death has been contested in the strongest manner, lamented by the whole empire, except by Alexis, whose brutal character rendered him incapable of appreciating her value. Brunswic Wolfenbuttel furnished the next instance in the person of Elizabeth, married in 1765, to the lateKing of Prussia, then only prince royal, divorced four years afterwards for her irregularities; confined at Stettin, where I have seen her in 1774, and relative to whose private history I could state from high authority, the most minute, as well as curious particulars, if I were not restrained by motives of respect and delicacy towards the illustrious persons who are connected with her by descent or by alliance. I believe she still survives, forgotten and unknown, in some part of the Prussian dominions, after having witnessed the temporary subversion of her own house and the calamities inflicted on that of Brandenburgh by Bonaparte. Caroline Matilda of Brunswic Lunen- burgh, posthumous daughter of Frederic, late Prince of Wales, and sister of George III., is the fourth in this enumeration. To her I had the honour of being well known, have dined frequently at her table, and was employed by her during the year preceding her decease in conducting negotiations of the deepest importance to her future greatness as well as felicity. Banished by a revolution from Denmark in 1772, effected in the name of Christian VII., her imbecile husband she only survived it about three years, terminating her short career in the prime of life, at Zell, in 1775. Augusta Caroline of Brunswic Wolfenbuttel, whose melancholy history and whose ambiguous end we have been surveying, continues, but does not terminate the list."

It should be mentioned that Mr. Carlyle, who had thoroughly studied the German records, bears testimony to Wraxall's accuracy, and distinctly declares him to be not -" mendacious " as it was the fashion to describe him. I

35

SECTION 35

could give innumerable instances of the accuracy of his " Secret History," which at the time was scouted.

After this disappearance many strange stories were afloat, but one night her sister, the Princess of Wales, equally unfortunate, entered on the subject with Lady Charlotte Campbell in a very interesting way, and her account may be accepted as accurate :

" She amused us very much," says Lady Charlotte, " by telling us the history of her sister, Princess Caroline. I asked her if it was true that the Duke of Wirtemberg had poisoned the princess. She said she did not believe it, and had even reasons for supposing she was still alive. The princess married at thirteen or fourteen years of age, and like all princesses and most other women, she did so in order to have an establishment, and be her own mistress. For some time she behaved well, though her sister said her husband was very jealous of her from the beginning, and beat her cruelly. At length they went to Russia, and there she became enamoured of a man who was supposed to have been the empress's lover, a circumstance which rendered the offence heinous, even though he was a cast-off lover."

After adding some scandal, the Princess of Wales went on to relate that: " The empress then informed her it was no longer possible for her to allow her to live under her roof, but that she might go to the Chateau de Kevelt, on the Baltic|that is to say, she *must* go: whither accordingly she was sent. The curious part of this story is, that Miss Saunders, the Princess of Wales's maid, at this time living with her, had a sister, which sister lived as maid to Princess Caroline, and she,after a time, came from the Chateau de Revelt back to Brunswick, saying her mistress was in perfect health, but had dismissed her from her service, as she no longer required her attendance. She gave her money and jewels, and, after vain entreaties to be allowed to remain with her royal mistress, to whom she was much attached, Miss Saunders's sister left the Princess Caroline.

" Not long after this, word was brought to the Duke of Brunswick that she died suddenly of some putrid disorder, which made it necessary to bury the body immediately, without waiting for any ceremonies due to the rank of the deceased. All further inquiries that were made ended in this account, and no light was thrown upon this business. Some years subsequently to this, a travelling Jew arrived at Brunswick, who swore that he saw the Princess Caroline at the opera at Leghorn. He was questioned, and declared that he could not be mistaken in her. I own, said the Princess of Wales, that from her sending away the person who was so much attached to her, and ' the only servant she had whom she loved and relied on, that I always hope she contrived to elope with her lover, and may still be alive."

After these vicissitudes we find that, in the year 1814, fresh rumours got abroad in London, which were reported to her son by Mrs. Harris :

"Another curious subject," she writes, "which is privately discussed is, the return to England, and to her former station, of the Queen of Wirtemberg. His majesty's first wife, it seems, has escaped from her confinement, and has thus proved herself to be alive, as boththe Duchess of Brunswick and the Princess of Wales were convinced was the case, when he married the second lady."

" I lived during several years in habits of familiar acquaintance with Sir John Dick, who retained at fourscore all the activity of middle life, together with the perfect possession of his memory and faculties. He was an agreeable, entertaining, and wellbred man, who had seen much of the world. Dining in a large company, at Mr. Thomas Hope's, in Berkeley Square, on Sunday, the 10th of February, 1799, I sat by Sir John Dick, and well knowing his intimacy with Alexis Orloff, I inquired of him where the count then was. ' He is,' answered Sir John Dick, ' at present at Leipsic, from which place he wrote to me only three weeks ago. The. Emperor Paul commanded him to travel, after having made him and Prince Baratinskoi, both of whom assisted in the termination of Peter IIL's life, assist likewise at the funeral ceremonies of that prince.' Encouraged by the frankness of his reply I ventured to ask him if he had read the narrative of the Princess TarrakanofFs seizure related in (Castera) ' Vie de Catherine Seconde ? ' ' I have certainly perused it,' said he, ' and not without some concern, as I am there accused by name, no less than my wife, of having been a party to the act of transporting by violence a young, unsuspecting, and innocent princess on board the Russian fleet. I will relate to you, as a man of veracity, all the part that I took, and all I know, relative to the pretended princess in question, who is there asserted to have been a daughter of Elizabeth, Empress of Russia.

" ' During the time that the Russian squadron lay inthe harbour of Leghorn, in 1771, Alexis Orloff, who was the admiral, resided frequently, if not principally, at

Pisa, where he hired a splendid house. One morning, about eleven o'clock, a Cossack who was in his service, and who acted as his courier, arrived at my door charged with a message to inform me that his master, with some company, in three carriages, meant to dine with me on that day. I accordingly ordered a dinner to be prepared for his reception. When he arrived he brought with him a lady whom he introduced to my wife and to myself; but he never named her, only calling her " *Questa Dama"* She was by no means handsome, though genteel in her figure, apparently thirty years of age, and had the air of a person who had suffered in her health. There seemed something mysterious about her which excited my curiosity, but which I could not penetrate. Considering her with attention it struck me forcibly that I had seen her before, and in England. Being determined, if possible, to satisfy myself on this point, as we stood leaning against the chimney-piece in my drawing-room before dinner, I said to her: " I believe, ma'am, you speak English ?" "I speak only one little," answered she. We sat down to dinner, and after the repast Alexis Orloff proposed to my wife, and to another lady who was there present, to accompany him and the female stranger on board his ship. They both declined it; Orloff took her with him in the evening. The boom, or chain, was then stretched across the harbour, but a boat came from the Russian admiral's ship, into which he put the lady, and accompanied her himself safe on board.

"' On the ensuing morning, when Orloff came onshore, he proceeded to my house. His eyes were violently inflamed, and his whole countenance betrayed much agitation. Without explaining to me the cause or the reason of his disorder, he owned that he had passed a very unpleasant night; and he requested me to let him have some of the most amusing books in my library, in order to divert the lady who was on board his ship. I never saw her again, but I know that soon afterwards she was sent by Alexis *in* a frigate to Cronstadt, where, without being ever landed, she was transferred up the Neva to the fortress of Schlusselbourg, at the mouth of the Lake Ladoga. Catherine there confined her, in the very room that Peter III. had caused to be constructed with intent to shut up herself in it. The lady unquestionably died in that prison of chagrin; but she was not drowned by the water of the Neva coming into her apartment, as is asserted in " La Vie de Catherine Seconde." Having stated to you,' continued Sir John Dick, 'these circumstances, I will now inform you who, and of what description, was the lady in question. Far from being, as is pretended, a daughter of Elizabeth, Empress of Russia, her father was a baker, of Nuremberg, in Franconia. If on this point my testimony should appear to you doubtful or suspicious, the present Margrave of Anspach, who is in this country, and who knew her well, is ready to testify the same fact. She lived during a short time both in Paris and here in London, at which last-mentioned city she had picked up a few words of English. Prince Nicholas Radzivil, who was driven out of Poland by the Russians, having met her, carried her with him into Italy. In order to revenge himself on Catherine, who had expelledhim from his native country and confiscated his immense estates in Lithuania, he resolved on calling her the Princess Tarrakanoff, pretending that she was Elizabeth's daughter. Such she was in fact considered to be by many who saw her, and the report gaining strength soon reached Petersburgh. Catherine, naturally alarmed at the existence of a female pretender who might lay claim to the very throne of Russia, thought that not a moment was to be lost in securing the person of so dangerous a rival. She issued private orders therefore to

Alexis Orloff, enjoining him to gain possession of the pretended princess at all events, and by every possible means, either of money or of violence. To so great a height did the empress's apprehensions rise that Orloff avowed to me he had received the positive commands of her majesty to pursue her even to Ragusa, if necessary, where it was understood she had retired ; to demand her from the Government of that small republic, and if they should refuse to give her up, to bombard the city and to lay it in ashes.'"

Other stories of mysterious disappearances connected with the Empress Catherine make the presumption of her having had a share in the disappearance of the princess rather strong. There is something almost romantic in the story of the Princess Tar-rakanoff, which was related as an after-dinner anecdote to Mr. Wraxall by a person who actually took part in it.

With such rumours abroad it was natural that the English Court should for a long time decline to favour the project. The Chevalier de Zeppeline, who represented the grand duke in London, found his position exceedingly delicate and disagreeable, and the prince

36

SECTION 36

complained bitterly to him of the unhandsome way he was treated under these sus-picions, " having to fly like a mendicant," he said, "from door to door," for leave to vindicate himself. The chevalier vainly prayed for an audience with the king, though he had laid before him proper proofs of his principal's innocence.

SIE J. HIPPESLEY TO LADY HAECOURT.

"My Dear Madam,

"The earnestness of Russia to make her *amende honorable* will give new weight, & as I before observed, effectually silences all Calumny from that quarter. The King may observe that the answers to his *Enquiries* are not so *favorable* as He could wish. To this His Majesty may be correctly answered in turn, that ' unless the same candid exposition of facts had been made abroad as we have seen made here by a reference to *authentic Documents, &c.,* it could hardly be supposed that any persons who had remained so long in error could have returned a favorable report.'

" If it is observed that even the Duchess of Brunswick *had* her prejudices as strong as anyone, the reply is, that until the Duke (who knew all the facts) *very lately undeceived* her Royal Highness, it was natural she should have had them; but the part she and the Duke have since taken is now the *best refutation.*

"In a word, can it be supposed that the Duke & Duchess of Brunswick, the Emperor & Empress Queen, would *all* enter into a *Conspiracy* to *impose on His Majesty*, & sacrifice the Princess Royal to a Prince soundeserving of Her Royal Highness ? How! if the *thousandth* part of what Vulgar error has asserted be to be credited !

At last, when the agent was actually recalled, the king gave way. But the sensitive prince was then aggrieved at receiving no present that he could show. It will be noted with what cool hauteur his demand was put aside.

Secret. "25th May.

"H.S.H. speaking to Sr in great confidence

last night, regretted that he had received *no present* from H.R.H. on Her marriage; as it is an invariable usage in Germany, & of so much consequence, that *He could wish the Hint to be given* to Her *R.H.,* tho' it ought not to come from *Himself or any one of His own family.*

"His S.H. mentioned this circumstance to Ly H' & myself with so much sollicitude, that it appears advisable that the Hint should be communicated to Her RH. The P. said that it would be one of the first *Questions* put to Him on His arrival, & He should really find himself mortified in replying to it. *Any thing,* however trivial, would answer the purpose. Perhaps

a *Hair Ring* set with Brilliants, which could get

set in *two* or three days. Her R.H. will forgive the zeal of Him who suggests this Hint, knowing it can only proceed from the Motive which has influenced His conduct through the whole of the negociation.

"The P extended His *Finger* in speaking to

Ly H saying: ' *not a ring to show, &c.'*"

Harcourt Papers, vi. 142.

The answer ran:

" I am very sensible of the zeal that induc'd you to write to me; & I hope you will allow my motives for refusing your request to be just. I hope too, that upon reflection, the P. will consider that every Country has its own customs ; & that it is as reasonable that he should at present be satisfied with those established here, as it will soon be for the Pss. to adopt those of the place she is going to."

The following is an account of the reception of the bridegroom:

" His highness, who had been invited by Sir Joseph Banks to partake of a collation, was met at Spring Grove by Lord Malmsbury and Sir Stephen Cottrell, his majesty's master of the ceremonies, and was by them conducted to London in one of his majesty's coaches, drawn by six horses, and repaired to his apartments at St. James's. Immediately after his arrival, his highness received a visit from the Marquess of Salisbury, lord chamberlain of his majesty's household. Their majesties and the royal family sent their compliments of welcome to his highness upon his arrival at St. James's ; and Mr. Charles Greville, vice-chamberlain of his majesty's household, who carried the compliments from his majesty, acquainted his highness that his majesty had appointed the ensuing day to receive his highness after the leve"e, when his highness waited on his majesty, and afterwards on the queen and on the royal family, at the times respectively appointed.

" Before the hour came for his highness to have access to the king, his highness received visits from their graces the archbishops of Canterbury and York, the lord chancellor, and other lords of his majesty's most honourable privy council, and from many of the nobility, and other persons of distinction, and from the foreign ministers, all of whom were presented to his highness. The following day, his highness again received visits from divers of the nobility, and went to the Drawing Room to pay his compliments to the queen. His highness afterwards paid his compliments to his majesty at the leve'e.

" The solemnity of the marriage of his highness Frederick William, hereditary prince of Wirtemberg- Stutgard, with Charlotte Augusta Matilda, Princess Royal of Great Britain, lady of the Imperial Order cf St. Catherine of Russia, and eldest daughter of King George III., was performed in the Chapel Royal by the Archbishop of Canterbury. After the ceremony, their majesties, with the rest of the royal family, passed into the great council-chamber, where the great officers, nobility, foreign ministers, and other persons of distinction, paid their compliments on the occasion, which were received by the bride and bridegroom in her majesty's apartment.

" The last interview between his majesty and his royal daughter was of the most affecting kind. The princess hung upon her father's neck, overwhelmed in grief, and it was not until her consort urged her to close the painful scene, that she could be prevailed upon to leave her father. The affectionate parent followed her to bid her farewell, but he was so overcome by the excess of his parental feelings, that he could not give utterance to his words, and his streaming eyes looked the last blessing, which his lips could not pronounce."

VOL. I.

The marriage at last took place, but on the eve of the departure of the royal pair, in May, 1797, an unlucky contretemps occurred. The frigate in which they were to embark was waiting at the Nore, but, owing to the mutiny which was then raging, it was not allowed to depart, and another vessel at Yarmouth had to be selected. That was to be the beginning'of a sad and disastrous life ; for, like her father, this new duchess was destined to a life of sore trials, in which she was, however, to acquit herself with all the fortitude of a daughter of her house.

After her marriage to the duke (afterwards, by the favour of Napoleon, King of Wirtemberg), she passed from the notice of the English public. But that she was person of character as well as of fortitude, and that under the severest of trials, is shown by her behaviour to Napoleon under circumstances of danger and humiliation, when she may be said to have saved her husband's kingdom. " I have heard her say," Miss Wynne relates, " ' it was of course very painful to me to receive him with civility, but I had no choice ; the least failure on my part might have been a sufficient pretence for depriving my husband and children of this kingdom. It was one of the occasions on which it was absolutely necessary to *faire bonne mine d mauvais gout.* To me he was always perfectly civil.' I have since heard that he gave her facilities for correspondence with her own family, at the time that the state of Europe would otherwise have made it nearly impossible.

" The Queen of Bavaria was not as wise, and upon some occasion when Napoleon was incensed at some slight from her, he said she should remember what shewas but for him, *la file d'un miserable petit Margrave* (Baden), and imitate the conduct of the Queen of Wirtemberg, *lajille du plus grand roi de la terre.*

The queen said that the great preparations made in the palaces at Stutgard Louisbourg for the reception of Napoleon were not with her approbation, and that she said to the king : ' *Mon ami, vous devriez faire le pauvre au lieu d'etaler vos richesses si vous ne voidez pas avoir des fortes contributions a payer.'* It was ridiculous enough to hear her say how, when Napoleon admired the Lyons embroidery and said, ' I cannot have such at the Tuileries,' she told him it was her work, adding, ' God forgive me, that was a lie.' When he made the same observation on some other instance of magnificence, she told him it was all done by the *due mon beaupere,* and in relating this added the same corrective. She said the manners of Napoleon were extremely *brusque,* even when he was making the civil. She had seen both Josephine and Marie Louise with him, and seems to have been less pleased with the manners of the former than most persons who saw her.

Connected with this matter was the " ogre's " treatment of another of the German royal ladies :

"December 1st, 1806.

". . . The old Dss. of Weimar has acted with great courage. She remained in Her own country, & in her own Palace; & when the wretch, Bonaparte, arrived, she received Him there. Supposing who she was, he said: ' Ah, Madame Weimar'|that is the way He has spoke to all people of birth in Germany|& added : ' I chuse to dine alone.' After dinner He sent for her, $ abusedthe K. & Q. of Prussia with the most horrid oaths, & the most dreadful language for a woman's ears; & theu told her he intended to destroy the town of Weimar by fire. She let him have his whole *say out,* & then most nobly said: ' If you chuse to punish the Duke of Weimar's family for his belonging to the K. of Prussia, we must submit; but to punish his innocent subjects, who have had nothing to do with it, will only injure yourself;' & after representing it in this manner, She nearly fainted away ; when she recovered, He promised her he would not burn the town, & would give counter orders. He then sent her away: & about two hours after, when his fury & rage were Subdued, he sent her word he would come & drink tea with her. He then talked of Vertu, Pictures, &c., & was very agreable. ..."

Miss Knight often visited this amiable princess at her Court, when all tongues were loud in praise of her goodness and high principle. The king, her stepson, spoke of her to Miss Knight with the highest esteem and the deepest gratitude. He said that during the fourteen years which had elapsed since the death of his father, he had never in one instance had reason to complain of his stepmother, but, on the contrary, had always experienced from her the kindest and most judicious conduct towards himself and his family.

Nothing is shown more distinctively marked than the characters of the royal princesses in their intimate correspondence. The Princess Royal's, and her sister the Princess Elizabeth's, were of a grave cast, and their communications marked with a reflective thought andgood sense. Princess Augusta seems full of impulse and affection for her friends, pouring her thoughts out with a spontaneous warmth which often lent a graphic literary power. The royal brothers could not be compared as letter writers with their sisters. Mrs. Harcourt writes :

" I really knew not such girls in any rank of life. They are all amiable in their different waysland they are very different. Princess Royal has excessive sensibility, a great sense of injury, a great sense of her own situation, much timidity; without wanting resolution she.wants presence of mind, from the extreme quickness of her feelings, which show themselves in her perpetual blushes. She has excellent judgment, wonderful memory, and great application. Certainly what may be called a strong understanding and perfectly good principle. She is unjustly considered pioud, and a peculiarity in her temper is mistaken for a less sweetness than it deserves. Her sense of injury and her humility are alike mistaken. But those she loves and who love her cannot be mistaken, and when she possesses friendship she is warm, constant, and affectionate."

This lady, wife of General Harcourt, like her sister-in-law, kept a pleasant Court diary, in which she recorded various conversations with members of the royal family. Her notes on the princesses show a genuine admiration of the characters of these noble ladies. That of the Princess Eoyal is very pleasing.

" Princess Elizabeth said some years ago her father had refused the Prince of Denmark for Princess Augusta, and Lady Harcourt told her he had also refused, some years ago, the Prince of Brunswick for Princess Royal; that a disposition to receive him had since been hinted,but not taken. At the Drawing Room I talked with the Duke of Gloucester about the prince's strange intention of settling them in England, with which he appeared particularly disgusted, and said he thought the king had not looked out for Continental alliances from a notion they would be unwilling to leave England. He fancied the Prince of Prussia would not have been accepted."

At a subsequent conversation, the Duke of Gloucester said : " The Duchess of Brunswick had long and ardently desired to see her son married to the Princess Royal, but the king had always disliked the idealhe had a strong prejudice against the alliance and against his sister. He had even lately said that one of her last letters was the pleasantest he had ever received from her, because there was no scheme in it. He doubted the Prince Royal of Prussia being disposed to any such alliance. He thought the Prince of Denmark a very desirable match, but doubted his disposition to marry. The King of Sweden's brother, Duke of Ostrogothland, was then mentioned. The duke had spent six months with him at Naples, and thought highly of his character. The duke said that the Duke of Saxe Gotha, a very good man, had, when in England, fallen in love with the Princess Royal, his own wife being then supposed dying, in which case he could have undoubtedly married her ; but though afflicted with fits, there was no prospect of a vacancy."

One day the Duke of Gloucester took occasion to expatiate to Mrs. Harcourt on his " wrongs," and the fashion in which he had been treated. In the course of this complaint he incidentally shows what was the position of the queen. " He said the unfortunate distanceat which he had been ever kept, and the little opportunity he had had of living with his own family, had been the original cause of throwing him into other society, and therefore of all the misfortunes of his life (meaning his unhappy marriage). The duke might, however, have considered that had it not been for that marriage, unhappy as it had proved, he should not have had the blessing of those two children he so passionately loves. He told me that in regard to the queen's former behaviour to him and the king's family, for she had been blamed as the cause of that distance, he much acquitted her, as he thought the retired life the king and queen led for the first many years of their marriage was entirely the king's doing. That it was not, as supposed, by the late Princess of Wales' (his mother's) desire. That too much blame had been laid on her on that account unjustly. That as far as regarded the king's education perhaps she deserved it, for it had been much confined. That he had been kept locked up till he married, and taught to have a bad opinion of the world, and almost to dread human honour. That he was therefore delighted with having entirely under his own training a young innocent girl of seventeen, for such was the queen when she arrived, and that he determined she should be wholly devoted to him alone, and should have no other friend or society. That he knew the king on her arrival told her this, and told her that even with the Princess of Wales she was to have as little communication as possible, and depend on him and him alone."

When the marriage of her niece, Princess Charlotte, was broken off, we find the princess writing : " I wish she had not allowed things to go so far before she changed her mind. Such things make a great noise, and hurt a young Lady in the Eyes of the World." Indeed, all her letters are models of good sense and propriety, and those to the governess of Princess Charlotte, quoted by Lady Harcourt, are admirable and instructive.

Then she speaks of her mother and sisters in this affectionate style. She is sure "that in few countries people meet with such an example as that which is set before them by the queen and my most admirable good sisters who, have sacrificed almost every earthly comfort to attend to their aged parents, and contribute to make their lives pleasant." Nothing could be more true. From the unfortunate year of the king's first seizure in 1789, during a period of twenty years, this life was one scene of oppression and misery, of family dissension and rebellion, which they vainly strove to soothe or avert. All through the memoirs and chronicles of the period are evidences of their unswerving devotion, and of the distraction of that unhappy royal household.

" You are," again writes the Princess Royal, " dear Lady Harcourt, perfectly right in saying that the Queen is the great link of the Chain; and I fear, should that one drop off, that much misery would ensue. In all numerous families there are a variety of opinions, which are softened when there is a person at the head of them whom all look up to. Through their influence a sort of friendly unanimity is preserved; but should they fail, all draw different ways, and outward union is no more to be thought of."

In 1818, when the queen's health was fast breaking up, she dwelt sadly on the impending loss.

" I join with you in looking on the day which will deprive us of the best of Mothers, as a most fatal one for Great Britain. Certainly the Queen's example has done inconceivable good; and I am the more convinced of this, by seeing daily how much mischief is done by those whose intentions are not bad, but from being quite inconsiderate, and from the desire of enlarging their circle, admit all sorts of people into their Society, which by degrees will, I am afraid, quite ruin the manners and morality of the Continent.

" It grieves me to hear that poor dear Sophia is so seriously ill; and I fear she will not long survive our beloved Mother. Her health has so long been delicate, that we must ever look on her as a Hot House plant which requires every care to prevent its being destroyed.

" Poor Augusta," she added, " from her great shyness, stands more in need of a real, steady friend than the rest of her Sisters. The account you are so good as to give me of Mary's Character gives me great satisfaction. I always thought her mild, good, and amiable; but from a variety of circumstances, I was less intimate with her than my other Sisters. I trust that her good Heart will lead her to exert her influence over the Regent for the advantage of Augusta and Sophia, who, however, I hope will determine on having separate establishments; as, though both amiable, their dispositions and tastes are too different for them to be perfectly comfortable if they were to live together."

When her mother's demise was close at hand, she wrote that: " The gracious affectionate Message our dear Mother has sent us is calculated to sooth our Minds, and to make us all doubly feel the very severe loss she will be, not only to her afflicted Children, but also to the Nation. The resignation and courage with which she hag bore the being acquainted with her very precarious situation is a great comfort to me; as I was quite wretched at her leaving this world without her mind being prepared for the awful change. Not that I am not convinced of the mercy of God to all His Creatures, and particularly to a Being who has led so exemplary a life as the dear Queen; but still the most innocent soul must be anxious to devote some time to Prayer before they Expire, and to take leave of their Children; as, of course, at such a moment every word of advice has double weight on the Soul of a Christian."

Further extracts will be interesting :

Description of the Rain.|" I am still in hopes of a few *lines from* you *to-day,* if the *Rain* has not turned the *Post Bag,* or rather *its contents* into *Pap ;* for such a *perpendicular, steady, quiet Rain* puts me in mind of what *I should think a Quaker's Grief must appear* to persons of a more lively Description."

Louis XVIII.|" He has a *v&ryjine manner,* and is very *Gracious.* He is a well informed man, speaks English very well, and understands it perfectly. He is very large, as large as Stephen Kemble. He converses in a Most agreeable manner; and generally walks up and down the Room in the hope of its keeping down His fat. His countenance is very good; and He makes a fine Bow without any Affectation."

Bonaparte.|"The Book gives a very accurate account of *the ' Monster 'from If is Childhood.* I must tell you what happened to me. I was reading to *myself,* and my Maid was in the *room;* and being very eager, I called out *d propox* of one of His very malicious acts as a *boy,* '0 ! *you Devil.'* To which She *said,' I know what you are reading for I read some of it this morning, and a more horrid Creature never existed.'* I was then shocked at having called Him Dll, it was an injustice to Beelzebub, who was a *fallen Angel;* for I believe Bonaparte to be *an indigenous Devil."*

The House of Lords.|" Lord Hobart's reply, very *neat,* very *determined,* but perfectly *cool,* & what a Minister *ought to say:* that *Every Body* is astonished at Lord *Carlisle,* who went down with the *language* and appearance of an *Oppositionist,* & changed all of a *sudden, no one knows why,* to a *Supporter."*

Finding of Charles I.'s Body.|" I can assure you it is a matter of great *joy to me* that so *good* and so *ill used* a man should lay close to *my family.* I was also greatly struck to-day *at Chapel,* that *(irith* the sight of this Excellent *man's earthly part,* for I *saw the bone,* which was fresh in my memory) the Psalms for *this Day,* the 2nd, were the 9, 10, 11, the very Psalms which were selected for His Martyrdom ; it certainly made a great impression upon me, and I am quite happy that *the only creditable Stuart* is *near us."*

Not less agreeable, and not less genuine, are her letters after all the troubles of her life had passed and she had become a mature elderly queen. There is the same ring of sympathy; and though on the death of her husband there appeared a certain anxiety about the.*placement* of her funds, later letters explain this and show that shewished her son, the new king, to have the benefit. These letters were addressed to Sir J. Cox Hippisley, a well-known diplomatist, and have been recently added to the British Museum.

THE QUEEN OF WIRTEMBERG TO *SIR J.* COX HIPPISLEY.

Stutgard, October 31, 1810.

As you were one of the trustees to my marriage settlements, and have on every occasion shown your attachment to the King of Wirtemberg, I think it right to acquaint you that I had the deep affliction to see him expire yesterday morning after an illness of a few days. Not knowing whether my late husband had named any fresh trustees I have written to my brother, the Prince Regent, to beg that he will name General Taylor, in addition to yourself and Lord Greuville. Not knowing how the money is placed, I must beg of you, sir, to have the goodness to give me some information on the subject. You will, sir, easily imagine how painful it is for me to write on business at a moment when I am in the deepest affliction. But the present king's kindness in sending a messenger to England makes me think it a duty to settle as soon as possible everything regarding pecuniary affairs. I believe that from the day of the king's death I am entitled to the whole interest of my fortune, but, not being sure of this, or of the sum my late beloved husband added to make up the sum of one hundred and sixty thousand pounds' stock, I beg you will send me an answer by return of the messenger. I believe never was anybody more attached to another than I was to the

late king. This affection, which, during our union was the happiness of my life, makes me look forward with impatience to the end of my life, when I trust through the mercy of Providence to be reunited to my husband in a better world. The present king behaves very kindly to me, and has shown the most dutiful affection to his late father.

Charlotte.

By The Same To The Same.

Louisberg, November 30, 181G. SIR,

After having troubled you with a letter yesterday I should not have been so very indiscreet as to write again this morning, had I not been informed of a circumstance which I am obliged to communicate to you, for to prevent your refusing to accept of the late king's drafts for the interest of my fortune. About five days before he was taken ill he was informed that the course of exchange on London was very high, and was, as I have since heard, induced to sell the drafts which were only due on January

5, 1817, to the royal bank at Stutgard. By this speculation he realised, I believe, the whole of the sum, which was, I believe, not quite according to the tenor of the marriage articles. Being, therefore, anxious to avoid anything which could in the least affect the memory of one I am so sincerely attached to, on receiving the statement from the bank I agreed to be repaid by the king's heirs the two months which, according to your account, belong to me, and shall this morning write to Lord Grenville on the same subject. I should be very much obliged to you, sir, if you wouldtalk over this business with his lordship, as it would be dreadful to me if the king's name was exposed to suffer from what, I am convinced, was an error, but is the custom abroad. As I am persuaded that you will enter into my feelings, I shall try to compose my feelings till I hear from you again, and remain, with esteem and

regard,

Sir, your friend,

Charlotte. Sir J, Cox Hippisley.

THE SAME TO THE SAME.

May 1, 1817. Sir,

I am afraid you have some reason to think me idle as I have so long delayed answering your last letter, but must plead in my defence frequent returns of indisposition which have prevented my expressing sooner my thanks for the trouble you were so good as to take, sir, that I might be authorised to receive the dividends due on January 5.

I am also very much obliged to you, sir, for the specimens of new silver coins which are beautifully executed.

I am the more anxious to trouble you with a few lines this morning, sir, as I wish to be the first to acquaint you that the King of Wirtemberg has followed your advice, appointed General de Neieffer his trustee in the place of the late Baron de Rieger. This gentleman will, of course, address himself to you to mention not only his nomination, but also that as the funds are at present very high I wish to avail myself of thearticles five and six of my marriage settlement, and sell out that part of my fortune which, according to those articles, I have the right to draw out of England and lay out on a mortgage on the King of Wirtemberg's dominions, and hope the trustees will approve of the plan, as the money will be laid out on the Crown lands, which are, of course, entailed. By this means I shall have an addition of near eight hundred a-year to my income, as the money will be placed at five per cent.

I thank God that the riots are over, and trust that by degrees the wretched spirit which reigns in Europe will be extinguished, at least in England; the various measures which Government has taken will, I hope, prevent its continuing to spread.

I beg my compliments to Lady Hippisley and the Misses Stuarts, and desire you to be convinced of the regard and esteem with which I remain,

Ever your friend,

Charlotte.

THE SAME TO THE SAME.

July 22, 1818. Sir,

I hasten 'to acknowledge the receipt of your obliging letter of the 22nd, and regret very much that you were prevented returning here again, as I should have been very glad to have had some conversation with you on many subjects, which it was impossible to touch on during the short time I had the pleasure of your company.

I beg you will, sir, present my compliments to Lady Hippisley and your children, who, I hope, will havetaken a sufficient liking to this country not to object to making me a second visit.

I am very sorry to hear of Lady Shaftesbury's unpleasant robbery, and hope that the property m,ay be recovered.

I enclose the letter from my dear Eliza, to whom I beg you will say everything kind and affectionate in my name. Her silence worries me, as I cannot understand her being ten days at Homburg without indulging me with one line. I must make many excuses for this scrawl my hand being much swelled, and a band being in the house on account of St. James' Day, which is an annual popular feast.

I shall not fail to mention to my daughter what you are so good as to say about her, but neither of us found, out your mistake ; and she was very much pleased to have made your acquaintance and Lady Hippisley's. Catherine left me yesterday morning to return to Schoenen.

I must now take my leave, and remain, with regard

and esteem,

Your friend,

Charlotte.

THE SAME TO THE SAME. .

Louisberg, May 28, 1821.

I hasten to return you thanks for the obliging letter you was so good as to send me by Mr. Hamilton, and am very glad to hear that on the whole both yourself and Lady Hippisley are in good health. You willeasily, sir, imagine how happy I am to have the hopes of enjoying the society of my dear sister Augusta for a few weeks, and shall be happy to make Lady Mary Taylor's acquaintance, as I have heard her spoken of as a most amiable young woman; her being a friend of yours and Lady Hippisley's is also a great recommendation in her favour.

As you have, sir, given up your seat in the present House of Commons, I suppose that you will again turn your thoughts to the Continent; and should this be the case, I hope you will not forget Louisberg, where all will be glad to receive you, and I shall rejoice in introducing you to my dear little grandchildren, who are really

well worth seeing. Mr. and Mrs. , who saw them

last year, will, I am sure, have given you a favourable account of these little angels, who they seemed much pleased with. It certainly is a great comfort to hear that the country is radically sound at present, and to see that by degrees the sad spirit which reigned last year has subsided. God grant that this state of things may go on improving, and that we may see Great Britain again loyal and happy as it was in former times, before the mania of democracy had more or less spread in every country in Europe. We are here, thank God, very quiet, and all seem much pleased and satisfied with the new Constitution. I will now take up no more of your time, only adding my compliments to Lady Hippisley and the young ladies.

Remaining, with regard and esteem,

Sir, your Friend,

Charlotte.

VOL. I. T

THE SAME TO THE SAME.

Louisberg, June *1*, 1824. SlB,

As I suppose that you are still in London, though you have given up your seat in the House of Commons, I will not neglect sending you a few lines by General de Neieffer, who is on his road to the Island of Madeira. Poor man! he flatters himself by spending two years in that climate to regain his strength. However, I think him wonderfully recovered to what he was when you saw him last, and therefore hope he may really receive benefit, should he be able to settle in that warm climate; but after all the accounts which have reached me of the revolutionary spirit which reigns in the King of Portugal's dominions, I dread the general will meet with many difficulties before he obtains his end.

I intend in about ten days to go for five weeks to

, and hope the baths and waters will do me good,

as I have been unwell the whole winter, and I am doubly anxious to regain a little strength that I can enjoy the society of my dear Augusta without any drawback. It has given me sincere pleasure to hear that the king has been received with great applause at all the theatres, and I trust that now this popularity will ever continue to increase. I beg my compliments to Lady Hippisley and your daughters, and flatter myself that the youngest Miss Hippisley is in better health than when you wrote to me last year, and that poor Mrs. Horneck has partially recovered her spirits from the loss of her children. Iwill now take up no more of your time, and remain, sir, with regard and esteem,

Your Friend,

Charlotte.

This amiable princess died October 6, 1828, and left no issue.

These and other letters of the same correspondent will be found in the British Museum, Eg. 2401.

37

SECTION 37

CHAPTER III.

PRINCESS ELIZABETH.

This princess, born in 1770, was one of the graver members of the royal family. Like the rest, she was affectionate to her friends and devoted to her parents, with whom she remained till her youth and prime had fled. This tardiness in providing alliances for the ladies of the family offers a curious contrast to the haste exhibited in our own times. Nor was she without a certain vivacity of description and enthusiasm, as a pleasant account of Strawberry Hill, written to her friend Lord Harcourt, shows :

"... I can never thank you enough for having persuaded Mama to go to Strawberry Hill; it was a morning passed after my own heart. . . . Portraits, Miniatures, Japans, enamels, china, & a thousand other beautiful things start up to claim one's attention; but of all the things I ever sav, what struck me the most, was that which I have heard you rave about, the famous Bell; which is really, in *my humble* opinion, the mostwonderful piece of workmanship I ever saw. If my time would allow me, I could run on in raptures about everything; but I will not leave the subject without a few words concerning the owner of this curious and interesting mansion, whose pleasing manners thoroughly gained the whole company. We hope that he will not have suffered from his great civility to us; it pained me to think that we were the cause of his exerting himself as he did; but if he could know how much his attentions were felt, I am sure he would be pleased.

" I wish I could be housekeeper there for a Fortnight. In case of your hearing that Lord 0. is in want of one, send to such a No., in such a place, near such a street, by such a Castle, in such a Lodge, you will find a discreet, steady young woman, who bears a tolerable good character, with the advantage of speaking a little french, who will be willing to enter into such a Capacity; She is a single woman. I beg I may be most kindly remembered to dear Lady Harcourt; & beg you to

believe me

" Your sincere friend,

" Eliza."

"25th July, 1794.

" It is a mistake *my* living at Court; it was certainly intended that I should have lived in the Country, & been a younger brother's Wife, for I do not understand *Court* quarrels ; Kiss & make friends, should be one of the mottos for a Palace. . . .

" Your most off

" Cinderella."

Of the Princess of Wales she wrote :

" Saturday night, going to Bed.

"... Think, my beloved Lady H., how things are changed, that / now pray to the Almighty to leave this country; turn which way we will all appears gloom, & melancholy stares one full in the face. The prospect we have to look forward to in the Wife of him who should be our protector in future times, is so dreadful, that I had rather far chuse the Deserts of Arabia than all the amusements of London, or the delights of the Country in England. Do pray for me, & wish for us all to be gone. My much beloved Mother knows a little how sincerely we all wish to be gone, but a daughter who loves her as truly as I do, must feel the indelicacy of speaking too openly on a subject which separates one from her ; but indeed, indeed it is most necessary. . . .

"... I fear every thing, nearly my own thought; but I trust in the mercy of God, who will with his mercy guard my conscience, & what I love almost best in the world, my Brother. If the world could know his perfections I should still be happy, but do get him to wish us all away. ..."

ON THE DEATH OP THE PRINCESS CHAELOTTE.

"How little, my dearest Lady Harcourt, can one ever look forward to the morrow, after what has happened; what an awfull visitation, what a blow to the whole family, & to the nation ! The hopes of all built upon this marriage, & the joy that all wereexpressing in the hopes of a Boy ! to see that in the first instance frustrated by its being a still born child. At the moment, one blessed God for the safety of the Mother, & naturally felt that so young we might look forward to that disaster being repaired next year."

" The mania, or hobby, denominated the *Porcelaini- mania,* raged in 1790, and it consisted in collecting old jugs, antique teapots, and indeed every kind of earthenware." It may be supposed that all the collectors, connoisseurs, and amateurs of virtu were immediately upon the alert, exploring the receptacles of broken pots and the shops of dealers in marine stores for some of these hidden treasures, which, in a little time, were destined to be promoted to a place in the cabinets of royalty. A collector of great celebrity, be it understood, of celebrity in imposing counterfeit articles for genuine ones, having heard that the Princess Elizabeth was seized with the mania, considered it a most eligible opportunity to gain the royal favour, by collecting a few of the valuables then so much in requisition. He set out upon his tour, and in a short time he had collected an unique assemblage of antiques. This selection was no sooner complete than a communication was made to the princess of the depôt of these valuables, and an invitation was given to inspect them. It was accepted, and the princess was in raptures with the view of such a multitude of curiosities. But still greater were her raptures when she was requested to accept of a few of the most rare and ancient. By degrees the stock of the princess was increased beyond her hopes, but no acknowledgment would the collectorreceive, he being amply rewarded by the condescension with which he was treated by the illustrious personage. At length, however, the cloven foot of this most disinterested and considerate virtuoso began to display itself, for having been informed that a situation was likely to fall vacant of about $1000 a-year, he packed up a most precious cargo of antique japan, amongst which were two most curious cracked caudle-cups from the depository of some celebrated lady of a Chinese mandarin, and the princess was astonished at this inestimable addition to her store. The princess insisted upon making him some remuneration, but he informed her that pecuniary reward was not the object of his ambition, but at the same time he presumed to mention to her royal highness the expected vacancy, and the princess lost no time in hastening to her father, urging her request that her valued friend might succeed to the expected vacancy. The king could not refrain from laughing, for he was too deeply read in the knowledge of man to be ignorant that the collector, in his gifts of jugs, tea-pots, and caudle-cups, had some other view than merely to please the taste of her royal highness. After much importuning, his majesty granted the request, adding: " Well, well, go along, your china merchant must be paid for his mugs and jugs.; but let me tell you, that the price is unconscionable."

It was during the time that her father and the family were so sorely afflicted that the disposition of this amiable woman was shown to most advantage. The extracts that follow reveal a character that was true, genuine, and earnest.

TO LADY HAKCOURT.

"... Yesterday was my day for going to Chapel. You may believe I was happy to be alone there, for it was a day of trial to one's feelings, & whilst my heart was full, & uplifted to God for every blessing for my Father, I recalled four years ago, when the day Shone bright, & the whole Country rejoicing in the Jubilee, with the finest weather that ever was seen. Yesterday the weather accorded with the day, very *grey*; but while the prayer was reading, the Sun shone so finely, that I could not help thinking of God's peculiar goodness in supporting us as He has mercifully done through this dreadful trial, giving us the blessing of knowing, that, tho' in a most melancholy State for *iis*, yet a happy one
for himself."

" November 9th, 1810.

"... We have been, & are severely tried; yet I trust that God, who never has forsaken my beloved Father, will still stand by Him; yet the occasion of this sad illness is so different from every other, that I trust all who really love him will but give us time. Aggri- vating subjects have been the causes of his former illnesses; this one is owing to the overflowing of his heart for his youngest & dearest Child; a child who had never caused him a pang, & who he literally doated upon.

".All this is natural; & I fairly own to you, had it pleased the Almighty in his wisdom to have released our sweet Angel three weeks back, I firmly believe this would never have happened. If I am presumptuous, *God forgive me.* ..."

"Yaff

" Eliza."

"July 18th, 1811.

"... The Doctors think that there is no amendment ; which is wretchedness to us, tho' they are right in telling the truth. The day, however, has been quieter; . . . but the mind is a blank to surrounding objects; the only nourishment, jellies ; all other eatables refused. We none of us dare think or look forwards, for everything is so black; we do what we can to support ourselves ; but, believe me, I see everything as I ought to see it, in fear & trembling, yet thoroughly trusting in God. ..."

"October llth, 1811.

"... The doctors think very ill of the case, & give it a term which is a dagger in our hearts; yet we ought to be grateful that everything has been *done that could,* & that he does not Suffer. . . . The going to Bed is dreadfull; the day otherwise is quiet, always thinking the room full, & amused the whole day ; they all say such a case was never seen or known before, for it is not the *common* kind of complaint; don't think me a fool, I cannot say the word, it is horror to me.

" Believe me y^{TM} aff7,

" Eliza."

" October 24th, 1811.

"... The first Question the Council put to Sir Henry Halford and Dr. Robert Willis was, ' Do you think that by throwing buckets of water upon your patient's head he would be cured ?'

" You may easily believe that they both answeredthese strange questions and proposals the same ; that no regular bred Physician would venture such an expedient, particularly my Father being blind ; & at his time of life they could not answer for the consequences. R. Willis quite Shuddred at it when he told it us; which He would not have done, had not my Mother forced it out of him "

"November 16th, 1811.

"... We have had a pretty tolerable night, which is a great comfort; for indeed I live in agony, & always think & dread its ending suddenly with my Father; tho' his, I believe, is the only instance that would not cause me horror; for when well, no man's life was ever more perfect than his, & therefore constantly prepared to meet His God ; otherwise, you well know my extreme wretchedness at the thought of such an end. . . .

" I fear you will find me very tiresome in my epistles, I so often go over the same ground ; but really my head is so full, & my whole thoughts absorbed in this one subject, that it quite kills me. . . ."

TO THE HON. MISS SCOTT.

"Windsor Castle, May 12th, 1812. "my Dear Madam,

" The Queen has commanded me to write you a few lines, which ought to have been written this morning, to inquire after the Chancellor: for, well knowing how deeply he feels, she greatly dreads that the shock of yesterday may have injured his health. It is impossible not to shrink with horror when onethinks of an Englishman committing murder, and doubly striking when one must ever mourn for the loss of so excellent a man as Mr. Perceval. We live in most awful times: for the loss, both public and private, must be equally felt. We really are so horror- struck, that it *is* impossible for me to describe our feelings. Your own good heart will better judge, than my pen relate, the agony and misery that was occasioned by my brother Adolphus's arrival last night. This Family have lost one who has ever proved real affection and attachment, and my beloved father has lost a most upright and conscientious Minister. Our only comfort in the midst of our own trial is, that my father is spared this affliction : for I verily believe, had it pleased the Almighty to have allowed of its being told him, it would have totally overset him.

"The ways of Providence are dark and intricate, and we too blind to understand. It is our duty to submit and trust in God's mercy. That He may mercifully watch over this country will be my fervent prayer.

"My mother commands me to add she would herself have written to the Lord Chancellor, but she thought it better to make me write, well knowing his time is precious, and that it was cruel to add to his troubles by desiring an answer. She begs you to explain this, and I trust you will forgive the length of this letter, which I am ashamed of; but the state of nerves I am in must plead my excuse, for literally I can think of nothing else.

" Yours very sincerely,

" Elizabeth."

Anticipating by some years, it may be told that the Princess Elizabeth remained with her family till she reached the mature age of forty-eight, when, in the sudden ardour for marriage that seized on the royal brothers and sisters, an unpleasing husband (in looks at least) was found for her in the Landgrave of Hesse Homburg. He was described as a gross corpulent German, of enormous dimensions, smelling always of tobacco, in days when the " weed " was detestable to most persons. His appearance and manners were ridiculed ; he was called " Humbug." He snored at the theatres. " You never saw such a disgusting object," one writes, and all wondered at the destiny which could consign a pleasing princess to such a being. A princess of England, Mary, daughter of George II., had in 1740 married another Landgrave of Homburg; and Princess Augusta, paying a visit in 1821 to her sister at Hombourg, was told the rather curious story of this lady, which she relates to her friend in the pleasing unaffected style that was common to all the princesses :

". . . At Wilhelmsbad the people were very curious to see *Eliza*, and *me;* as they are so attached to the memory of the Landgravine Mary, a Princess of England. You may have heard that after Her youngest Son was born, Her Husband left Her for a long time. Nobody knew where He was gone to ; when at last He wrote to His Wife, to say that, previous to His having married Her, He was attached to a Catholic Lady of very great family. That He had wanted to marry Her; but that She could not agree to it, as He was a Protestant. She entreated Him to espouse the Catholick faith. He, being fearfull of His Country being offended, held outfor a long time. Then He was sent for by King George the 2nd to Hanover, who settled the marriage with His Daughter. As soon as He left Hanover, He went to the lady, having previously written to inform Her of the King of England's intention that He should become His Son-in-law in a few weeks. This Lady shut the door upon Him, and forbad Him the House; but He then wrote to entreat that if He was ill, and really given over, She would come and *Shut His Eyes;* and. that *He* would promise to do the same by Her, if She would permit it.

" Accordingly *one letter* passed to Seal this promise. Prom that hour they had no more interviews ; but just after the Landgravine's Confinement, He was sent for by this Lady, who was dying. And on Her Death bed She asked Him whether He would become a Catholick, that their *Souls might be united* in Heaven; He *gave Consent* at that moment, and became a very violent *Bigot.* He theu wrote to His Wife, who shortly after received a peremptory Command from King George the 2nd to return to England, and never to live with Her Husband Auu, She replied that it was Her Duty to remain in the situation in which it had pleased God to place Her ; Wt that she would make her *own twins* for the sake of Vt kU as they were brought up Protestant."

Mr, Rush, the American minister, was present at , wamage, and thus describes the scene :

X|U 8, 1818. The Princess Elizabeth was mar- - V$| tfwuing to the Prince of Hesse Homberg. The inwts, foreign ambassadors and ministers, of titt royal household, persons in the suites of 'al IWksa aud Princesses, the Archbishops ofCanterbury and York, the Bishop of London, the Lord Chancellor, the Lord Chief Justice were present. The Prince Regent was not there, being ill. Our invitation was from the Queen, given through the Earl of Win- chelsea, nearly three weeks before. We got to the palace at seven o'clock. Pages were on the stairs to conduct us to the rooms. The ceremony took place in the throne-room. Before the throne was an altar covered with crimson velvet. A profusion of golden plate was upon it. There was a salver of great size on which was represented the Lord's Supper. The company being assembled, the bridegroom entered, with his attendants Then came the Queen, with the bride and royal family. All approached the altar. Her majesty sat; the rest stood. The marriage service was read by the Archbishop of Canterbury. The Duke of York gave the bride away. The whole was according to the forms of the church, and performed with great solemnity. A record of the marriage was made. When all was finished, the bride knelt before the Queen to receive her blessing.

" Soon after the service was performed the bride and bridegroom set off for Windsor. The company remained. The evening passed in high ceremony, without excluding social ease. From the members of the royal family the guests had every measure of courtesy. The conduct of the Queen was remarkable. This venerable personage, the head of a large family|her children then clustering about her|the female head of a great empire, in the seventy-sixth year of her age, went the rounds of the company, speaking to all. There was a kindliness in her manner from which time had struck away useless forms. No one did she omit. Around her neck hunga miniature portrait of the King. He was absent, scathed by the hand of Heaven; a marriage going on in one of his palaces; he, the lonely, suffering tenant of another. But the portrait was a token superior to a crown ! It bespoke the natural glory of wife and mother, eclipsing the artificial glory of queen. For more than fifty years this royal pair had lived together in affection. The scene would have been one of interest anywhere. May it not be noticed on a throne ?

" Tea was handed. The Queen continued to stand, or move about the rooms. In one was a table of refreshments. I went to it with Major-General Sir Henry Torrens, distinguished by service and wounds, whose acquaintance I had made at Lord Bathurst's. He was of the establishment of the Duke of York. On the table were urns and tea-kettles of fretted gold. Sir Henry recommended me to a glass of what I supposed wine, in a flagon near me; but he called it king's *cup,* given only at royal weddings.

" Returning to the chief rooms, the Princess Sophia Matilda pointed out to Mrs. Rush and myself the paintings, the representation of a bird from India formed of precious stones so as to resemble beautiful plumage, with, other objects of curiosity or taste. She did more. She spoke of Washington. She paid a spontaneous tribute to his virtues. None but Americans can know how this would fall upon the heart. To hear his immortal name pronounced with praise in a palace of George III., had a high and touching value. Mentioning this Princess, I add, that myself and family afterwards experienced her obliging attentions in ways the remembrance of which is cherished with grateful pleasure. At ten the company came away."

There was something pathetic in this scene. The old queen, now near the close of her long and honourable life, had bravely determined to take part in it, though scarcely able to move.

"The Princess of Hesse Homburg," wrote Mrs. Trench, " will redeem the character of good behaviour in the conjugal bonds, lost or mislaid by her family. She is delighted with her *hero, as* she calls him. In his way from the scene of the marriage ceremony to the Regent's Cottage, where, to his great annoyance, they were destined to pass the first quarter of the honeymoon, he was sick, from being unused to a close carriage, and forced to leave her for the dickey, and put Baron O'Naghten in his place. He said he was not so much *ennuye* at the Cottage as he expected, having passed all his time in his dressing-gown and slippers, smoking in the conservatory."

Princess Augusta, as we have seen, set off in 1821 on a visit to both her sisters, the Landgravine and the Queen of Wirtemberg, whom she had not seen for years.

"... I have passed," she wrote home on September 27, 1821, "a very happy time at Louisbourg, which is a very fine Palace. My Sister's apartments are very beautifully situated in a fine Garden, and overlooking a fine country ; they are prettily furnished, and are very comfortable. She leads a very pleasant, happy, rational life. She rises early, either goes up to Her Grand-daughters at ten, or they come to Her with their masters, and stay together till twelve. Then,

VOL. L U

if any body wants particularly to see Her, or speak to Her, She admits them till near *one,* when She dines. She has a very delightfull Society, both of Ladies and Gentlemen. She occasionally invites the King's Ministers and the English Bureau to dinner. At half- past ten She retires to Her own room; if any body wishes to see Her upon business, they are admitted then. Eight months in the year She drives out after dinner, and generally alone. At Seven o'Clock She goes into the Drawing room, where she has three or four Tables for the different amusements of the Company, Work, Cards, and Music. Here we have had little dancing Parties, impromptu, for the little Princesses; very interesting, from the excessive innocence and happiness of all the young party, and the *esctasies* of the Parents and Elderly people, and of the *adopted Aunt;* for I was quite *the Aunt* of the two little darling Girls. The last dances were two quadrilles, and an English country dance; and I hope that my Sister will give one *regular ball* to the Dear Children before I leave Her. We are very comfortable, and very happy here; and I shall ever look back on this week with very great pleasure.
. . .

" I found my Sister very much altered at first; and had I not had Her picture previous to seeing Her, I should not have guessed it was Her. But she was at the Window of the *Inn* where I was *last* to change Herses. I flew upstairs to Her directly ; and by degrees I have quite *retraced* Her features and Countenance. She is very large & bulky. Her face is very broad and fat, which makes Her features appear quite small and distended. But what strikes the most is, that from.not wearing the least bit of Corset, Her Stomach and Her Hips are something quite extraordinary. Her face is *not at all old*; and though she commonly has to drive a foot's pace, she is very active in the House. She goes out every day, the whole winter through, in Her open Carriage ; and generally by Herself, reading all the while. She is uncommonly cheerful; and I may say has every reason to be as perfectly happy as she appears to be. She is universally respected by the whole Country; and the good she does is incalculable. She walks sometimes ; but as she can only go a very slow pace, it chills Her in cold weather. She can always wrap up in the open carriage; therefore she never catches cold. Her little Grand-daughters are a great subject of delight and interest to Her; and She does Her duty most thoroughly by them. ..."

Princess Elizabeth wrote on September 9th, 1818, entreating Lady Harcourt to let her know of her sisters, and of " everything concerning them ; and if my adored Mother is still in existence. What a loss ! what a blow to us all, & to the Nation! You have often heard me say, ' no one will thoroughly know the value of my Mother till they have lost her.'

" I am very unfit to write, but I have no one to assist me; & all my exertions will be necessary to bear up under my present trial. You, who know how I ever loved my Mother, may well conceive how very much I am afflicted. The blow *is deep,* & the sorrow rankles at my heart; I shall keep much to myself, & will do all I can to support myself, yet you must recollect that tho' the spirit is willing, the flesh is weak. Excuse this hasty note; the Prince is so kind as to take it toFrankfort to go by the post. He says he is sure you will be charitable, & forgive me. We both know that no one will feel more than yourself. My husband desires his kind compliments to you. Y^{TM} affy, Eliza."

"Hombourg, January 21st, 1821.

"You will be glad to hear, my dear Lady Harcourt, that I am got safe home to that dear & blessed home, which, if possible, becomes more valuable to me every hour. You may suppose that I enjoyed my five weeks with my Sister beyond words, & that my beloved Husband's absence was softened to me by her kindness ; for no words can do justice to the friendship, affection, & attention of every sort that she shewed me. We literally were never asunder. I arrived the 12th of December, & staid with her till the 18th of this month. It was a great comfort to us both, as we had much to talk over. You would be enchanted to see my Sister so thoroughly alive to all that is passing of your side the water, quite as if she had left it yesterday. . . .

"I have so very many things to be thankful for, that I ever feel I cannot do too much to prove my feelings both towards God, & my excellent Husband. Tho' I lived in a degree of magnificence & splendour whilst with my Sister, I can with truth say that I was thoroughly happy to see my own dear little Hombourg
again.

" You would have enjoyed the Christmas eve, when my Sister gave all her presents. It was done quite *en Heine,* for there is not an inch about her which is not a Queen."

The amiable princess having to go away, declared that " she had really been so very comfortable here, and so delighted to see dear Eliza so perfectly and reasonably happy. But I shall leave her with *less regret on that account."*

Visitors to Homburg will recall the old-fashioned tumble-down Schloss on the rising hill, with its quaint towers and English garden. Here dwelt the English princess, and here she received her sister.

"At the top of the old high street of Homburg," wrote a pleasant traveller in the *Pall Mall Gazette,* " leading up to the Schloss, there is a gateway of beautiful hammered ironwork, through which any visitor can pass into the old-fashioned grounds that surround the Castle. You wander through the garden, pass the fountain, across the little bridge over the lake, and then under the plum trees of the orchard, till a wicket-gate takes you out on the high road that, lined with enormous poplars, leads straight away apparently up to the summit of the Taunus range. But, at one side of the dusty road, another wicket gives access to some grounds beautifully laid out and well known in Homburg, and known there, too, for several generations, as 'The English Garden.' It is laid out in the formal style of the past century, with walks and grottoes and alleys, planted thick with shrubs and old-fashioned flowers. Hundreds of the *habitues* of Homburg, who wandered last year (1881) under itstrellised vines, will learn with regret that by the next time they visit the little place the grounds will have passed into other hands, the wicket-gate will be closed, and the English Garden will have become a tradition.

" This English Garden at Homburg had a history of its own. You pass through the courtyard of the Schloss, with its great white watch-tower, seen for miles all round, on your way to the little wicket-gate. In the Schloss lived the Landgravela bankrupt kind of prince, whose revenue in the year 1853 was 374,000 florins, and whose expenditure in the same year was 377,000. When Thackeray was at Homburg he went over the old Sehloss. He was shown the apartments of the English princess, whose life was spent in that scene of faded feudal splendour. She was one of the fifteen children of our George

III., and late in life married the Landgrave. They showed you, too, in the Schloss the rooms she occupied, the books she used to read, her English- made furniture, and the portraits of her royal brothers of England. Thackeray saw an old clock hanging on the wall of her bedroom, and noted the name of the Windsor maker on its face. She died childless, in 1840, the year before M. Blanc set up his gaming-tables, having survived her husband about ten years. The English Garden was of her planting and laying out.

" A few years ago a dealer in old curiosities used to exhibit in his window priceless bits of Frankenthal or Hochst 'from the collection of the Princess Elizabeth/ The English princess died in 1840, and at that time neither the wells nor the tables of Homburg had been opened. It was not long afterwards M. Blanc acquired the land, and the arrangement which shut up his rooms and compensated him for their loss in no way interfered with his title to them. The English Garden, after his. death, belonged to his widow, who set up in the midstof it a monument to recall the memory of the dynasty that had become extinct."

Miss Knight was on the most intimate terms with this princess, and paid her many visits at her castle.

" I was much pleased," she says, " with the Landgrave. He had a noble frankness of character, and a patriarchal kindness for his family, which, added to his generous and humane care of his subjects, rendered him truly worthy of being beloved by all who knew him. There was a chapel in the castle in which service was performed twice a day every Sunday, alternately in the Calvinist and Lutheran manner. He had chaplains for each, who dined in turns with him; and we went to both services. There were several Catholics in Homburg, who had a chapel of their own, to which the Landgrave had contributed. He not only found physicians for the sick, but paid for all their medicines, and usually visited them during their illness. He often, too, attended funerals, and was, indeed, the father of his people. He spoke and wrote French with great correctness, and without any unpleasant accent. He was well versed in history and geography, and had a good library of books of that description, and a great number of engravings, all of which he was most willing to lend me. He was remarkably neat in his person, and never came into company without changing his dress if he had been smoking. He was then about fifty-four."

Of the daily life at Homburg she gives this agreeable and lively account:

" One day very much resembled another. This is the ordinary routine. At seven the drum beats a re"veil;a few minutes afterwards the stoves are lighted. At half-past eight the servant brings hot water; and at nine, coffee, boiled milk, a small white loaf, a piece of brown bread, a slice of butter, a salt-cellar, and in a saucer ten small lumps of sugar. At a quarter or half- past twelve, if tolerably fine, we go out in a drosky, and afterwards walk, returning home by a quarter before two, when the trumpet sounds for dress. At two it sounds again to serve up dinner. I then go through a long passage, down twenty-five steps and up twenty- five steps, which lead me to another long passage, and that to the drawing-room, where I find two or three more guests. The door opens, and the gentleman esteemed the most considerable gives me his arm. We walk into the dining-room, and stand still till the other door is thrown open, when the grand maltre d'hotel, with a white wand and hat in hand, enters, preceding the Landgrave and Landgravine, followed by the aide-de-camp of the former and the maids of honour of the latter. All sit down to table, the Landgrave having made me a sign to sit down beside him on his left hand. Three or four times in the week the band plays during dinner, after which the brother gives his arm to the Landgravine, and the Landgrave his to me. During all these movements the ladies curtsey and the gentlemen bow down to the ground. We walk into the drawing-room ; the Landgrave and his brother stand at one window; the Landgravine and the ladies sit near another; the gentlemen stand at the other end of the room, unless any one happens to be addressed by the Landgrave. Coffee is served; after which the Landgrave and

Landgravine leave the room, making bows and curtseys, which are answered by profound bows from all present. A maid of honour throws a shawl over the Landgravine's shoulders and walks after her, first turning to salute the company. The aide-de-camp does the same, and follows the Landgrave, after which everybody retires. The drum beats soon after as a salute to the Landgrave and Landgravine as they drive out in a drosky, returning before six. About half-past six the Landgravine sends for me. A servant with a lantern lights me down stairs to her apartment, and I sit with her in her boudoir till eight o'clock strikes. The servant then lights me through the passages and up the twenty-five steps, and I arrive at the drawing-room, where I find a maid of honour at the tea-table, and, about a quarter of an hour later, the door flies open, and the Landgrave and Landgravine enter. The former takes his tea, and then desires the card parties to be formed; he playing at one table and the Landgravine at another. At a quarter before nine the other door opens, and Prince Ferdinand, the Landgrave's youngest brother, comes in, and bows to the company. He walks up and down and looks at the players, at a little distance; then sits down, and then walks again. I sit at the corner of the Landgravine's table. A few minutes after, the drum beats for some time. At half- past nine the aide-de-camp and a captain, who is always in waiting, come in with low bows, and almost immediately afterwards a servant enters, goes up to the grand maitre, and announces supper. He is probably playing at the Landgrave's table ; but, as soon as the game will permit, he rises, takes his white wand and hat from the chair on which he had deposited them, and comes up to the Landgravine's table, where he stands till he catches her eye. He then announces supper, makes a bow, and retires. As soon as the parties break up, all go to supper, as before to dinner. The Landgrave and Landgravine retire as soon as it is over; so do the company; and a crowd of servants and kitchen-maids rush in to put out the lights and carry away the plates and dishes. The guard is relieved every two hours: at one, three, five, etc. At eleven at night a man blows a horn eleven times, once at one, and three times at three. On Sundays we dine at three. The Princes and officers all in full-dress uniforms, and company, to the number of thirty to thirty-five."

Such is a quaint and curious picture of the peaceful life for which the princess had exchanged her English home.

Almost the last appearance of the aged queen was at the marriages of her sons. Indeed, the closing of her long and respectable reign was of a sad and disastrous nature. On one of the latest occasions when she repaired to her son's Court she was set upon by the mob, and, as she describes it, " sphit on." But she behaved with true courage under such a trial.

After Mr. Rush's account of one of Queen Charlotte's last Drawing Rooms in 1818, one begins to see how sadly the old Court ceremonials have fallen away, and how shorn of splendour are the Drawing Rooms of our time, which attract an attenuated line of unpretending equipages stretching, perhaps, from Buckingham Palace Gate to St. James's.

" February 27.

" Yesterday her Majesty held a Drawing Room. It was in celebration of her birthday. My wife was presented by Lady Castlereagh. The weather was fine with a brilliant sun. A permit had been sent from the Board of Green Cloth for my carriage to pass into St. James's Park, through the gate on Constitution Hill. Going through Hyde Park I found the whole way from Tyburn to Piccadilly (about a mile) filled with private carriages, standing still. Persons were in them who had adopted this mode of seeing those who went to Court. Tenfold the number went by other approaches, and every approach, I was told, was thronged with double rows of equipages, filled with spectators. I was to be set down with the rest of the diplomatic corps and others having the *entree* at a door assigned, within the court-yard of the palace. Arrived in its vicinity, my carriage was stopped by those before it. Here we saw, through the trees and avenues of the park, other carriages rapidly coming up, in two regular lines from the Horse Guards and St. James's. Another line, that had been up, was turning slowly off, towards the Birdcage Walk. Foreigners agreed that the united capitals of Europe could not match the sight. The horses were all in the highest condition, and, under heavy emblazoned harness, seemed like war-horses, to move proudly. Trumpets were sounding, and the Park and Tower guns firing. There were ranks of cavalry in scarlet, with their bright helmets and jet black horses; the same, we were told, men and horses, that had been at Waterloo.

" We were soon set down, and entered the great hall. What a contrast! The day before I had gone up the staircase alone. Now, what did I see ? We were not out of time, for, by appointment, my carriage reached the palace with Lord Castlereagh's ; but whilst hundreds were still arriving, hundreds were endeavouring to come away. The staircase branched off at the first landing into two arms. It was wide enough to admit a partition, which was let in. The company ascending took one channel, those descending the other, and both were full. The whole group stood motionless. The openings through the carved balusters brought all under view at once, whilst the paintings on the walls heightened the effect. The hoop dresses of the ladies sparkling with lama ; their plumes, their lappets, the fanciful attitudes which the hoops occasioned, some getting out of position as when in Addison's time they were adjusted to shoot a door; the various costumes of the gentlemen as they stood pinioning their elbows and holding in their swords ; the common hilarity from the common dilemma; the bland recognitions passing between those above and below, made up, altogether, an exhibition so picturesque that a painter might give it as illustrative, so far, of the Court of that era. Without pausing to describe the incidents during our progress upwards, it may be sufficient to say that the party to which I was attached, and of which Lady Castlereagh, towering in her bloom, was the pioneer, reached the summit of the staircase in about three quarters of an hour.

" Four rooms were allotted to the ceremony. In the second was the queen. She sat on a velvet chair and cushion, a little raised up. Near her were the princesses, and ladies in waiting. The general company,as they reached the corridor by one arm of the staircase, passed on to the queen. Bowing to her, they regained it, after passing through all the rooms, by an outlet that led to the other arm; which they descended. When my wife was presented, her majesty addressed some conversation to her, as a stranger. This she could not do to all, time not permitting. The regent was there, and the royal family ; cabinet ministers and their ladies; foreign ambassadors and ministers with theirs. These, having the *entree* remained, if they chose, in the room with the queen. A numerous portion of the nobility were present, their wives and daughters ; with others distinguished in life, though bearing neither title nor station. Conversation you got as you could, in so great and rich a throng.

" If the scene in the hall was picturesque, the one upstairs transcended it. The doors of the rooms were all open. You saw in them a thousand ladies richly dressed. All the colours of nature were mingling their rays together. It was the first occasion of laying by mourning for the Princess Charlotte; so that it was like the bursting out of spring, No lady was without her plume. The whole was a waving field of feathers. Some were blue, like the sky; some tinged with red; here you saw violet and yellow; there, shades of green. But the most were like tufts of snow. The diamonds encircling them caught the sun through the windows, and threw dazzling beams around. Then the hoops ! I cannot describe these. They should be seen. To see one is nothing. But to see a thousand land their thousand wearers ! I afterwards sat in the ambassadors' box at a coronation. That sight faded before this.

Each lady seemed to rise out of a gilded little barricade, or one of silvery texture. This, topped by her plume, and the "face divine" interposing, gave to the whole an effect so unique, so fraught with feminine grace and grandeur, that it seemed as if a curtain had risen to show a pageant in another sphere. It was brilliant and joyous. Now I saw, radiating on all sides, British beauty. My own country I believed was destined to a just measure of the two first; and I had the inward assurance that my countrywomen were the inheritresses of the last. *Matre pulchrd flia pulchrior.* So appeared the Drawing Room of Queen Charlotte.

" The ceremonies of the day being ended, as far as myself and suite were concerned, we sought the corridor to come away. In good time we reached the head of the descending channel. We got down stairs in about the same time it took to get up. As we waited in the hall for our carriage, military bands were playing in the court-yard, some mounted, some on foot; amidst the strains of which we drove off."

38

SECTION 38

CHAPTER IV.

PRINCESS AUGUSTA.

It has been mentioned that there was a prevailing impression that most of the princesses were secretly married. That six such young and unattractive women (with the exception of the Princess Royal), have been studiously kept till they had grown elderly, without any attempt at arranging marriages for them, was extraordinary. Some excuse, no doubt, was found in the wretched affliction that overtook their father, and perhaps made them disinclined to seek alliances. Something also must be placed to the account of the difficulties of this united family and the sorrows of the queen. It is certain that two at least were married. ThK state of things suggested to the Princess Royal these sensible reflections:

" The more I reflect on Mary's situation and mine, the more I regret my other Sisters not having been equally fortunate; as I am convinced they would all have been happier had they been properly established;and they are so good and amiable in their different ways, that they would have been a blessing in every family."

See the author's Life of George IV., where this matter is discussed.

Attached to the Court as reader was an excitable French clergyman (Mr. Gif-fardiere), who was always making love to the ladies, and who was free enough to carry his admiration to the feet of the princesses. One evening the following scene occurred :

" The Princess Augusta came, during coffee, for a knotting shuttle of the Queen's. While she was speaking to me, he stood behind and exclaimed, *d demi voix,* as if to himself, ' *Comme elle est jolie ce soir, son Altesse Royale!'* And then, seeing her blush extremely, he clasped his hands, in high pretended confusion, and, hiding his head, called out, ' *Que ferai-je ?* The Princess has heard me !'

" ' Pray, Mr. Turbulent,' cried she, hastily, ' what play are you to read to-night ?'

"'You shall choose, ma'am; either *La Coquette corrigee,* or ' pie named another that I have forgotten.]

" ' Oh no !' cried she, ' that last is shocking ; don't let me hear that !'

" ' I understand you, ma'am. You fix, then, upon *La Coquette? La Coquette* is your Royal Highness's taste ?'

" ' No, indeed; I am sure I did not say that.'

" ' Yes, ma'am ; by implication. And certainly, therefore, I will read it, to please your Royal Highness !'

' No, pray don't; for I like none of them !'

" ' None of them, ina'am ?'

'"No, none ; no *French plays* at all I'

" And away she was running, with a droll air, that acknowledged she had said something to provoke him.

"' This is a declaration, ma'am, I must beg you to explain!' cried he, gliding adroitly between the Princess and the door, and shutting it with his back.

" ' No, no, I can't explain it; so pray do open the door.'

"' Not for the world, ma'am, with such a stain uncleared upon your royal highness's taste and feeling !'

" She told him she positively could not stay, and begged him to let her pass instantly.

"But he would hear her no more than he has heard me, protesting he was too much shocked for her, to suffer her to depart without clearing her own credit!

" He conquered at last, and thus forced to speak, she turned round to us, and said :

" ' Well, if I must then, I will appeal to these ladies, who understand such things far better than I do, and ask them if it is not true about these French plays, that they are all so like one to another, that to hear them in this manner every night is enough to tire one?'

" ' Pray, then, madam,' cried he, ' if French plays have the misfortune to displease you, what *National* plays have the honour of your preference ?'

" I saw he meant something that she understood

VOL. I. X

better than me, for she blushed again, and called out: ' Pray open the door at once! I can stay no longer.'

" ' Name it, ma'am, name it,' he exclaimed; ' name but the *chosen nation !'* And then, fixing her with the most provoking eyes, ' *Est-ce la. Danemarc ?'* he cried.

"She coloured violently, and, quite angry with him, called out : ' Mr. Turbulent, how can you be such a fool!'

"And now I found .... the Prince Royal of Denmark was in his meaning and in her understanding. He bowed to the ground in gratitude for the term *fool,* but added, with pretending submission to her will : ' Very well, ma'am, *s'il ne faut lire que les comedies Danoises.'*

" ' Do let me go !' cried she, seriously ; and then he made way, with a profound bow as she passed, saying:

" ' Very well, ma'am, *La Coquette,* then ? Your Royal Highness chooses *La Coquette corrigee?'*

" ' *Corrigee ?* That never was done !' cried she with all her sweet good-humour, the moment she got out; and off she ran, like lightning, to the queen's apartments.

" For my part, I was greatly surprised. I had not imagined any man, but the king and Prince of Wales, had ever ventured at a *badinage* of this sort with any of the Princesses; nor do I suppose any other man ever did. Mr. Turbulent is so great a favourite with all the royal family, that he safely ventures upon whatever he pleases; and doubtless they find, in his courage and his rhodomontading, a novelty extremely amusing to them, or they would not fail to bring about a change."

Of Lord Melville's fall she wrote : " What a sad and melancholy reverse; from having been the leading man in the House of Commons to appear as a culprit there ! Indeed I feel sadly for Him; but I never saw such injustice in my life. The Dear King said, ' Good God, it is not like the English Character to Murder a man that is *down;'* but I fear the mischief will not end here."

Here is a charming letter, dwelling on their enjoyment of the ever favourite Nuneham, from this princess:

" Windsor Castle, June 29, 1805.

" My Dearest Lady Harcourt,

"Everybody is delighted with the very Comfortable manner in which you have settled everything for us. The King will certainly inhabit your room ; but He still begs He may have His small bed: and I will let you know about His sheets.

" With respect to Mary and myself, we are very much obliged to you; and as there is a dressing-room to the Bed Chamber, we would prefer there being a bed in the dressing-room for one of us. But this is only for your *private ear,* for where it would be inconvenient to have us separate, we are perfectly contented to be together; and as for our Maids we are not used to have them near us, therefore they will be quite as well in the Atticks.

" We are to be three Weeks on our Tour, which is a good thing; and the King is determined to be very

careful not to hurt Himself, particularly on account of His Eyes, which have been very bad of late. He has seen Phipps, who has ordered Him Spectacles of black crape, and a large Shade, which He finds soothing to His Eyes.

"We passed a very pleasant Day yesterday at Cashibury, notwithstanding that it rained the whole time we were there; but, on the King's account, I am glad it rained, for He could not have seen anything had we gone out; but He was perfectly contented, and His Sweet Amiable heart said that He should have enjoyment enough if He knew we were amused. Indeed, I have been wretched about Him ; but I must hope His Eyes really are some little better. He was certainly in very good Spirits about Himself yesterday. Our party at Cashibury was very pleasant. The Dowager Lady Essex, Mr. & Mrs. Darner, Mr. & Mra. Stanhope, and Lord S'. Helen's. We took Lady Bath, Lady Radnor, and Lady Crawley with us. There was much to see in the House, which is a very Excellent one indeed.

" Wyatt has shewn His power, His skill, and His Judgment, by making a very old, awkward, inconvenient House into a very handsome and Comfortable Habitation. Some of the Rooms are Magnificent; but the whole is not kept up in style. All is Elegant and Good; but there is a mixture of taste, and it is rather *Gaudy.* There are some very fine Pictures, and some Capital Old China. It was indeed a very pleasant party. We staid *six* hours together, and nothing flagged; the whole of the time being spent in seeing the House, and in a variety of 'pleasant and General Conversation. . . ."

FROM THE SAME.

"Sept. 7th, 1807. " My Dearest Lord Harcourt,

"... The King asked many questions about you all separately; and was quite happy at the good account we gave Him. He has not forgotten anything in the House nor the flower Garden; and I told Him what a loss you had met with in the three fine *Elm Trees.* He ended a long Series of interesting questions and kind remarks upon Nuneham by saying, ' *it is the most enjoyable place I know.*' He is delighted with the good news ; and not a little pleased that *our invaluable* friend, *General Spencer,* took possession of the Dock Yard and Citadel of Copenhagen. Nothing could have given me so much real pleasure. I was also quite glad for Sir Home Popham and Sir David Baird (neither of which I know), that they served on this occasion; for they have in truth many Enemies. . . .

" Yours very truly affectionate,

"A. S. . . ."

The reader will note the affectionately earnest strain of these letters, of which one would be tempted to give many more. Thus, when the dear, very attached friend of the family, Lady Harcourt, died, how sincere is her grief:

PRINCESS AUQDSTA TO THE ARCHBISHOP OF YORK.

" Bagshot Park, February 12th, 1826. "My Lord,

" It is impossible to say what my Heart felt, and does feel, for the contents of the enclosure,|The trulykind and affectionate remembrance of Dearest Lady Harcourt expressed to my Sisters and myself! We *all loved* and *respected* Her ; nor can we ever expect to *sec Her like again!* It is gratifying to our feelings that She names the *number of years* our uninterrupted friendship existed; and indeed it was as *Sincere* as it was *long* in years.

". . . . Every day brings Dear lady Harcourt to my mind, as it *ever* did; but formerly it was with the *anticipated* pleasure of seeing Her, or the *hope* of having that blessing. All is over! but the *Memory* of *Her,* and of Her Dear affection, kindness, and good advice, are Engraven on my Heart; and I thank God that I had such a friend spared to me for so many years.

" I hope Lady Anne and all your family are quite well

" Believe me, my lord,

" Your very sincere friend,

" Augusta."

FROM PRINCESS AUGUSTA.

" October, 1809.

" We have such an example of good humour and of Patience in the beloved King, who bears up against his infirmity with such resignation that we can never be sufficiently thankfull for his present cheerfulness under such a heavy affliction. It can only proceed from the Piety and Goodness of his *most perfect mind.* To think that yesterday he went up to London and did not return till twenty minutes before nine, and at 71 years of age was the life and joy of our Common party, quite *alive* and *gay* from *pure goodness* of Heart; it was a delight to see Him and hear Him. . . .

" Your *old and. faithful friend,*

" Augusta."

On May, 1824, a meeting was arranged at Lady Donegal's between Moore and three of the princesses| Princess Augusta, Princess Mary Duchess of Gloucester, and Princess Sophia of Gloucester. The poet of all circles first sang his own songs for them, then Princess Augusta went to the piano and flattered him extremely by playing some new airs she had composed to his words, "The wreath you wore" (" Rather pretty," says Mr. Moore) and " The Legacy." She next performed a March which she said " she had composed for Frederic ' (Mr. Moore was much pleased at this familiar way of speaking of her relation before him) with some waltzes. He then sat down and gave his rebel song, " Where's the Slave?" It was no small triumph to be chorused in it by the favourite sister of his majesty George IV. If his majesty had heard of it he would probably not have been so pleased. Of the party were Mr. Jekyl, the official wit, and a Lady Poultney. Jekyl told stories about Lord Kenyon's stinginess, how he died of eating pie-crust at breakfast to save muffins, which the pleasant princesses matched with others as good, relating how the king used maliciously to send the Despatches tohim after half-past seven when he knew he was in bed, the judge being accustomed to go to bed at that hour to save candlelight. "Altogether," says Moore, "the report went off very agreeably."

The last survivor of these princesses who impressed their contemporaries as "fine handsome young women," was this Princess, who died unmarried, September 22, 1840.

the Jourth. THE BRUNSWICK FAMILY.

39

SECTION 39

CHAPTER I.

THE BRUNSWICK FAMILY.

The intimate connection that has existed between the English Royal House and that of Brunswick, and the disastrous alliance of George the Third's son and heir with Caroline of Brunswick, renders some account of her line specially interesting to the English reader.

Lord Malmesbury's account of his visit to the Court of Brunswick to demand the Princess Caroline's hand, a most vivacious and amusing one, is remarkable for its observations of character, and its minutely accurate report of remarks and conversations. It is evident, however, that he had many grave forebodings as to the levity of the princess's character, and the sort of recklessness with which she uttered " whatever came into her head." But if we sought an excuse for the follies that were to succeed, it is mainly to be found in the fact that her father's mistress was actually installed under

The author has given at length an account of Caroline of Brunswick and her marriage in his "Life of George IV." What follows is chiefly intended to supplement her account, and not to go over the ground again.

40

SECTION 40

the same roof, though relegated to a wing of the palace, with herself and her mother !

"On Dec. 31, 1799," writes the envoy, "at six went to the duchess's casino, so they call an undress ball. She received me with the most winning condescension. It is impossible not to be delighted with the ease, good humour, and familiarity of her deportment. She has great fluency in her own conversation, and is very- attentive to that of others, evidently showing her approbation when anything is said that strikes or pleases her. She is a fair, well-looking woman, with what we call a very good countenance, and I think when young must have been handsome. She is now a great deal too large, and her dress made her appear more so, being a thick buff-coloured satin chemise, with long sleeves entirely lined, as she told me, with fleecy hosiery. The duchess invited me to sup at her table with a party of about ten, and placed me by her. The Duke of Brunswick is a tall military-looking man, with a fine penetrating countenance; his manners polite, but imposing and dignified even to a degree of state-liness.

"*Jan.* 1, 1800.|Dined and supped with the duchess, and sat by the hereditary prince each time. At dinner he was wonderfully affectionate, considering we had not been acquainted twenty-four hours. At supper, when time had improved our knowledge of each other sufficiently for such a confidence, he assured me I was the most interesting person he had ever met, and that nothing could make him so happy as being able to prevail on me to stay at Brunswick. This was accompanied with many sighs, *doux yeux,* and exclamations,to all which I answered with low bows and *audible* expressions of gratitude. I could not refrain from this *malice,* as everything of the soft kind was said in so very low a whisper that I saw nothing could be more unwelcome, or more likely to stop such declarations, than thus making them public. In the course of the evening I was presented to the Dowager Duchess, a wonderful woman of eighty-five. She is granddaughter to George I., whom she says she remembers seeing when she was eight years old, and grandmother to the Princess of Wales, so is doubly connected with England. She is sister to the great Frederick, whose pictures she resembles, has great sharpness in her eyes, and peculiar animation in her remarkably small features. Her address is pleasing, and there is a neatness, a purity, if I may so express myself, in her whole appearance, that one contemplates with satisfaction. I played Commerce at her table, putting a florin in the pool, a strong contrast to the high play of London.

" *Jan.* 2.|In the evening went to a concert at the reigning duchess's. I do not find an atom of that form I was taught to expect in all German courts. Not only the duchess, but the ladies who played *raco* with her, worked in the intervals of the game. At another table there was a large party employed in knotting, netting, embroidery, and even the homely occupation of knitting stockings ; while the hereditary princess, and those idlers who had no regular work, were busy making lint for the hospital.

" The ceremonial of the dinner at Court on the ordinary days is as follows: You go about three, dressed as you like, except that you must not appearin a hat, bonnet, shawl, or muff. You find the duchess standing at the door of an inner apartment, her maids of honour being in the next. The whole company stand till dinner time (the duke and duchess never sit except when their company can do so too). The chamberlain announces to the duchess that it is on the table, and hands her out. She makes a low curtsey to the duke and the company. The ladies follow, also curtseying to the duke, according to their rank; except foreigners, who, even when untitled, take place of all others going in and out of the rooms and also at table. At dinner the duchess sits at the middle of one side, and the duke opposite to her. This situation, as far as I have seen, answers to the head and foot in England. The ladies are all ranged on one side, and the gentlemen on the other, excepting princes, who are allowed to mix with the ladies. The Prince de Salm generally fell to my lot, and once Prince George. The Prince de Salm is rather above par in address, appearance, and understanding. At dinner there are every day forty people, and the conversation, of course, is seldom general. Once only it turned on politics. Some of the company expressed their expectations that monarchy would be re-established in France. " *Je le desire,"* said the duke, *"plus que je ne l'espere."* He speaks well, in the subdued voice of good sense, and has a stoop which takes nothing away from the dignity of his appearance. I have never seen him converse with a woman. There is an apparent coldness in his manner to the duchess, and in hers to him a degree of constraint which it is evident she tries to conceal. (Her rival, a woman of birth and fashion, is lodged in the palace! and he

dines with her on a fixed day in every week.) Some time after dinner the company all remove to the drawing-room, where tea and coffee occupy a few minutes; no one sits down. The duchess takes leave of her company about half-past five; the ladies curtsey to the duke, and return home, even though they may be engaged for the evening party which begins at a little after six. The duchess one evening invited me to retire with her at this time to her private apartment, which is a particular favour. She spoke with great gratitude of the affection the English had shown to her daughter, and with great delicacy of the Prince of Wales, yet in a manner which showed she felt his conduct."

Of this unhappy family|unhappy or ill-fated in so many of its members|Mrs. Trench, who was on her travels in 1799, and stayed at the Court for a short time, gives some curious sketches in her pleasant memoirs:

This family seemed to be doomed to misfortune, as hardly a single member of it escaped a disastrous career or disastrous end.

" Prince Leopold of Brunswick (the brother-in-law of the King of England) lost his life in endeavouring to relieve the inhabitants of a village that was overflowed at Frankfort-on-the-Oder. While the prince was standing at the side of the river a woman threw herself at his feet, beseeching him to give orders for some persons to go to the rescue of her children, whom, bewildered by the sudden danger, she had left behind her in the house ; some soldiers, who were also in the same place, were crying out for help. The prince endeavoured to procure a flat-bottomed boat, but no one could be found toventure across the river, even though he offered large sums of money. At last, moved by the cries of the unfortunate inhabitants of the suburb, he took the resolution of going to their assistance himself; those who were about him endeavoured to dissuade him, but he replied ; " What am I more than either you or they ? I am a man like yourselves, and nothing ought to be attended to here but the voice of humanity." He immediately embarked with three watermen in a small boat, and crossed the river. The boat had not gone above three lengths from the bank when it struck against a tree, and in an instant all disappeared. A few minutes after the prince rose again, and supported himself a short time by taking hold of a tree; but the violence of the current soon bore him down, and he never rose more. The boatmen, more fortunate, were every one saved, and the prince alone became the victim of his own humanity. Had it not been for the rapidity of the current he would no doubt have been saved, as he was an excellent swimmer. "

Brought up in such a family, and with such examples before her, it is not surprising that her sister-in-law, the Duchess of Wirtemberg, should thus write in extenuation of her later follies :

" She is to be pitied for her bad education ; indeed, her relations are unpardonable for allowing those about her to treat her with such cruel severity. Will you believe it, at thirteen years old she had a governess who would not allow her to go to the window ; she was seldom or never permitted to dine at table, or even come downstairs when there was any company; if she did, her eyes were always full of tears, and her motherinstead of either speaking kindly to her or leaving her alone, always bid her go on crying, for it was only her naughtiness that made her so passionate. Was that the way either to soften her manner or do her heart good ? Poor thing! the moment she obtained her liberty, having not the strength of principles to govern her passions, she allowed all her little evil impulses to get the better."

Driven from this country the Brunswick family were completely dispersed, the duke taking command of armies, his wife obliged to fly to London, where she found herself in a false position, obliged to keep the Prince of Wales in good humour, and yet look on at the treatment her daughter had to endure. An amusing picture of the pressure put on the poor old lady is given by Lady C. Campbell.

" On one of her visits to the princess she said to her lady-in-waiting in her blunt way: "Madame de Haeckle, you may have a day to yourself on Wednesday next, for the prince has invited me to dine at Carlton House, and he will not suffer any lady-attendants to go there ; and as my son accompanies me I shall not want you." This speech was followed by a general cessation of all conversation, Madame de Haeckle only looking dismayed. The Duchess of Brunswick first broke silence by turning suddenly to her daughter and saying: " Do you think I should be carried upstairs on my cushion " To which the princess, with a curious presence of mind, replied coolly : " There is no upstairs, I believe the apartments are all on one floor." " Oh, charming, that is delightful!" rejoined the duchess; and with a few more queries, to which the princess always replied with

VOL. I. T

the greatest self-possession and *sangfroid,* as though she was not in the least hurt, this strange royal farce ended. The Duke of Brunswick, however, came to the princess his sister, and said : "This must not be. You must not suffer her to think of going." Accordingly,

Lady G was despatched the next morning with

a long letter written by the princess to her mother explaining to her that if she went to Carlton House her presence there would seem like a tacit acknowledgment that she was satisfied with the prince's conduct to her daughter; but the duchess was immovable in her intention, and persisted in going. " No," said she, " I see the business quite in another point of view from what you do; I love my daughter above all things, and would do anything in the world for her, but I must go to

Carlton House." Lady G continued in earnest

converse and entreaty with her for two hours, but nothing appeared to move the old lady from her determination ; when weary and worn the ambassadress was about to depart, the duchess cried out: " No, no ; tell her I love her of all things, but give her no hopes upon this subject. The princess has a jewel in you; you have done your embassy well; but give her no hopes." ' *Eh bien!*" said the princess, continuing her narration of this curious scene, and drawing her breath as she usually does when she is angry, " I gave the matter up, and thought, like many other things, it could not be helped; when the next day I received a letter from my mother, saying: ' Far be it from me to do anything contrary to your interests; and hearing that there is a doubt upon the subject I shall not go to Carlton House.'"

41

SECTION 41

Before her death the unhappy Princess of Wales was destined to lose even the few relations she had left to her. Her mother, the Duchess of Brunswick, never returned to her dominions, and during her last days had been quite intimidated by the regent. The poor exiled lady could not contend against the Court, and dared not take part with her daughter. A little scene, vivaciously described by Lady C. Campbell, gives a striking picture of the relations of the family.

At Princess Charlotte's.

" After luncheon I accompanied the princess (attended by her lady-in-waiting) to town, to the Duchess of Brunswick's. The Duke of Gloucester was there; he received the princess very heartily. The conversation between these three royal personages put me exactly in mind of the Margravine of Bareith's Memoirs, and I think all accounts of Courts and the petty transactions therein must have precisely the same stamp. The old duchess talked chiefly of the queen and the princesses having visited herlupon which her daughter, the Princess of Wales, addressed herself as loud as she could across her mother to the Duke of Gloucester, not liking to hear her enemies, as she conceives them, so dwelt upon, and with such complacency. Then they talked of the death of Lady Ailesbury, and immediately of who would get her place in *this wwld;* then of the death of a Mrs. Fielding, and who would get her place, upon which the Princess of Wales rolled her eyes in signal of being weary ; though, in talking of the places she intends to bestow if ever she has the power, she isnot at all aware that to those not particularly on the look-out, it must be equally tiresome. Then they mentioned the new theatre, and the duke said : ' Nobody but Mr. Whitbread could have done so clever a thing.' ' Why,' said the old duchess, ' is he an architect ? I thought he was only a brewer.' Not so bad as that, but she meant, in the simplicity of her heart, merely to say, ' How the devil got the apple in ?' Duke : ' No, ma'am, only no one but he could have had so much taste and ingenuity.' Then their royal highnesses made a joke on the conveniences attached to the private boxes ; after which the conference broke up|the kiss of peace was given and the princess came back here."

§ *The Duke of Brunswick.*

The Duke of Brunswick|her son|some years later came to England, viz. in 1810. This ill-fated prince, who had the spirit of his race, was destined to a death of glory and even romance, and was celebrated by Byron in some stirring verses. Pursuing a romantic affair in one of the country towns, his foreign appearance caused him to be taken for a French spy, and he was arrested, and with difficulty released.

When in England he was vainly pressing ministers to equip him for the war, to give him a command, but in vain. No one would attend to him. At last, weary and disgusted, he determined to leave England and seek his fortune abroad. The morning he came to see the Princess of Wales he is thus sketched by Lady Charlotta Campbell:

" Her royal highness was very injudiciously attired|wrapped in a pink dressing-gown. Lady C n

was with her ; she seemed dead tired of the latter, who in truth appears to be a dull woman, and there is an expression in her features of something very like deceit, and a sneer.

" The Duke of Brunswick is," she goes on to say, "very near being a handsome man; his figure is light and graceful; and were it not that he carries his head ill, he would be a noble-looking creature. His eyes are deep sunk in his head, more so than I ever saw in anyone, and his brows are remarkably prominent, with shaggy eyebrows. This circumstance gives him a sombre expression, and indeed, the whole cast of his countenance is gloomy, but his features are regular; and when he smiles, there is a transitory sweetness which is very striking, by the contrast to his usual severity of expression. In manner he is very reserved|stiff and Germanic. He remained some time conversing with his sister in German, eyeing the lady-in-waiting occasionally askance. He seemed glad to take his leave.

" Her royal highness, the old Duchess of Brunswick next arrived. The duchess appears kindhearted; the tears rolled down her cheeks as she said the poor Princess Amelia cannot live : she seemed really affected. I take her to be a kindhearted upright woman, but not in the least clever, very slow in her speech and in her comprehension, whereas her daughter is precisely the reverse, and has no patience with the repetition of phrases, and the lengthiness of histories, for which, in fact, she feels no interest.

" There is no company at the Duchess of Brunswick's|but old women of the last century, and naturally the princess calls this *dullification.*

" The Duke of Brunswick came to take leave of his sister, her royal highness. He detailed to his sister the whole particulars of the conversations he had had with the ministers, the Prince Regent, etc., he mimicked them all admirably, particularly Lord Castlereagh, so well as to make us all laugh; and he gave the substance of what had passed between himself and those persons, with admirable precision, in a kind of question - and - answer colloquy that was quite dramatic.

"The princess heard all that he said in a kind of sullen silence, while the tears were in several of the bystanders' eyes. How could this be so ? At length, when the Duke of Brunswick said: ' The ministers- refused me all assistance; they would promise me neither money nor arms. But I care not; I will go straight to Hamburg: I hear there are some brave young men there who await my coming; and if I have only my orders from the Prince Regent *to act,* I will go without either money or arms, and gain both.' ' Perfectly right,' replied the princess, with some enthusiasm in her voice and manner. ' How did Bonaparte conquer the greater part of Europe ?' (the duke continued); ' he had neither money nor arms, but he *took* them. And if *he* did that, why should not I who have so much more just a cause to defend ? ' The duke then proceeded to state how the ministers and the regent were all at variance, and how he had obtained from the latter an order which he could not obtain from the ministers. After some further con-

versatiou he took leave of his sister|she did not embrace him. When the duke was fairly gone, however, she shed a few tears, and said emphatically: ' I shall never see him more.' "

PEINCESS CHARLOTTE TO LADY C. CAMPBELL, ON THE DEATH OP THIS DUKE OP BRUNSWICK.

"August, 1815.

"... I cannot close this letter without returning my best acknowledgments for your condolence with, and inquiries after me, in consequence of the fall of my glorious (as well as much-loved) uncle. I bore it as, I trust, a Christian ought, bowing to the will of the all-wise Being; but it was a grievous circumstance|a dreadful, irremediable loss to me, for the great possess a few real friends. In him I had a warm and constant one, allied, too, by the closest ties of blood. I loved him with the fondest affection, and am confident he returned the sentiment. His death was so glorious|so completely what he always desired for himself|that if it was decreed that he should so early in life quit this world, he could not close his career more gloriously or more worthy of a hero, as he was, and of that father and that blood he descended from.

"Pardon me if I seem enthusiastic in my expressions ; but I confess this is a topic which warms every feeling of my heart and mind. You knew him [a word illegible] impartially if I say too much in his favour. My health I do not think has suffered from this shock; but I have not been really well for some time past.

" I was much better for so doing last year, and trust I may derive equal benefit this; but I am still complaining, though I am not the least fanciful about my health; that is a weakness I do not allow myself to indulge in, though there are some which cannot be avoided by the wisest. I less regret than I otherwise should do your remaining abroad, for two reasons : the first is [illegible]; secondly, there is at present so little chance, I may say none, indeed, of our meeting, that it would only be tantalizing. Time, which is the sweet healer of all sorrows, has mitigated and softened down my previous afflictions and distresses to a gentle mild melancholy and resignation; but the recollection of them cannot be effaced. What was at first (as you sensibly remark) the aggravation of my sorrow is now my consolation.

" I trust my mother continues well, and that she has not been very much shocked by the death of her brother. I hope she has got a letter. *I was permitted to wtite to her* on the sad event, etc.

" (Signed) Charlotte."

Soon the poor old duchess closed her troubled career in England. " The Duchess of Brunswick is dead," wrote one of the princess's friends. " The Princess of Wales, poor soul! is much vexed at the carelessness of all the royal family in never having condoled with her on the

occasion. Miss H told me she was much affected

on first hearing of the duchess's death, which I can believe. When she heard the news, she said to a friend: ' There is no one alive now who cares for me except my daughter, and her they will not suffer to loveme as she ought or is inclined to do. True, my moder behave ill to me several times, and did eat humble pie to the queen and the prince, yet she only did so from cowardice ; she was grown old and was soon *terrified,* but she love me for all that.' The little property she was able to leave she has bequeathed to the Princess of Wales."

The death of her father occurred some years later, and " losset" her, as she would say, another friend. Her brother, the more famous Duke of Brunswick, fell at Quatre Bras, and her daughter was to die in childbirth.

But there was yet another Duke of Brunswick, more familiar to our generation, whose career deserves a special chapter.

42

SECTION 42

CHAPTER II.

DUKE CHAELES OF BRUNSWICK.

There were heroic Dukes of Brunswick, whose careers were chivalrous, with whom many have become acquainted through the aid of Mr. Millais's well-known picture of the Black Brunswicker. But there was another who died recently, whose career was anything but chivalrouslDuke Charles.

This strange being was the nephew of the unfortunate Queen Caroline, and ward of George IV., who became .his guardian, and to whom he gave much trouble. The hero of Quatre Bras left two sonsl Charles and Williamlwhom Napoleon, enraged at the escape of their father from his grasp, in 1809, tried to seize. Their mother died in 1808, and the Regent became their guardian. Driven from his duchy by the Revolution, and thenceforward making one of the band of the dethroned, he set up in business in an extraordinary Monte Christo fashion, being remarkable for diamonds, uniforms, Eastern dressing-gowns, and wigs of the most resplendent brown. For about five-and-twenty years Europe was entertained with hissingular and eccentric proceedings. Even during the reign of George IV., when he was a little boy, he gave that monarch much trouble. But when William IV. came to the throne a more serious step was taken. On the 6th and 18th March, 1831, his majesty and his cousin, Prince William, joined in a declaration that he was insane, and took his private property into their keeping, appointing the guardians of his person and affairs. What more immediately led to this was his conduct under these circumstances. An actor, as a jest, had the curtain of the theatre drawn up, which revealed the duke to the audience as paying his addresses to one of the female performers. It was actually said|I know not with what truth|that he had the man put to death.

Another episode of his singular career was connected with the attacks of a well-known scurrilous assassin of reputations, who pursued him in his paper with the grossest charges. In *TJie Age* and *The Satirist* were to be read the most dreadful calumnies of the duke and his friends, who was driven to bring him before the Courts of Law. One of these enemies, however, having withdrawn from this species of profession, determined to embrace the stage, for which he had real talent, and the duke, smarting under his injuries, actually hired emissaries to repair to the theatre to hoot him down. For this he was in his turn brought before the Courts and cast.

This gave occasion to constant appeals for justice to the British Parliament, the French Courts, and other tribunals, who all declined to interfere. In this country he seems to have incurred the dislike of the Press generally, and was often engaged in actions for libel,when he made long rambling speeches to the juries, enumerating his wrongs. It is curious that the most general topic of ridicule should have been his wearing a beard.

Not many may have heard of the extraordinary- bargain concluded between him and Louis Napoleon, then in Ham Prison, and his equally singular treaty concluded with the well-known Mr. Duncombe ("Tommy "), sometime member for Finsbury.

The strangest part of this story was the treaty signed and sealed in Ham, by the "Prisoner "of that place, in which both parties solemnly swore on the holy Gospels, that whichever first came to power should aid the other to recover his rights with arms and money. This arrangement was made in 1845, in presence of G. T. Smith, Mr. Duncombe's secretary.

This document runs thus :

i Ham, 1845.

Nous C. F. A. G., D. of Bk., nous Prince Napoleon Louis Buonaparte, convenons et arretons ce qui suit:

Art. I.|Nous promettons et jurons sur notre honneur et sur le St. Evangile de nous aider l'un et l'autre, nous *C. D. of Bk.,* a rentrer en possession du Duche' de Bk.. et a faire s'il se peut de tout l'Allemagne une seule nation unie, et a lui donner une constitution adapted a ses moaurs, & ses besoins, et au progres de l'dpoque; et nous *P. N. L. Buonaparte* & faire rentrer la France dans le plein exercice de la souveraineW nationale dont elle a e'te' approuve'e en 1830, et a la mettre a meme de se prononcer librement sur la forme de gouvernement que lui convient de se donner.

Art. II.|Celui d'entre nous qui le premier arriverait au pouvoir supreme, sous quelque titre que ce soit, s'engage a fournir a l'autre, en armes et en argent, les secours que lui sont ne'cessaires pour atteindre le but qu'il se propose; et de plus, a autoriser et faciliter l'cnrolement volontaire d'un nombre d'hommes suffisant pour l'exe'cution de ce projet.

Art. III.|Tant que durera l'exile qui pese sur nous, nous engageons a nous aider reciproquement en toute occasion, a fin de rentrer en possession des droits politiques qui nous ont 6t6 ravis; et en supposant que l'un de nous peut rentrer dans sa patrie, l'autre s'engage a soutenir la cause de son allie' par tous les moyens possibles.

Art. IV.|Nous engageons en outre a ne jamais promettrc, faire, et signer aucune re'nonciation, abdication en detriment de nos droits politiques ou civiles; mais, au contraire, a nous consulter et a nous soutenir en frere dans toutes les circonstances de notre vie.

Art. V.|Si par la suite et lorsque jouissant de notre pleine libertt), nous jugerons convenable d'apporter au present Traite' des modifications, dictees soit par notre position respective, soit par l'inte're t commun, nous nous engageons a les faire d'un commun accord, et a reviser les dispositions de cette convention dans tout ce qu'elle contienne de defective par suite des circonstances sous lesquelles elle a e'te' faite.

Approuve', etc. etc.,

In the presence of G. T. Smith, and Count Orsl

These two persons, indeed, now entered on a most extraordinary *rdle*, devoting themselves to the cause of this strange potentate, and in the year following secured a last will and testament, solemnly drawn up, in which " all and everything " was left to the member for Finsbury, and $30,000 to the worthy G. T. Smith.

" I, Charles Frederick Augustus William, Sovereign Duke of Brunswick and Luneburg, now residing at Brunswick House (late Harley House), Brunswick Place, New Road, Regent's Park, in the parish of Marylebone, in the county of Middlesex, being in sound mind and health of body, do declare this to be my last will and testament. I do hereby revoke all other wills and testamentary papers by me heretofore made. I desire, after my death, that my executors hereinafter named shall cause my body to be examined by three or more proper surgeons or physicians, to ascertain that I have not been poisoned ; and thereupon to report in writing the cause of my decease; then to be embalmed, and if found advisable for the conservation of my body, I wish to be petrified according to the printed paper enclosed with this my will. I further desire that my funeral shall be conducted with all the ceremony and splendour becoming my legitimate position as Sovereign Duke of Brunswick, as far as the same may be allowed or is permitted in England ; and that I may be deposited in a mausoleum to be erected of marble in Kensal Green Cemetery, and whereupon a statue and monument shall also be erected, according to the drawing to be hereafter annexed to or enclosed in this my said will; and that my executors shall cause the said statue and monument, or mausoleum, to be erected and made of the materials described in the document so annexed or enclosed, and that the work of art thus described shall be executed by some of the first artists in England. And I also direct that all my just debts, funeral, and testamentary expenses, be paid and satisfied by my executors hereinafter mentioned *as soon* as conveniently may be after my decease, and subject to the condition that they shall enter into no compromise of any sort with my unnatural relatives (the usurper, William of Brunswick, the King of Hanover, the Duke of Cambridge), or any of my family, their servants, agents, or anyone else ; but on the contrary, I direct my said executors to use all means, both legal and parliamentary, to possess and recover my property in Brunswick and elsewhere after having seized that in England; and subject to their respecting and carrying out any codicil or codicils I may further leave in favour of those who may console my last moments. And whereas, Thomas Slingsby Duncombe, Esq., M.P. for the borough of Finsbury, and George Thomas Smith, Private Secretary to the said Thomas Slingsby Duncombe, having severally afforded me great assistance in prosecuting my case in the House of Commons, for the purpose of vindicating my character from the vile aspersions and slander which has been so industriously promulgated by the members of my family, and taking the above into my consideration, as well as any further valuable trouble and perhaps necessary outlay, in executing this my last will and testament, I do hereby give and bequeath unto the said George Thomas Smith the sum of thirty thousand pounds, sterling money, from my general personal estate, to be paid to him, the said George Thomas Smith,free from legacy duty, immediately after my decease, for his own absolute use and benefit. And further, I do hereby give and devise unto the said Thomas Slingsby Duncombe, *all* and everylthe castle, houses, messuages, lands, tenements, hereditaments, whatsoever and wheresoever situate; my diamonds, jewels, plate, pictures, horses, carriages, china, household furniture, linen, wearing apparel, books, papers, correspondence," etc. "And I declare this to be my last will and

testament.

" In witness, etc.

"Dated this 18th day of December, 1846.

"Witnessed by

" Me. Chas. F. Arundell, solicitor.

" Mr. Walter E. Wm. Goatley, solicitor, and

" Mr. John Miles, clerk to Mr. Arundell,

3, Cork Street, Burlington Gardena"

To the former, by way of whetting his zeal, was given a detailed list of the jewels and bonds, amounting to close on a million sterling in value. In March, 1848, the gems, bonds, etc., were actually entrusted to G. T. Smith. His account reads like a page of Dumas.

"On Saturday night I was occupied for five hours making a catalogue of the bonds, etc., now in my care. I have money to the amount of two hundred thousand pounds, and gems, etc., to the amount of ninety thousand pounds, and all was safe at my house this morning when I left, and I hope will be there when I return. Where the sixty thousand Louisiana are I know notl at least, I could not ask him too much, or he would

43

SECTION 43

have got frightened. I have only one saddle-bag, Number Four, and if your brother Henry will lend me his brougham to go in, I will show him all. Now, then, for your assistance. After he had decided what he would entrust me with, he started; in fact, he told me that before then his fear had been of my house being destroyed by fire, and the paper-money thereby lost. I, fearing to lose the opportunity, said I had got (which I have) an iron chest; but alas ! mine is too small, and I am compelled to keep the saddle-bag in a cupboard perfectly safe, except against fire. I want your permission to move your iron chest, till I deliver up the treasure again. My reason for making this curious request is this : he might perchance come to my house to look and see that it was all safely deposited in iron. I fear, on looking at your iron box, that I shall not be able to get the saddle, bag in, but I may the money, etc., by packing close. One thing is a fact; that I have in genuine good securities a tolerable good sum now in my house, and really if he would allow all the large loans (and which he does not for the present purpose think of changing) to be at my house it would be a grand thing for us at his death, and they would be just as safe as with him, for I would not touch one shilling until I felt I was entitled to it by his death. After all, he cannot be so suspicious as we fancy, else why should he trust me with so large a sum ? I left his house at one o'clock after midnight, and was compelled to walk to Oxford Street before I could get a cab.

When in the cab my fancy ran upon the excitement I should feel if the bags with the treasure had been with me in a cab under different circumstances, viz. the starting to join you. I cannot but think it a Vol.

good omen that some of it should be with us, and it must, I am sure, please you to think that his confidence has not in the least diminished. Pray don't forget to say whether I may use the iron box at my house; there is nothing in it but the will, and where so fit a place as that which contains the documentary powers of disposing of the money, for the money ? "

Another custodian of the property was Baron Andlau, and it is amusing to see how he tantalised the expected heirs by appetising assignments which were mere Barmecide feasts, and revocable at any moment. Each expectant was formally kept *au courant* of the disposition of the property, so that there could be no jealousy.

" The Sovereign Duke of Brunswick has this day informed us that he has left in the hands of the Baron Andlau the following bonds and securities, viz. :

50 Bonds Russian English Loan, 5 per Cent., of

$1036 each. 5 Bonds Russian English Loan, 4$ per Cent., of

$1000 each. 45 Bonds Danish Loan, 1849, 5 per Cent., of $1000

each. 15 Bonds Danish Loan, 1850, 5 per Cent., of $1000

each.

2,000,000 francs, 5 per Cent. French Rentes; as also a sealed portfolio. And his Sovereign Highness has been pleased to command that in the event of his death the Baron Andlau shall take therefrom the sum of twenty thousand pounds sterling money as a legacy ; and whichdonation we promise to respect as his Highness's testamentary executors.

"London, this 15th day of March, 1851.

(Signed) "T. S. D.

G. T. S."

"The Sovereign Duke of Brunswick has this day informed us that he has left in the hands of Mademoiselle Lucie Victorine Bordier six bank notes of $100 each as a legacy in case of his death, which donation we promise to respect as his Highness's testamentary executors.

" London, this 15th day of March, 1851.

(Signed) "T. S. D.

G. T. S."

The duke's proceedings in London were of the most singular kind. He lived at Brunswick House with an enormous establishment of servants and horses, where he affected to consider himself a sovereign prince and above the law. Judgment having been obtained against him for some debt which he refused to pay, the sheriff's officer obtained admission by a stratagem. An immense iron chest containing the duke's food being brought inside the gates with due precautions|for he affected to dread poisoning|the officers rushed in with it. The alarm was raised. The duke appeared with his pistols. Men and bloodhounds were set on the unfortunate officers, who were flung out with broken legs and other

serious injuries. Yet he succeeded in obtaining one thousand pounds damages for violation of domicile.

An earnest appeal to Lord Palmerston only produced the following characteristic reply :

My Dear Buncombe,

I am sorry to say we cannot assist the Duke of Brunswick in the matter mentioned in your note. Foreign princes are, like our own, liable to the laws of this country while they are in it, and the Government has no power to interfere in regard to legal proceedings in which a foreign prince is concerned, or to stay those proceedings on the ground of his royal birth and position. Neither has the Government any power to send a foreign prince out of the country. In fact, the legal position of a prince of a foreign royal family, while resident in this country, is exactly the same as the legal position of a British subject.

Yours sincerely,

Palmerston.

Prince Louis Napoleon had now come to be president, but found difficulties in carrying out his part of the treaty. He, indeed, put off its execution until he should have full power in the state, but he never did anything serious to restore his friend.

Mr. Smith was despatched to Paris in 1849, to remind the president of the " treaty," taking with him a silver eagle as a present from the duke.

" I have this instant," wrote Smith to Duncomhe, " left the president. I have settled the treaty matter I have arranged for the letter of invite I have gotback the ' national shares,' and on which there is $200 to receive on the 15th instant; and, in fact, I have done all but raise troops, which, being the point most wanted, will be the most difficult to satisfy Him upon. However, L. N. has, I say, behaved very well. He has pointed out to me how little power he has while the present chamber exists ; for they are as *puissant* as him, and can make laws and issue *ordonnances* without him. Therefore, he says, until it is dissolved he can do nothing respecting the treaty."

Meantime the duke was entrusting his other secretary, Baron D'Andlau, with bags of money, who was posting to Paris with forty thousand pounds, to be invested there; for this shifting of his property from state to state was a mania of the duke's. He had also charge of large plaques of pure gold, into which form the duke had a fancy for converting his hoards.

Meanwhile, the position of the legatees, " Tommy " Duncombe, and G. T. Smith " The Treasurer-General," as he is described was becoming more and more precarious. His royal highness was flourishing; and though he once fell sick and was attended by the latter, the potentate, suspicious as he was, seems to have had perfect confidence in his English attendant. At one time Mr. Smith put twenty leeches on his head, and was about to put twenty more on. " Strange to say, he will not have a doctor, but trusts me a very unpleasant responsibility." Later he wrote to his friend more hopeful news.

" I have taken an opinion with regard to D. B., and it is thought to be a breaking up of the constitution: they say, at his age, he runs a great risk of a severe attack. Last night the conversation between H.R.H. and self was the subject of the will; and he said to me : ' If anything happens to me during this illness, over and above what you have by the will, I give you fifty thousand Sardinians as a gift; and as there are one hundred and fifty-six thousand in the packet, it

would be well to send Mr. D over the same amount,

and place the remaining fifty thousand in some secure place, to pay your joint law expenses which you would incur in insisting upon the whole of my Brunswick property being placed at your disposal.' I then said (having a good opportunity) : ' Are you quite sure that the will is in perfect order to satisfy the French law ?' He said : ' I have always understood so.' "

The contentions between these hopes and the sense of decent propriety is amusing enough. The situation was certainly a tantalising one, and would try the stoicism of a philosopher. The awkwardness, too, was that there could be no anticipating the inheritance, as all was precarious; and any eagerness, even as to current expenses, might overset all. For the duke was sensitive even to these, and would haggle over details.

" Thus, on our return, we arranged that my travelling accounts should be paid, as I was to quit the next day. Accordingly I made out my account, he deducting the carriage to Godstone, which he said he did not ask me to take, and then settled to the sou. He then hum'd and hah'd a good deal, and at last counted out ten sovereigns, which he handed over to me saying: ' This will pay for your white gloves ;' and he said: ' Allow me to seize this opportunity of telling you that I have long since felt that I have very inadequatelyremunerated you for many things you have done for me.' He then entered fully into the history of the visit to Ham; how many times he had seen you, etc.; vhat you had done for him ; and finished by saying: ' As a collateral remuneration, I have made my will in your favour jointly with Mr. Duncombe; and should I have the strength to see you before I die, I will, independent of that will, make you a present worthy of your acceptance.'"

In 1851 the duke left England suddenly for Paris, choosing, as an eccentric mode of conveyance, Mr. Green's balloon, the Nassau, in which he ascended from Vauxhall. He arrived in Paris with his enormous baggage, some chests of which were reasonably detained at the custom-house, owing to the suspicious circumstance of their containing uniforms which caused great excitement. After the *coup d'etat* our duke established himself in the Champs Elyse.es, at Lola Montes's Hotel, which he gradually transformed into a sort of Eastern palace, full of extraordinary caprices and devices out of the " Arabian Nights." But under the blaze of gold and decorations which adorned his bedroom, everything was of iron, to guard against assassination|floor, ceiling, and door|so that it was in fact an iron cage in which this unhappy sultan lay down to rest. The various portions were entrusted to different sets of workmen, so that the whole combination was a secret. In the wall was contrived a recess, opened by a key which was always attached to his person, where was hung by chains an enormous coffer, which a touch allowed to sink into a deep well that reached far below the very foundations of the hotel Here were stored hisbonds, jewels, and golden tablets, some of which were cast in the shape of chocolate slabs. The whole house was as gorgeous as money and extravagance could make it. Forty horses were in the stables, and as man; servants waited on him. The visitor, after innumerab'e precautions, was seated in a rich chair, which carried him aloft to the upper floors, which, in the days before " lifts" were familiar, was considered something out of the fairy tales. But the old idea of being poisoned cling to him, the very milk arriving from the country uader locks and bolts. His regular dinner he partook of not at home, but at the cafe's and restaurants.

At the theatres and on the boulevards for manT years the spectacle of this strange duke became familior. He was always carefully painted and bewigged for the day; and the story ran that he had a room full of waxen images of his own face, tinted in different fashions, according to which he would colour his own. A " Nubian slave" always attended him. One night, at a party given by Prince Jerome, the duke, impatient at not being able to get through the crowd of empire magnificoes who blocked the way, called out fiercely to his black: " Make a passage for me. Use your sword *I*"

His grand passions were lawsuits and diamonds. He went to law with a wash-erwoman for a bill of seven francs, he went to law with his architects, upholsterers, gardeners. His rage for jewels was extraordinary, and when he appeared on some grand gala, bearing all his treasures, he was a sight to see. He wore two epaulets of large yellow diamonds, each worth forty thousand pounds, while his chest was encrusted with a dozenjewelled orders, from the Golden Fleece to the Lion and Sun.

Mr. Smith reports some proceedings of the duke, which show that his brain was somewhat unsettled :

"The duke, when I saw him the other day, was quite well, but very busy making a large bracelet, which he wants me to try to show to the queen. It will be the finest bracelet in the world; and will be of an immense value when finished, and I have got it in my possession. The duke was rather in high spirits, for it appears that Austria wishing, *sub rosa,* to have the power of deciding the question of the German (*i.e.* Prussian) Bund, and feeling desirous not to show her teeth without being sure of being supported by the minor German Powers, has been proposing terms to our duke something to the following effect, viz. that she, Austria, will be very glad to allow him to reside in Vienna, and receive him as a sovereign ; that she will undertake the settlement of his claim upon the following terms : first, that he shall marry; and, secondly, that he shall at once see his brother William, and forgive and forget all animosities.

" The duke's reply to the Austrian Government was to this effect, viz. that he had no objection to marry; that he most decidedly objected to being in any way bound, and would not be, to any act which would compromise his having the power to punish his brother William both as an usurper as well as a traitor ; that he claimed that right as sovereign *de facto,* although by his brother's usurpation not *de jure;* that the punishment for such offences was death by the axe-man, and that he called upon them not to interfere in any way with the"jurisprudence" of Brunswick, and that he begged, if the matter was to be at all entertained, that no interference should take place with respect to the sentence he should pass on his brother ; that if he could not find him, he should condemn him and punish him *par contumace,* and should carry the final sentence into execution whenever he could catch him; that he should not quit this country without having under his command six thousand troops, natives of Ireland, all officered, and to be called his body-guard."

But in 1864 this satrap was to receive a severe blow. His daughter had married against his wishes the Count de Civry, and had moreover changed her religion. With a strange rancour he refused to forgive, see, or support her, and after many ineffectual advances she had to appeal to the French courts. When he saw that in spite of all his protests a French court was going to entertain a question which referred to Brunswick, he suddenly broke up his vast establishment, and taking all his bonds, and selling his French stock, he left nothing to be seized, and retired to the Hague, where he lived two years. Then growing weary of this banishment he returned to Paris, and under the advice of counsel invoked the French law, which, after a series of appeals was in his favour. The duke therefore triumphed, and was once more established in his Elysian Fields hotel.

But, alas! in the year 1861 a significant matter occurred which must have shaken Mr. Duncombe's hopes, if he had not resigned them altogether, or grown indifferent, for he was near his end, and was to die in that year. The secretary was sent for to Paris.

"His highness said: 'This is a bad day, 17th,

and you have arrived twice lately on a 7.' I replied : ' I think, your royal highness, I was in the house before twelve o'clock last night.' The valet said it was ten minutes past twelve. His royal highness then said : ' My reason for sending for you is, that I thought you would not care to run about Paris with the large sum of money you have, and although I am not ready to settle accounts with you' (he being in bed), 'you can seal up the packet, or how you like, and we will settle by-and- by. I have been thinking a great deal about my testament lately, and I intend to change it, as to its legality, and you must get my testament back from Mr. Duncombe.' I replied : ' Your royal highness, that requires an authority from your royal highness.' He then said, speaking in the plural : ' You would have less difficulty with a French will than with an English one here in France.' The conversation here ended, and I, having some important appointments, left his royal highness. I may safely say that is all that passed."

The next stage was a new testament. Accordingly he " cut off" his old friends ! This strange duke, it seems, delighted with the favourable view taken of his case by the French tribunals, had determined to choose a Frenchman for his heir, and selected the son of his old ally, the Emperor Napoleon ; to whom, by a fresh " Act," he bequeathed all his immense possessions. But by-and- by came the crash of 1870. The duke had to fly from Paris, and established himself at Geneva, leaving his magnificent hotel to the besieged and to the invaders.

On the news of the general disasters he completely turned against his lately-named legatees, casting them and the French nation off altogether. On March 5 he

44

SECTION 44

destroyed his will, and prepared another. " We bequeath our fortune|that is to say, our castles, demesnes, forests, lands, mines, salt-works, hotels, houses, parks, libraries, gardens, quarries, diamonds, jewels, silver, pictures, horses, carriages, china, furniture, cash, bonds, stocks, notes, and especially that portion of our fortune of which we were stripped in 1830, with interest accruing, all to the Town of Geneva."

But amid all these dispositions there was another he did not accurately make account of. He himself was to be disposed of. On the evening of August 18, 1873, he was playing chess, and rose to go to his room, leaving the game as it stood. "Don't rob me," were his words |and his last words. He was found dead in his room.

All his instructions were strictly followed, but the "petrifaction" process failed. The society of "Funeral Pomps" from Paris undertook it, bringing all their magnificent cars, etc. Then the city began to lay out the inheritance. The costly tomb is finished ; so is a magnificent opera-house, costing together about half-a- million. The town rather handsomely allotted annuities to some of the faithful attendants|including the hardworking Mr. Smith|the duke had so selfishly passed over. To make the whole grotesque even to the end, he courts of Brunswick, now that the money is half spent, have decided that the will is void.

CHAPTER III.

THE PRINCESS OF WALES.

The history of this unhappy lady, Caroline, Princess of Wales, who for a short time was Queen of England, is certainly one of the most extraordinary in the annals of the royal family of England. The outlines of it are well known, and it has been recently detailed in several works.

From the day of her landing in England to that of her death at Brunswickla period of some thirty years la series of scandals attended her course.

Much angry debate equally attended her on the question as to who was responsible for these, whether husband or wife. But, whatever be the merits of the case, she might fairly plead that a woman who was cast off by her husband within a few weeks of the wedding-day, simply on the ground of her being distasteful to him, was likely enough to have met with similar cruel treatment subsequently.

A more interesting view, however, may be taken of her social character as displayed among her friends and companions in her conversations and letters ; and these exhibit a certain power and vivacity for which she hasnot generally been given credit. She had gifts of quick observation for character and oddity; she loved fun and frolic, and could write with a pleasant shrewdness and gaiety. Neither was she without sagacity in her action, though too often hurried on by passion and impulse. But at the bottom of all was the incurable *gamin* temperla taste for low society and flatterers, and that greedy welcome of scandal and abuse directed against those whom she disliked.

I shall therefore select from a large number of her letters a number of characteristic specimens which display her peculiar tone and temper at various stages- of her course. It will be noted how a strain of reckless vivacity is often alternated with something like desperation; and with what acute and pleasant observation and even wit she "touches off "the scenes and characters that pass before her.

" *0 tempera, 0 mores!* Since Saturday I am hi town again; and I feel myself much more comfortable from having performed my arduous tasks at the royal menagerie. Lady Westmoreland called on me one morning, and is going abroad directly. She is always going somewhere or anoder. I call her de perpetual motion. A Mr. Malcolm sent me a second edition of his ' Sorrows of Love,' for which I had paid him years ago; and also two copies for the Regent and Princess Charlotte, both of which I sent to her ; and desired Mr. Malcolm to write to the Duchess of Leeds to get paid. I certainly never shall give him another shilling for his trash of poetry. He should send a fourth volume to Lady Hertford, as I think, in the present predicament,.it would be acceptable, as it contains the ' Sorrows of

Love.'

" Pray believe me ever your affectionate

(Signed) "C. P ."

"Thom. Sheridan, I hear, is gone abroad, dying. I never knew much of him ; for he also was one of the great Mahomed's favourites, to whom, by-the-way, the latter has not behaved with the most loyal bounty, or steady friendship.

"As to myself, I have nothing agreeable to tell you,

dear . I hear plenty of ill-natured stories, put about

by dat old witch de Queen ; but I say to dose who tell them, you do me no good by repeating these reports. You do not gain favour with me either by so doing, I assure you. When I answered Lady Oxford in this fashion de oder day, she did look quite *ebahie,* and

ashamed of herself. 'Tis true, my dear , 'pon

honour, I never wish to be told these things. I know them to be said. I know quite enough, God knows, and wish never to know more, if I can help it.

" I did much regret your absence from my little party last night, for we were all very merry. The Gell, Berry, Sidney Smith, Lewis, Lady Oxford *(De Miscellany Harleyan,* as all de world does call her now), and Milord Byron, did make it very pleasant; and we all laugh till we cry. Lewis did play de part of Cupidon, which amuse us, as you will suppose. He is grown so embonpoint, he is more droll than ever in dat character; but he tink himself charming, and look so happy when he make *les yeux doux* to the pretty ladies, dat it is cruel to tell him: ' You are inde paradise of de fools, ' so me let him sigh on to my Lady Oxford, which .do torment Lord Byron, who wanted to talk wid her, and never could contrive it. Lady Anne is *en petite sante* just now; she is truly interesting; yet, as your song says : ' Nobody's coming to marry her,' nor I fear never will; so I and Joan shall live and die together, like two turtle-doves, or rather like dem two foolish women, Lady Eleanor Butler and Mile. Ponsonby, who must be mad, I should tink, to choose to leave the world, and set up in a hermitage in Wales|*mais chacun a son gofit*|it would not be

mine. My dear , I do dread being married to

a lady friend. Men are tyrants, *mais* de women- heaven help us ! dey are *wais Neros* over those they rule. No, no|give me my sweet prince, rather than a female governess.

"A princess, and no princess. A married woman, and no husband, or worse than none!|never was there a poor devil in such a plight as I am. Lady Euphemia Stewart, that old *commdre,* talked to me till I thought my ears never would be able to hear again. She thought I listened. Well, no matter. What think you I did ? I dare say they all said I was mad. I sent them all away, ordered the carriages, and set off wid a chosen few to the play. The first one made me cry; and, strange to tell you, I felt a satisfaction in being able to weep. And den de second piece was a farce, and it made me laugh ; so dat amusement compensated for the dullification of the first part of the night. Little Lewis came into the box : he affected to be sentimental; dat is always laughable in him, and I quizzed him- I do not think he enjoyed the fun."

FROM THE PRINCESS OF WALES TO THE SAME.

I shall see Mr. Brougham next Sunday, as he is my counsellor and chief adviser. He thinks it his duty first to inform me of it before he gives his final answer in the newspapers.

Many thanks for the interest you have taken in the unexpected event of my brother's death. It was a happy release for him, as he was in a delicate state of health from his cradle. My mother has not suffered in the least from this occurrence.

I have just been calling at Lady Oxford's door to inquire for her and the new-born little ruffian; both are doing well. The only news I can tell you is, that the Duchess of R|| is going to lie in of a marvellous child. Her husband is as old as de hills; but no one says any harm of her; indeed she is universally extolled.

I have been much amused with your remark

concerning husbands, and I trust, dear , you will

retain the same sentiment for ever, as I all my life thought husbands were only a creditable evil, and men in general a necessary plague. But so much about nothing.

I must tell you an unpleasant circumstance which occurred to me the other evening. I was in the anteroom ; Mr. M and Lord L were talking

together in the drawing-room, waiting for me, and I

heard Lord L say: ' The princess is so vain and

foolish, no one can do her any good; her English is the most ridiculous language any one ever made use of, and I could scarcely help laughing the other night, when she said to me : " Give me my wails."

Vol. i 2 A

I did not stay to listen to any more of what these treacherous " friends " of mine might have to say about me, but I thought to myself, Then why do you come so often to my dinners ? etc.land I determined they shoukl not be asked again in a hurry. However, I went in to them, and tried to be as civil as I could, but I felt furious when they made me fine compliments, and I soon dismissed them. So much for courtiers. I send you Madame De Stael's pamphlet, and remain

yours,

C. P.

THE PRINCESS OF WALES TO THE SAME. MY DEAR ,

I have been busy all this week trying to make

up a match for Lady A. H . I have set my heart

on getting her married somehow or other to some man ; she would be so much more agreeable if she was married; at present she is so full of old maid's whims and prudery, it is quite tiresome to be under her surveillance.

Lady Oxford has no thought but for Lord Byron. I wonder if she will succeed in captivating him. She *can* be very agreeable when she pleases, but she has not pleased to come near me for this long time past; she has quite forgotten that Kensington Palace used to be a convenient place to see certain folks, and be seen by them; *n'importe, ga m'est bien dgal;* she does not make *la pluie ou le beau temps* to me, only it shows what her friendship is worth, and how little gratitude there is in her nature. Lord Rivers, I think, is a little mad, but very interesting. Lady is in a greatfright that Sir W. G is falling in love with her.

I do not see the tender passion growing, but perhaps I

am shortsighted : Lady is not apt to be vain. I

wish you good-night, my dear; my eyes are beginning to gather straws, as you English say, so no more from yours, etc.

C. P.

THE PRINCESS OF WALES TO THE SAME.

Last night I gathered together, my dear, a room full of people, and when I did look round at them I said to myself, *d quoi bon* this dull assemblage of tiresome people ? And it so happened they were all ugly, and I longed to get them out of my sight, yet I could not send dem away, having made them come. De fact is, I know not what to do."

She often read aloud to her ladies, though it was difficult to understand " her Germanised French, and, still more, her composite English," and thus once read aloud the whole of " Candide." She passed this criticism on it:

" The persiflage which reigns throughout is not consonant to my taste or understanding. Vicious subjects ought not to be treated lightly, they merit the coarsest clothing. But the whole work seems designed to turn vice into virtue. Either it has no aim or end, or it has one which should be loathed. It must be confessed, however, that the tripping levity of its self-assurance and the sarcastic drollery of its phrase excite laughter; but it is a poor prerogative after all."

" All the news I can offer you, my dear , is

a most dreadful blunder which that wonderful woman, Madame De Stael, has committed. She was in some

party several evenings ago, and mistook old Mrs. B

for the Marchioness of Hertford. She began by assuring her ' *que la renommee avoit vante* sa *beaute et* son *esprit par tout le continent\|que ses portraits etoient graves, et faisaient les charmes et l'ornement de tons les palais.*' Of course, you may imagine that this event has been the laughing-stock of these last eight-and- forty hours."

There is a strange chapter in the social life of the time, viz. the power of literary assassins, who now " lived and throve" by a terrible system of " blackmailing." The princess herself was surrounded by a set of low, unscrupulous persons, the least worthy of whom were eager for their own interests, and to turn her misfortunes to their profit. The princess herself, under bad advisers, often planned giving to the press papers of a private and secret nature : and there is mentioned in Lord Brougham's " Memoirs," as well as in Lady Charlotte Campbell's " Diary," a plan of this kind. Thus she writes to a friend of " our plan about our mutual friend's letters to be published. I have some particular reasons that the title should be ' Genuine Documents found among the Papers of the ever-to-be-lamented Chancellor of the Exchequer,' and that in the year 1806, on June H, Mr. Perceval undertook the charge of very valuable letters and papers which were in the princess's posses

sion."

45

SECTION 45

The history of the well-known " Book " is instructive in this view.

When she had finally made up her mind to go abroad, allured by the offer of a handsome allowance and the prospect of amusement, she did so with the best intentions of regularity and propriety. This will be seen from her thoughtful and decorous letters, hitherto unpublished, to her man of business.

PRINCESS OF WALES TO MR. HOPES.

" Sompting Abbey, July 31, 1814.

" The Princess of Wales desires Mr. Hoper not to enter info any particulars with Mr. Sicard concerning the servants, which has been settled between Mr. Hoperand the princess, as she must be the chief judge how far her income will permit her to be generous or not, and no one has a right to tax her or to make unnecessary demands on her too well-known generosity, for which reason people may think they have a right to impose upon her. The princess thinks it is much more fair that, after the princess has embarked, and the servants returned to town to the apartments at Kensington Palace which will be allotted to them, Mr. Hoper will be so good to inform them who is to receive their *pension for life,* and who is to receive from Michaelmas twelvemonth their salary for one year, as it would offer them the opportunity to find another situation sooner and not to be out of service the whole year; and that it be well understood that the salaries should be paid the same for a year, if even they get situations before the expiration of that time."

This was written by Mr. Perceval, and suppressed and destroyed, only half-a-dozen copies being preserved. A wretched creature named Ashe, or Captain Ashe, has written some revelations of the blackmailing system. " From Mr. Lindsell, of Wimpole Street, I learned that he was employed by Mr. Perceval to print two thousand copies of a certain work, but on no account to publish or sell a single copy till he had further instructions from his employer. This information was not cast away upon me. I discovered the printer, Mr. Edwards, the celebrated author of the Diamond Testament, and I obtained from one of his compositors a sight of the rough sheets in succession as they were printed off. At the conclusion of the printing, however, seals were set upon Mr. Edwards's office, the workmen were sworn to the number of copies printed, and the whole of the immense edition, with the exception of six copies withdrawn by Mr. Perceval, and six more purloined by the persons employed on the press, was committed to the flames. This conflagration was by order, and in the presence of Mr. Perceval, the proprietor, compiler, and editor of the work! ! ! *The Plunnix*, which I conducted, was the instrument I employed. In a number of that paper, published August the fifth, 1810, I inserted the following notice :

"the Book."

" To this universal conflagration there were some few exceptions : six rough copies had been purloined, and gone abroad. To correct this lamentable error, Mr. Perceval applied to the Chancellor to send injunctions to the holders not to dare to publish them, and to discover the holders, rewards were offered for the extant copies to a very large amount. Such being the case, and the importance of " The Book," the Editor of *TlwPhceuix*, who has access to one of the extant copies, is determined to give extracts from it in this paper, and to investigate the spirit and principles of the proceeding in such a manner as must eventually bring the whole question before the public eye.

" Immediately after the publication of this notice, an injunction was sent into *The Pluznix* office not to print the extracts alluded to, and Mr. Swan, the proprietor, was first menaced, and then debauched to change the principles of his paper, or to abandon me to my usual evil destiny. He abandoned me, and I retired to Brighton, where I came to the resolution of writing " The Spirit of the Book," and of convincing Mr. Perceval how absurd it was to call himself an upright minister or an honest man, before he had burnt my evidence of his life, and put out the eyes of his judge."

A publisher was found, and " The Spirit of the Book," and " The Book " itself had an enormous sale.

In another letter she shows a creditable anxiety that her servants should have their pensions, " though," she says, " all English servants are only mercenaries. Poor old Davis at Blackheath has not received anything ; you must give him twelve pounds every quarter, and to my two old maids who are at Kensington. Naples is a charming situation, and, besides, reasonable. I shall make a much greater figure here than the Queen of England in London."

She then describes a *fete* she gave to the king and queen, with fireworks, and the gardens illuminated, for $150. "In short, Naples is the only place to *leave* on a most agreeable footing, for people who have not a great fortune. I bought three fin *gawns,* one in satin and two in velvet, for $20."

Again:

"dear Mr. Hoper,

' I give you a commission to execute, which is to send me 50 Bottells of Colley's Chemical Cream, from 132, Oxford Street, each bottle costing one guinea."

But early in 1815 her tone changed. She began to complain of not getting money, of new debts that had to be discharged in England. " The cheapness is certainly true at Naples, but as the princess has very extravagant gentlemen at her Court, who make most exorbitant pretensions, and after all never *satisfait,* she is obliged to draw for $2000 in the course of the two months."

By April a supply of $4000 came in from the sale of Brunswick House, and she announced that "as to the pensions of her servants she only intended them to be paid until they were provided with situations; and she now begged of Hoper to inform this to all the servants/' excepting the old ones now not able to do their duty. The new pensions to be paid|$50 a quarter to Sir W. Cell, and $50 every quarter to Lady Eliz. Forbes."

Her letters from abroad to other persons were always in a strain of reckless gaiety.

" Thank you a thousand times, my dear ,

your kind inquiries after my health, which has suffered as little as I could expect from my late misfortune. I .cannot at dis moment inform you where I shall go to; my plan depends on letters from England, about dat vile money, who do always annoy me. As to my household, I hear people are meddling wid it, and saying it is improper. In de first place what would they have me do ? All de fine English folk leave me. I not send them away, though, by-the-by, some of dem not behave as civil as I could like. No matter| I wud have had patience wid them, but dey choose to go, so I not prevent them; but I must have some one to attend me, and I make my choice of some very agreeable persons, in every way fit to be my attendants ;though de jealous English beggars, such as Miss -,

It is curious that at the present date there should be still some servants of her late majesty Queen Charlotte, as well as her husband, in the receipt of pensions. Of the Civil List pensioners of George III-, who died in 1820, there are still living a sufficient number to represent in the accounts an annual sum of $1156 14s. 8d.; while George *iV.'s* pensioners figure for $3200 10s.

and one or two more of our acquaintance, dear, wud have liked to have had the situation which La Comtesse Oldi now fills to her and my great satisfaction. Her hrother is also a very intelligent and gentlemanlike person. Dey are of a decayed nobleman's family, much

better born and bred than William B l. But -I

know people are very ill-natured, and choose to abuse me for the choice I have made in my household. No matter, I not care|from henceforth I will do just as I please, that I will. Since de English neither give me de great honour of being a Princesse de Galle, I will be Caroline|a happy merry soul; but, *simplement,*

what do you tink, my dear ? Just before I and

Lady ‖ parted, I hope never to meet again, I gave her a very pretty cast of an antique. I should have been proud of it in my room. Well, a day or two after she broke it, *purposely* I know, and had de impudence to come and say to me: ' Oh ! ma'am, dat figure your royal highness bought for a bronze is only

plaster;' to which I reply : ' I knew that, Lady

very well, when I gave it to you. Dat is so like de English people; dey always ask, when one make them a *souvenir,* how much it cost ? how much it worth ?

You are a true English, my dear Lady , there

can be no mistake.'

" She laughed, but I saw she looked ashamed of herself. I cannot say I regret any one of my old household. I have been disappointed in dem all, and am much happier now I have no longer *des espions* about me, such as Lady A. H., watching me into every place where it is possible for a human beingto set foot. I must conclude, my dear , wishing

you well, and remain ever your sincere friend,

"C. P."

" PS.‖When you have any amusing news from England, I should like to hear it if you will favour me wid some."

It is clear from this that she was growing more and more unsettled, as there is a folly here verging on disordered intellect. At the same time, Lady C. Campbell says truly that the affected singularity of the letter was assumed to hide the soreness of her heart, and to make her forget her misery.

Then followed her reckless proceedings, and the scandal of the trial, all too familiar.

QUEEN CAROLINE TO LADY C. CAMPBELL ON HER ACQUITTAL.

" I assure you, my dear , no one's congratulations have been more welcome to me than yours. I do indeed feel thankful at having put my enemies to confusion, and received the justice my conduct andcharacter deserved. *Mais helas!* it comes too late,

It will be curious to note what the regent's unseemly contest with his wife cost the nation. I take its total from the MS. accounts in the British Museum.

Amount of all monies expended touching any proceedings had respecting her majesty the queen, from the year 1817 to 1821. Presented to House of Lords":

$ *s. d.* Secret service monies for commencement of proceedings 18,100 15 0

Total sum to Solicitor of Treasury 46,000 0 0

To Mr. Vizard, the Queen's Solicitor .... 60,000 0 0 To the King's Great Chamberlain for expenses . . 2,250 0 0 To Magistrate for expenses towards keeping peace . . 3,103 10 0

129,454. 5 0

dear . Her who would have rejoiced wid me

at her moder's triumph is losset to me; but she is in a much better world dan de present, and we shall meet soon, I trust, for to tell you de truth I cannot expect much comfort nowhere so long as I shall live. No one, in fact, care for me; and this business has been more cared for as a political affair, dan as de cause of a poor forlorn woman. *Mais riimporte!* I ought to be grateful; and I reflect on dese proceedings wid astonishment‖car *Us sont vraiment merveilleux.* That I should have been saved out of the Philistines' hands is truly a miracle, considering de power of my enemies and deir chiefs, for noting was left undone- dat could be done to destroy my character for evermore. I could tell you somethingIoh! *mein Gott!* some day I willIbut I cannot write dem. I feel very unwell, fatigued, and *ebaye*; I wonder my head is not quite bewildered wid all I have sufferedIand it is not over yet wid me. Dat cruel personage will never let me have peace so long as I stay in dis country: his *rancune* is boundless against me.

" I was sure you would rejoice at my glory, dear

; no one has been more true to me dan yourself

at all times, and you have not wasted your interest on an ingrate, I assure you.

" Poor Joan of Arc has really proved herself true to de name I used to give her *pour me inoquer d'elle*. She has staid wid me through it all, and God he knows dat was no small trial. Poor soul! I hope He will reward her for her courage.

"Many people call on me now who never didbefore. The is one of those who has made me

l'amende honorable. I will not quarrel with their respect, though it is shown me rather late in de day, and when they cannot well help it.

" I could prose for an hour to you, dear , but

will spare your patience, and my own eyes and head, which are both aching.

" So adieu, and believe me truly and affectionately yours, " Caroline."

We need not enter on the unsavoury subject of the charges against her. It must be owned that the case against her was strong, for it will be remembered that there had been already another indictment, one vulgarly known as the " delicate investigation;" and again, her education must have been fatal to all modesty. On the other hand, she is entitled to the benefit of the failure of the harsh and cruel persecution directed against her. It was a disastrous chapter in English History.

gook the Jifth.

PRINCESS CHARLOTTE,

46

SECTION 46

CHAPTER I.

PRINCESS CHARLOTTE.

One of the most interesting figures of the royal family of George III. was the young and only child of the Prince Regent, the Princess Charlotte, long the spoiled child of her circle, the " nation's hope."

This amiable and engaging creature was reared under conditions that might have shipwrecked one less gifted ; but her character, naturally open and generous, faithfully withstood the trials of an internecine discord that raged between her father and mother, between her grandfather and her father, between her grandmother and her mother, and was firm against the insidious advances of partisans, who tried to use her for their own ends.

The evil example, too, of a dissipated father, and of a deplorably foolish (if not corrupted) mother, were equally ineffectual to destroy the bloom of her innocence, and she ended her short career a charming and affectionate wife, bewailed by the whole nation. All this would make her story an interesting one; but from her earliest childhood she had to endure trials and harsh persecution, to make her take a part against her mother, which was

47

SECTION 47

carried on even to the prejudice of her health. It was attempted to force her into a marriage that was distasteful to her, with a view to drive her from the country where her popularity interfered or overshadowed such little favour as her father enjoyed. She was indeed destined to a short and troubled life.

It was at first thought that worthy Mrs. Hannah More, who had written a highly popular book, " Hints for the Education of a Young Princess," would have been selected as governess. But, as she put it to herself, " Am I fit for the situation ? I understand there is to be a governess, a sub-governess, and an assistant- governess. I have not rank for the first, or qualification for the second, and I am too old for the third." She, however, gives a pleasing little sketch of the royal infant:

" Lady Elgin brought the princess to chapel here yesterday; she is certainly a wonderful little creature. She has taken a great liking to the bishop, and always desires to walk alone with him. Yesterday she desired to repeat a hymn to him, and repeated one of yours. I have heard some things of her lately, which lead me to believe she has a thinking mind, uncommon for a child of her age. Did I tell you of the princess's soliloquy on reading the second chapter of St. Matthew ? ' I think,' says she, ' Joseph ought not to have been afraid of returning into Judea, when God had told him by an angel that he might return; but I leave that to be settled by the Bishop of London and Lady Elgin.'"

Miss Hayman was the first of her sub-governesses, and to her we owe little sketches of the young pupil, |1-| little more than an infant. This was in 1797.

"She soon began to notice me, showed all her treasures, and played all her little antics, which are numerous. She is the merriest little thing I ever saw |pepper-hot, too : if contradicted she kicks her little feet about in a great rage, but the cry ends in a laugh before you well know which it is."

Again: "I have just returned from the Queen's House, and have seen the whole royal family assembled. The king took Princess Charlotte from her nurse and carried her away into another room, which produced the first cry I have heard ; however, she soon recovered her good-humour, and played with her grandpapa on the carpet a long while. All seem to dote on her. You would have laughed to see the little child doing the popular all day as she has done; we drove twice up and down the park in returning from the Queen's House, to show her to the crowd assembled there, and she huzzaed and kissed her hand the whole time, and the people looked extremely delighted, running with the coach all the way. This evening she has been doing the same from the window for a full hour, to a great mob and all the procession of mail coaches."

Her mother supplies a further sketch of the infant:

Carlton House, 7 o'clock.

" Madam," she writes, " I went up stairs when my dear little Charlott was undressed, and stayed till she was in bed, and the dear little Angle was remarkable well. I am much obliged to you for your great attention to her, and hope you will not return at Eight o'clock ifit is not convenient to yourselflas I am quite alone with my ladieslso I can go upstairs if anything should be the matter, and then I will let you know. Hope to have the pleasure of seeing you much better to-morrow.

These and other extracts are from Lady Eose Weigall's pleasing little volume, written with the approbation of her majesty, who supplied materials.

VOL. I.

" I am,

" Caroline."

Princess Charlotte's Account Book, Written In A Child's Round-hand.

1802.

February.

In hand .

Received for playing a new

lesson .

Received

Received

Received

to lay out .

guinea and 14 shillings.

1802. *s. d.* February..i. 11 120. A poor Frenchman .26newTo a chalk pencil .02. 1 025. A poor man .10. 5 0March. . 6 51. A poor woman10. 10 65. Poor man1 7. A lame man .10 13. To seeing a house .2II A poor man .1" To two men last weeko" 22. To 3 different poor .2C 30. To poor .36 To do. paid by Mr. Lyong .34 April. To the old woman with the asso 6. An old soldier10 The old sailor twice20 A man and boy with a hand organ40 The poor this week30$ 14 0$1130 April 3.| f-tte *s. d. .d. .* 10 62 Pictures20 December. n gold 17. Poor30ings.13. Poor10 2 men on the hill .20 The man in the cart .10

In these entries, taken from Lady volume|" The old woman with the $ sailor twice," "The man in the cart quaint simplicity.

Again, the princess thus wrote to her

TO MY DEAR FRIEND, DOWAQER LADY

Windsor, U My Dearest Lady Elgin,

May every blessing attend daughter|believe me my true and f attend her wedding, and I reflect with as you have been the means to make instilling such Christian principles in her happiness and felicity, both here and he also render you happy by following t through life|in which none can ever rejoice than Your affectionat

A letter has been preserved, written Princess Royal, which is in a natural A large, schoolgirl's hand, almost as large addressed to the late Princess Royal o Queen of Wirtemberg.

Shrewsbury Lodge, Ai

My Dear Aunt,

I am very happy to find by 1 that you are so good to love me I assure you I love you very dearly- great deal about you from Lady Elgin,to resemble you in everything. I am very anxious to write better, that I may let you know how I go on in my learning. I am very busy, and I try to be very good. I hope to go to Windsor soon, and see my dear grandpapa and grandmama. I love very much to go and play with my aunts. Mama comes very often to see me, and then we play at all merry games|Colin Maillard|

I am much obliged to you for sending me so many pretty things, and wish you and the Elector were here. and would bring my cousin, Princess Theresa, with you. Adieu, my dear Aunt, and believe me Your ever affectionate and dutiful niece,

Charlotte.

PS.|My duty to the Elector.

One of the elements of discord in 'the unhappy quarrels of the prince and his wife, was the partiality shown by the king to the Princess of Wales and her daughter. The queen was on indifferent terms with her son, but disliked the Princess of Wales heartily, -who reciprocated the feeling with more than heartiness, and did all she could to retain the favour of so useful a protector as the king. In my " Life of George *I*T." this crisis has been fully set out, so the ground need not be gone over again. Late, however, in the year 1804, a sort of reconciliation was planned between the kinc; and his son, and it was arranged that he was to go to Windsor to see his father. On the eve of the reconciliation he discovered that the princess was to be consulted in the scheme for the education of his daughter, which so inflamed him, that he abruptly refused to seehis father. A curious side light is thrown upon this matter by an unpublished letter to Queen Charlotte, from Lady Elgin, governess of the little princess, and which shows what factions the Court was divided into, and

what trivial stories were used to fan the discord.

LADY ELCJIN TO THE QUEEN.

Shrewsbury Lodge, Sept. 4, 1804.

I have waited, my dear madam, till you were settled
at Weymouth before I troubled your majesty with a
letter, which, in every respect, is one of the most painful
I ever wrote; one which I beg you never will mention
to anyone. The communication is entirely for your
majesty; so trusting to your goodness in granting my
request, I shall candidly relate the most extraordinary
scene I was ever involved in, and which so agitated me,
that I really believe I shall never recover it. The simple
story is this :

The Princess of Wales's return from Southend occasioned the usual intercourse. Her royal highness was here, and Princess Charlotte was at Blackheath. But on Sunday, 19th August, H.R.H. arrived in great spirits here, calling from her carriage that she had great news to tell us; and desired that we would guess what would make us happiest. Princess Charlotte exclaimed : " Going to Windsor." Her royal highness replied : " Not just that, but you are going to Kew. The king has wrote me to go to Kew and bring you with me to-morrow at one o'clock to take leave of us before he goes to Wey mouth." I was surprised, not knowing your majesties were going to the seaside. The Princessof Wales continued in high spirits and staid to luncheon. She repeated her invitation after, and enjoined me not to be too late. Her royal highness even said we might go with her, but I declined that honour on account of Princess Charlotte's very nervous tendency, and the necessity of keeping H.R.H. quiet before any exertion. Before the princess went I became uneasyIt was very odd the verbal invitation from the king, not a note from any of the princessesIand trembled that I never had carried Princess Charlotte to your majesty's presence without your commands conveyed by one of the princesses.

This curious unpublished letter will be found, Brit. Mus. 449 h. 16.

The moment the Princess of Wales left us, I convinced myself your majesty was displeased with me. I had not had a line of inquiry ever since the 7th of July. Hotv could I carry the little princess and present her and myself without being more particularly desired ? Yet I could not decline the Princess of Wales's command. It was too late to send to Windsor. Most fortunately I saw in the newspapers that the Prince of Wales was to be in town about that time. I wrote to H.R.H. merely to say I had received an invitation different from the usual mode, and was going to take Princess Charlotte to Kew in consequence. This, I thought, would save me from any suspicion, and I flattered myself when I told your majesty you would laugh at my timidity. On our arrival, ten minutes before the time, the good kin received Princess Charlotte with the greatest kindness, and me also. His majesty took me into the dining- room, but no words can describe my astonishment when his majesty said he was alone, and that he came merely to see the Princess of Wales and the dear little girl before he went to Weymouth. Soon after his majestysaid he was to have Princess Charlotte all to himself. The Princess of Wales wished it, but we could say nothing on the subject till he returned to Windsor. His majesty assured me your majesty and all the princesses were well. The Princess of Wales came in ten minutes. The king went to receive her, and took her into another room, and soon sent Princess Charlotte to desire I would take her and Mrs. Lisle into the garden. When I looked about me and saw no person I well knew, but Miss Mustall standing like a statue by the door of the opposite room, where she then remained Ifor I could not speaklyour majesty cannot form an idea of my feelings ; I really never was in such a state. At dinner his majesty revived me a little by giving me the comfort of seeing him eat his dinner heartilylof pudding and dumpling. Talked much of Weymouth. I was much afraid of his overexerting. In vain did I offer my poor services. His majesty made even his coffee himself. But without you, my dear madam, and his charming supporters, I was so completely wretched that I was quite stupid. I resolved on perfect silence when I came away till I should hear from Windsor. But on Wednesday morning I received the Prince of Wales's commands to let him know what passed at my visit. I tried to write, and could not express myself so as to prevent constructions being put on my expressions different perhaps from my meaning, therefore I said I wished much to see Sir Walter Farquhar on my son's account, and would call at Carl ton House on my way up street, and if his royal highness wished to ask me any questions I would answer him and no one else. For the first time in my life I left my dear Princess Charlotte alone with Mrs. Gagarin. I went in my own carriage, and wastold there was no message for me at Carlton House, and after calling on Sir Walter went to a small room, where my little matters are kept, till the horses should rest. I was just going away when a servant of the Prince of Wales came to me to desire me to go to the prince, as it was then three o'clock. I was introduced to his royal highness, whom, alas I I found in the most violent agitation and distress of mind and body. His royal highness had a violent cramp and a bowel complaint, occasioned by this misery, which, after asking me a few questions which I could answer, without occasioning him any irritationlthank God !lhe informed me of such dreadful cruel things as well might put him in the state he was in; and, he added, the terrible infirmities he had got had stopped his attending a meeting that was to have been at Kew at twelve o'clock, when the blessing so long prayed for by the nation was, it seems, to have taken place. But the anguish the prince was in, and his affectionate regard to your majesty, occasioned in him a warmth of temper that I dreaded would throw him into a fever. Thank God he was better before he left town, as I heard by accident, as the name of the royal family seldom passes my lips. The prince asked me if I meant to write your majesty, and his royal highness said I need not He would inform you he had seen me, and I am glad to add he seemed pleased with my conduct. I have, however, found it uncomfortable not writing your majesty on this occasion, having always communicated every circumstance of importance since I have been so connected and so truly attached to your majesty, whom I have long considered as my true and best friend. If I have done wrong I trust the motive will secure me your forgiveness.

OF THE FAMILY OF GEORGE III. 377

God grant you may find the king recovering every

day in health and strength, and attain yourself, my dear
madam, that peace and quietness God has so long
deprived you of. We must all have tribulation in this
world, and the next line is." be of good cheer." Often
have I thought your majesty understood that passage
better than anybody. Many times have I seen you
cheerful and gay when you were in much anguish, and the
same merciful assistance will, I trust, be granted to your
majesty in every time of need. I can enter on no other
subject this morning, but merely say that dear Princess
Charlotte is well, and that I have the honour to be,
My dearest Madam,
Your grateful and ever faithful Subject,

M. Elgin, Dowager.

In 1805, when she was nine years old, a change in her governess was made, the
result of a protracted dispute between the king and his son. Lady Elgin was displaced,
and Lady de Clifford, a relation of Lord Albemarle, then at school, was appointed
to succeed her. The difficulties of such a situation were enormous, for the lady in
charge was expected to please all concerned, to hinder too much intercourse between
the child and her mother, never to let her out of her sight, and, above all, to satisfy the
prince and the king. One of these official and strictly watched visits to the Princess of
Wales is thus described:

" The Princess Charlotte," says Lady Campbell, " always dines with her mother
on Saturdays ; this day, her royal highness came with Lady de Clifford and the Duke
of Brunswick. As soon as she grows intimate with anyone, she gives way to her
natural feelings, and there is an openness and candour in her conversation which is
very captivating.

" Lady de Clifford seems to be a good-natured, commonplace person, and the
young princess appears attached to her, which is a good indication of her ladyship's
temper. The dinner over, which always weighs heavy on the princess when composed
of a family party only, her royal highness recovered her natural gaiety as soon as
she returned to the drawing-room, and began talking eagerly to Lady de Clifford, *en
tete-d- tdte*. The Princess Charlotte ran from one end of the room to the other to fetch
herself a chair. I rose and said how shocked I was, that her royal highness had not
commanded me to do her bidding. ' Oh!' said her mother, ' I assure you she likes it;
it is an amusement for her; she is kept so very strict, it is like feeling herself at liberty
to fly about lis it not, Lady de Clifford ?' To which the latter replied sharply: ' I assure
your royal highness, the Princess Charlotte has liberty enough with me.' This retort
again produced a stiffness, and the time seemed to drag on heavily until the Princess
Charlotte and the Duke of Brunswick withdrew, when we went to the Opera. Mr.
Ward, Lord H. Fitzgerald, Mr. Luttrell, Mr. Lewis, Mr. North, and Mr. Macdonald
came to pay their respects in her box. Mr. Lewis, the author of ' The Monk,' was not,
however, a very suitable attendant upon royalty. Mr. Ward was clever and pleasing;

but her royal highness was not, upon the whole, much flattered by her visitors, neither had she much cause to be so."

"To Lady de Clifford," Lord Albemarle tells us, "she was a source of constant anxiety and annoyance. Often when in obedience to the king's commands, my grandmother took her young charge to the Charlton Villa, the Princess of Wales would behave with a levity of manner and language that the presence of her child and her child's governess was insufficient to restrain. On more than one occasion, Lady de Clifford was obliged to threaten her with making such a representation to the king as would tend to deprive her altogether of the Princess Charlotte's society. These remonstrances were always taken in good part and produced promises of amendment."

The rudeness of the regent soon drove out Lady de Clifford, and a new staff of preceptors and governesses was appointed. The secret of these changes was, that the persons were chosen by the regent, but were too independent to become his creatures, and " bully" the young creature into submission to his wishes. A further ezperiment was made with the Duchess of Leeds.

Young Keppel, the present Lord Albemarle, was at this time a young schoolboy at AVestminster, and his pleasant love of frolic excited the young princess's interest. They were almost playfellows. He thus recalls an amusing scene, which shows the high spirits and keen sense of enjoyment of the princess :

" The house at Earl's Court, Brompton," says Lord Albemarle, " which my father occupied, is next door to what was then a villa residence of Mr. Gunter, the confectioner, nicknamed by us children ' Currant-Jelly Hall.' In her visits to Earl's Court the princess usually came in my grandmother's carriage, but on this occasionin her own. The scarlet liveries soon brought opposite to the entrance-gate a crowd of people anxious to get a glimpse of the heiress presumptive to the throne. Soon after her arrival at Earl's Court I happened to pass outside the gates. I was asked by the bystanders, ' Where is the princess ?' I told her how desirous the people were to have a sight of her. ' They shall soon have that pleasure,' was the reply. Slipping out of the garden-gate into the road, she ran in among the crowd from the rear, and appeared more anxious than anyone to have a peep at the princess. I would fain have stopped her, but she was in boisterous spirits, and would have her own way. She proceeded to the stable entrance, saddled and bridled my father's hack herself, and, armed with the groom's heavy riding-whip, led the animal through the subterranean passage to the garden gravel walk. She now told me to mount. I, nothing loath, obeyed. But before I could grasp the reins or get my feet through the stirrup-leathers, she gave the horse a tremendous cut with the whip on the hindquarters. Off set the animal at full gallop, I on his back, or rather on his neck, holding on by the mane and roaring lustily. The noise only quickened his pace. I clung on till I came to the plot in front of the drawing-room windows, when the brute threw his heels into the air and sent me flying over his head. At the same moment the princess emerged from the rose-bushes, panting for breath. She had hoped, by making a short cut, to intercept the horse and its rider before they came into view. My cries brought the whole family on to the lawn. Of course the princess got a tremendous scolding from Lady de Clifford. That she was used to, and took coolly enough. In a short time quiet wasrestored, and my people returned to the house. But no sooner were the princess and I alone again, than the heavy riding-whip was once more put into requisition, and she treated my father's son exactly as she had just been treating my father's horse."

With the new governess came Dr. Fisher, the Bishop of Salisbury, and Dr. Short, the tutor. The former the young girl could not resist turning into ridicule, with infinite frolic; and her playfellow, the young Keppel, gives some amusing sketches of her high spirits and love of frolic. He thus draws the bishop :

" A dull solemn-looking man with a severe expression of countenance, to which a projecting under-lip contributed not a little. He was a good classical scholar, but had no more knowledge of mankind than was to be acquired in the quadrangle of a college, where he had passed much of his life. He was precise in dress and formal in manner. In language he was a thorough pedant, seeming to consider the force of words to be in proportion to the number of syllables they contained."

PRINCESS CHARLOTTE TO THE DOWAGER LADY DE CLIFFORD.

My Dearest Lady De C.,

A thousand thousand thanks for your very kind letter. I should have answered it directly, but the real truth was I miscalculated a day|that means, lost a day.

We go on pretty well, considering all things, without you. Heaven knows how very much I long to see you.Never have you been out of my mind since we parted. Our dear Duke sat of *(sic)* his picture yesterday, which was Saturday. It is coming on very well indeed. He dined with us and stayed till ten. I should have been quite happy if you had been with me. He asked very kindly after you, and hoped when I heard last you was well. He sends his kind remembrances.

I have this moment received a line from my dear mother, who sends her kind love and quite approves of your plan. She begged me to tell you that *the Duke* means to have the *babes with him in town* on purpose that the Duchess may come up to town. Mamma is determined to come up to town, I believe on the 25th.

When you saw him (Duke of Brunswick) you took leave of his dear beard : it is all cut off, and he looks like an Englishman. I took leave of it Saturday. I will tell you what will make you laugh. We were driving in Hyde Park yesterday (Sunday), and a man in a plain black coat, round hat, etc. etc., on horseback rode up close to the carriage and looked into it. I said to Mrs. U., " What a very impertinent fellow this is ! " when what should I hear but " *Vous ne me connais (sic) pas ?* " The carriage of course stopped; and we spoke, the Duke so changed you would not know him again.

As you were so good as to be anxious about everything that concerns me, I cannot help telling you that *I have lost my dear Puff.* We have advertised him at two guineas reward. I hope I shall find him. But papa has made me a beautiful present of a beautiful white Italian greyhound, with cropt ears, etc. Captain Lake took a ship in which the dog was, which dog belonged to the Empress Napoleon, and was going to some gentleman as a present from her. He took the ship and brought the dog as an offering to papa. But he said, " I don't care for dogs, I will send it to Charlotte who loves them." He did and by Dupaque..

I send you a letter I have had from the *great U. P.,* aiid one for you I took the liberty to open. When we meet I want to tell you about the picture Bloomfield has got. I am rather in an embarra *(sic)* about it.

Pray let me know how dear Elizabeth is. Pray give my kindest love to her and remembrances to Sophia, Augustus, etc., and my kind compliments to my Lord.

God bless you, my dearest Lady. Forgive this long letter, and believe me ever your very sincerely

attached and gratefully obliged,

Charlotte.

Mrs. U. sends her love to you. *Au sujet, louche dose*I always find when I write or see you that I have volumes to say. Let me know how poor Parsons' child is. My remembrances to her. When I answered the Bishop's letter *I did all I could to make it over waite.* I hope I succeeded.

She was very fond of her young playfellow, and would thus "lecture him":

PRINCESS CHARLOTTE TO MB. KBPPEL (NOW LORD ALBEMARLE).

My Dear Keppel,

You know me well enough to suppose that I never will refuse you a thing when there is no harm in it. But though I send you the money, still I must give you a little reprimand. You will, I hope, dear boy, love me as well tho' I do sometimes find fault with you.You will, if you go on asking for money and speriding it in so quick a manner, get such a habit of it that when you grow up you will be a very extravagant man, and get into dept *(sic),* etc. etc.

Your grandmamma de Clifford allows me $10 a month. But, though I spend it, I take care never to go further than my sum will allow. Now, dear George, if you do the same you will never want for money; say you have a guinea, well then, never go beyond it, and in time you will save up. That is the way everybody does, and so never get into dept *(sic).*

If you call at Warwick- House, my porter, Mr. Moore, will give you half-a-guinea. If you use that well and give me an exact account how you spend it, I will give you something more. I wish you was here. Write to me often, and believe that no one loves you better than I do, nor will be more happy to help you in all troubles than I. We have very fine weather, and your mamma is here and is pretty welL Gramma de Clifford sends her love to you, and I

remain,

Dear George,

Your very sincere and affectionate

Charlotte.

END OF VOL. I.

Lightning Source UK Ltd.
Milton Keynes UK
19 May 2010

154435UK00001B/52/P